ON BECOMING ME:

Memoir of an 80's Teenager

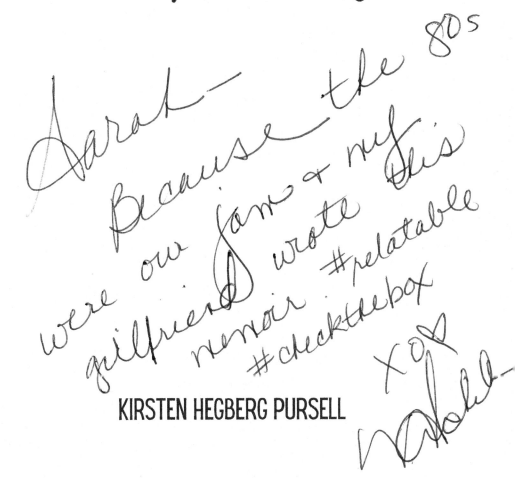

Sarah —
Because the 80s were our jam + my girlfriend wrote this memoir. #relatable #checkthebox
xo
Natalie

KIRSTEN HEGBERG PURSELL

Color photos and bonus content can be found at
www.kirstenpursell.com.

Cover design by Kirsten Hegberg Pursell

ISBN (paperback) 978-1-7377705-0-3
ISBN (digital) 978-1-7377705-1-0

Dedicated to
becoming the best versions of ourselves
during the hardest years of our lives.

CONTENTS

INTRODUCTION

Much of what we remember is often how we choose to remember it. But when you write it all down, it is like going back in that moment, reliving it as the 1980's all over again; reminding us how powerful the mind can be in changing the memory's narrative.

My story is not special or unique, but it is mine. It could easily be anyone's story. It is the teenage angst, joys, fears, discoveries, heartache, and growth that most of us have had in some form.

I have pulled out the diaries and journals over the years and quickly put them away likely mortified by my words and behaviors. Every so often I would come back to the thought that I should publish them so that whoever the audience might be could read that those feelings transcend time. But I had my own children and the thought of them doing things that I did or reading about them might make them see me in a different light.

I recently rediscovered the journals. It made me realize that time has distorted my memories. Some of the memories were more painful than I remember. Others were not as dramatic as I played them out on repeat in my head. And then there were some that were so raw and honest I tucked them away so deep I forgot the magnitude of those moments on my life. But they were all real and by having written it down then it was like going back in time and watching my life's movie play out in front of me. I have been loved and I have loved in return. As I reflect, I feel lucky to have had all those experiences.

I look back and remember the break-ups more than the highs I felt during those times. Because I was always the one breaking up, I am sure it is how I reconciled my actions. My journals reminded me I was quick to change my mind about those boys. I wish I would have handled those break-ups better for the sake of the boys I was running from. The ones who were willing to love me were the ones I hurt the most. I wonder in hindsight, knowing myself as I did and do, if it was that I was too afraid to let myself love/like them as much as they loved/liked me. I had such a love-hate relationship with myself, and they bore the brunt of that.

I have kept my journals since I started writing in fourth grade. I have kept every letter I was ever written. Those have been the most powerful reminders that I was loved and that I had friends I could turn to and count on during tough times. I also wrote poetry to convey my feelings on a deeper, more metaphorical level.

My friendships and struggles to keep them do not fail to make the pages. The battles with my parents were real. Figuring out who I was without my sport that had defined every part of me was especially grueling. But my story was never unique. We have all lived our own versions.

As I read and reread the journals to write this, I struggle with how much of myself to put out there. I read it thinking how bi-polar I sounded. I was happy one day, sad the next. I complimented myself here, hated myself there. My weight, my skin, my obsession with celebrities played out in fantasies, crushing on boys that made no sense. I beat myself up often. And I question why my friendships were so volatile. I am struck by how I chose to remember things versus how I wrote about them. And I am so glad I was able to find my inner strength in every moment and experience. Those experiences shaped who I became. It does not mean that even now there are not days I still struggle with that identity.

There is much I do not remember. And much I remember differently than I wrote. Those were the hardest years of my life, as they were for most of us. I have found this a beautiful journey back in time realizing that reality was not always what I recall and that I was not alone in my feelings. The struggles were real. Running away from people and emotions were just ways of avoiding vulnerability.

I remember feeling like no one ever liked me, that I was too ugly or too fat or too damaged to like. But reading back, I realize there were boys who were interested in me; I just didn't share the interest. We do not always fall for the people who fall for us. I became so focused on my feelings not being reciprocated by those I liked, ultimately fueling a sense that I was not worthy of others' affections.

People tell me now how they thought I was constantly smiling and seemed happy, that they secretly admired that, and wished they had half the confidence I did in high school. Clearly, what we project is not always what we believe.

Sometimes as I was transcribing my entries, I found myself wanting to yell at the words I was writing, wanting to tell myself to stop it, just hang in there as things are about to change. Or just let him love you instead of trying to make him hate you. If I just had the power of hindsight, being in the moment could have been so much more than anticipating what might be in the end.

I spent too much time in my own head. Judging myself. Worried how others saw me. I look at that person now and do not see the person I became. I have always been my own person sometimes marching to the beat of a different drummer, sometimes not. What I have somehow managed to seamlessly project to the world my entire life is not always what my brain is reflecting inside me. But if any of us were truly that transparent there would never be a story to tell.

The following pages are non-fiction. They are my words exactly as I wrote them. They are my thoughts, fantasies, fears, failures, triumphs, loves, and experiences as I lived them. They are my poems, and they are the notes and letters that went with those time periods.

I have been asked why I would want to publish my innermost thoughts and experiences. It opens you up to scrutiny. It exposes parts of yourself that you worked so hard to overcome. But it also shows the human side of growing up. I kept all my writings, maybe that is why I was encouraged to put it out there. Growing up is never easy. I know there will be people that see themselves in these pages not just because they were part of my story but because parts of their story were not really that different than mine. A friend asked what I hope to accomplish doing this? I do not have an answer. On a personal level, it has been a gut-wrenching, heart-warming, cathartic trip down a sometimes very dark hole. You will laugh, you might even cry. Those of you who know me might even be surprised. But I have put myself out there. Enjoy the ride. I did.

The Red Diary: The Very Beginning
(1977-1980)

The beginning of my writing in a diary was sporadic at best. My first entries are from 1977. I would be ten that year. Glimpses into my life would tell you that it consisted of obsessing over boys, brief mentions of time with friends, and swimming. In early 1977, I was still playing with Barbies, watching the Mouseketeers on TV, and pretending to be the Bionic Woman; however, I was already taking a strong interest in boys. I definitely had no qualms with letting my affections for boys be known. I even made-up afflictions for boys such as "Larryingitis" - after a boy named appropriately enough Larry. First notes and even a love letter followed in 1979. Glimpses of the foundation for my future mind are clear. If nothing else, it is a humorous perspective on how I viewed my life in the years before it got complicated.

The inside of the red diary reads:

> *Dear Diary, I really have never had a Diary before so these things might sound sorda weird, ok? -Kirsten*

> *Dear Kirsten, It is ok. I understand. -Diary.*

August 18, 1977: Dear Diary, I had a fun day. I'm starting to have crushes on boys.

August 19, 1977: Dear Diary, I have a new boyfriend. He's 16 oh so cute. His name is Joe but I'm too young for him, but I love him.

January 1, 1979: Dear Diary, Today I drank a ½ can of beer. I stayed up to 12:00

A boy named Todd

January 2, 1979: Dear Diary: Today was great. Todd kept getting notes from me. He's so cute. He's supposed to give me a note back.

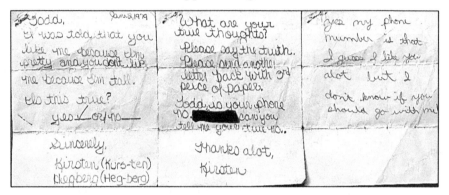

January 3, 1979: Dear Diary, Todd said he likes me. He doesn't want us going together yet. He's so neat. A lot of girls are jealous.

January 4, 1979: Dear Diary: I called Todd up today. He didn't even tell me to call. I could kill Michelle. I still have a mad crush on him.

January 5, 1979: Dear Diary: Todd waved to me and smiled at me. Diana was gonna ask him his address. And if he was gonna ask me to go with him.

January 8, 1979: Dear Diary: Today was a good day. Saw Todd a lot. I love the kid. I wish he was mine.

January 10, 1979: Dear Diary: I'm loving Todd more and more. I'm sitting in his seat now for reading. I played tetherball a little today.

January 11, 1979: Dear Diary, I played Todd a little in tetherball. I love him even more now. I'm gonna play hard at tetherball tomorrow.

January 12, 1979: Dear Diary: I let Todd have cuts in tetherball. I still love the kid. I hope he'll always be mine. I can't get over how cute he is.

January 13, 1979: Dear Diary: Today I had a swim meet. Did pretty good. I saw my old boyfriend Jim B. He's still cute. I'll always remember him.

April 21, 1979: Dear Diary, a lot has happened between Jan 13 and today. First off from Todd he finally did ask me. I said "no." Then I went to Jim again to ask him to go with me. He said he was going with someone else. Then came Mike N who I also asked. He said no because I bug him too much. It was because Tara told me to call him. Then came Marco. He's so cute. Still think he's cute but I want Mike no one else but Jim B. I like Mike's eyes so much. We're going to Germany this summer. I can hardly wait. Swimming is really great now.

A boy named Marco

April 29, 1979: A whole week has gone by. Marco likes me, I think.

May 1, 1979: Hi! Don't get mad. Maybe Marco doesn't like me. But I think when he breaks-up with Stephanie I think he'll ask me (hopefully). I hope he will ask me. He says he doesn't know how to French kiss and he kissed this girl for 10 sec. Now don't you call that Frenching? Yep! (your answer). He's so indescribable. I know his phone number by heart.

May 2, 1979: Hi! I think Marco is beginning to like me. Stephanie says he'll probably break-up soon. I hope so. He got his hair cut. Stephanie does not like him as much now that his hair is cut. I still like him though. He's such a babe. A friend says he's worse than Todd. You know getting fresh. I think I like guys like that.

May 4, 1979: Hi! Marco does like me. Well, I think he does? Because he was looking at me almost all day. I think because I was wearing this slightly sexy dress. I think he'll break up with Stephanie pretty soon. If I go with him I hope we both will learn how to French! Me and Tara have a bet on the 1st one to get a guy. A $2 ice cream.

May 6, 1979: Hi! I did good at the meet May 5. I got 1st in the 11 year old division. Debbie, a good swimmer, says she thinks Jim B. likes me again. I don't like him as a boyfriend though. I like Marco and tomorrow's school again and he might ask me. I think he will sometime this week. I hope he learns to French if I go with him.

May 10, 1979: Howdy! Sorry for not writing. Nothing great happened till today. No, he didn't ask me! I wrote him a letter asking some questions and here are his answers. Age: 12. Birthday: May 26. He has 1 brother 2 sisters. And he thinks I write OK. Stephanie says don't be surprised if you're going with him next week.

May 11, 1979: Hi! Marco hasn't asked me yet, unfortunately! He's such a doll. He's also nice. I think he's gonna ask me soon hopefully. Today we had a school track meet. I came in first in the broad jump. I saw Marco all day. And I fell more in LOVE with him. Only a few more weeks till we leave for Germany. I'm gonna miss Marco when we go. If he asks me, I hope he kisses me on the lips.

May 20, 1979: Dear Diary, sorry for not writing for a while. I had a track meet. I made 2nd place and Marco my friend. I think he hasn't asked me because I think he thought I was too popular or something. We became good friends at the track meet. I think Marco will ask sometime this week. Had swim meet today and yesterday, did pretty good for goofing off in practice.

May 31, 1979: I'm never gonna ever go with him (I think). I don't like him as much. I'm back to Jim*. Only 8 more days till we leave for Germany. I'm gonna miss dad. I love my family so. I wish dad could come and Heike (*our dog*).

[*Jim B.: my forever crush who never really ever paid much attention to me.]

June 6, 1979: He asked me!! I couldn't believe it. We were at graduation (a skating rink) and he asked me. I think we're gonna go with each other during summer. He is so neat. He asked me at 11:15am. Yesterday he called but I was asleep. We skated together holding hands. I hope we go with each other thru the summer.

June 8, 1979: It's been 2 days since he asked me. And today we're leaving for Germany. Marco kissed me goodbye, on the lips. It was so neat. I didn't even expect it. I also got his picture. We're gonna keep in touch. I like him.

June 9, 1979: My third day going with Marco and I miss him so much. I hope we go with each other all summer...Me and Marco like each other so much. I still can't believe we kissed (*I drew lips*). Wow!

June 10, 1979: Another boring day without Marco. I wrote him a letter, though. It said, "...I miss you, a lot! Sealed with a kiss!" ...so on. I like him so much.

June 11, 1979: Today was better than yesterday. I didn't miss Marco as much, but I still miss him. He's such a sweetheart...I think I love him.

June 12, 1979: You know what? I think I most miss Marco's lips, hug, and hand more now than before. The meaning holding.

[*Lisa/Leaky was my best friend from first grade. She sent me all the letters I had written her over the years, including this gem.*]

Hi Leaky,   June 13, 1979

Marco asked me! It's been ~~yet~~ exactly a week today! On Friday when we left for Germany he kissed me "Good-bye" on the ~~lips~~! We plane on goin' with each other thru the summer!

How's it goin' on your side of the world? It's great here except for the ~~weather~~!

The plane trip was ~~very, very~~ boring!

Marco asked me at a graduation party. A skating rink!

Gotta go,
Friends,
Kirsten

P.S.
Please write.
Over for address! →

9

June 15, 1979: Marco's still in my head, but Oliver is even more. I'd never 2 time a boy…Here you're allowed to buy cigarettes when you're young. Me and Ina (my cousin) are gonna smoke Tues. Maybe!?

June 19, 1979: [*My Oma confronted me about the smoking. I denied it. I came clean in this note I wrote her in my best German.*]

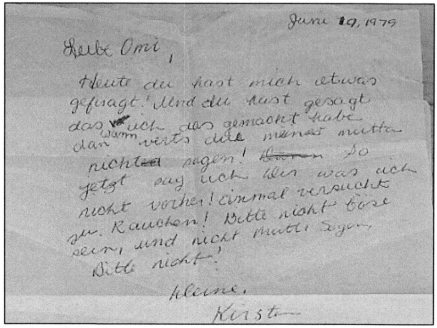

(*Dear Omi, Today you asked me something. And you said that if I did it you would not tell my mom. So now I am telling you what I did not before. I tried smoking one time. Please don't be mad and don't tell my mom. Please don't. Yours, Kirsten*)

June 20, 1979: 2 weeks ago today he asked me. That was probably the most important day of my life other than that Friday when we kissed. I like him so. Still…Saw Oliver today at courts. I wish he knew how much I like him. I'd never take him though cause I have someone much better.

June 22, 1979: 2 weeks since he kissed me and 16 days since he asked me. I like him, a lot. And I'd like him and my friends more if they wrote. Ina and I smoked today. That was my 3rd cigarette this day. Got my period 2 days ago.

June 24, 1979: I've been seriously thinking of breaking up with Marco. I just can't take it you know not seeing him and all. But down inside I really like him, so much.

June 25, 1979: It's almost 3 weeks that we've been together. I don't know how I could stand it without Marco. Going with him and not seeing him! And when I like Oliver and a 15 year old likes me I think. I also think a lot of other boys like me. I just think! I think I quit smoking. I think!

June 27, 1979: Today I got mad at my cousin and mom. And tomorrow I think I'm gonna break-up! Hopefully he'll write me saying he wants to break-up. Then I'd feel a lot better not going with him. If it was at home and we saw each other a lot and we broke-up I'd be very down and depressed.

June 28, 1979: Today I broke-up! I'm glad too because I can't hack it not seeing him and all. I got a letter from him. Which I think was too mushy. All it said was my <u>Love</u>! I have my lovers here. And I'll find others next time. I don't even think Marco went with me to make me happy, he really liked me.

(Letter dated June 22, 1979.)

Dear Kirsten,

Your letter came in the 21 of June. I have felt very happy because your letter came in. I thought you weren't going to write to me. I think that picture you gave me is the loveliest picture I've ever had. Since you left you don't know how much I've missed you my <u>Love</u>. But you will be back my <u>Love</u>. That very same day you left I missed you. It is really boring down here there's nothing to do but think about you. I think this is the best thing to do for both of us.

My Love
You don't know how much I miss you.
Your remembrance keeps me alive.
When I'm sad I remember you.
When I'm happy I remember you.
And I will keep remembering you.
Love,
Marco (last name)

June 29, 1979: I was joking around yesterday. Even if I did break-up, then tore up the letter, he would have never known. Tomorrow are the state championships.

June 30, 1979: Today I had the state champ. I did lousy except in 200 and 400 free *(long course meters in Germany)*. My time in 200 free was 2:23.6 tie for first. Then in 400 free I did a 5:04.9 and came in first. 200 back was cruddy and 7 sec off my best time and 200 IM 3 sec of my best time.

July 1, 1979: We're visiting relatives in Munich next week. The swim meet today was OK. I did better 1 time by 2 sec in the 100 back and did a 1:20.9 I think. And placed 4th. I got 3rd in the 100 free.

July 11, 1979: Today's our 5th anniversary. 5 weeks we've been together. Saturday I have the German national championships. I'm seeded 5th in the 400 free. Only 8 more days until we go home. I don't want to leave the swim team here.

July 16, 1979: Saturday I placed 8th in Cologne. I worsened my time 3 seconds. My picture was in the paper. I'm looking forward to home. But I'll miss them here. This coming Sat and Sun I have the JOs in California.

July 21, 1979: BREAK UP! (NO JOKE) Dear Diary, Today I broke-up! I mean Dana talked for me because I didn't want to talk to him. I saw Jim again. We always make these faces at each other. He's always looking at me. I hope I see him in Oceanside once in a while. I guess I'll probably always like him. There's probably a possibility I'll go with him at one time. Good night.

July 22, 1979: Dear Diary, I'm back in (sorda) love. With that butthole who I can't stand "Jim B."! I'm not really in love. I just like him. I think?????etc...that he sort of likes me. You should see us together at swim meets. We act or we do hate each other so that we always snicker at each other and end up laughing. He's so sweet and bratty.

July 29, 1979: Dear Diary...I can't stop thinking about Jim. I just think of us together. I really don't like him as a boyfriend just as a friend that I like so much. Whenever I hear neat music, I think of us in a field kissing. It's a strange feeling!

July 30, 1979: Dear Diary...I still think about Jim and me together at swim meets kissing or in a field. I LIKE to dream about him. I don't know why I still like him after about a year and a half and not having gone with him.

August 13, 1979: My first day here wasn't so bad*. Especially at swimming. This new guy joined our club. He is either 13 or 14. What a BABE! He swam in my lane. He's a pretty fast swimmer. But that's not the best part about him!

[*My family had gone on vacation, and I wanted to stay back and train for the end of summer meet. I stayed at my friend Chris's house. We were such good friends. I might have even had a small crush on him at some point, but I think in hindsight we both knew he didn't like girls as anything more than friends, and I loved being his friend.]

August 23, 1979: It's been forever since I wrote last. Now I have something to tell you. I got drunk Sunday. Dana and Tara were the ones who really got drunk. Believe me I'm never gonna drink again! And I hope my children don't ever drink!!!!

[Well, that didn't happen. Both counts.]

Advice from a coach

I started swimming when I was eight years old. I loved swimming with all my heart; I loved everything about it. All it took was one time for Coach Cheney to kick me down to the pool with kids my own age to make me realize I wanted to be better than they were. I was back the next day pushing myself to swim with much older kids because I could.

Swimming became my identity. I lived for that sport. I would sometimes sleep in my suit. I even occasionally wore it to school under my clothes. I learned a lot of life lessons; some were harder than others. I learned early on that people want to be your friend when you are good at something and you are dispensable when you fall from the pedestal. I had my highest highs and lowest lows in and around the pool.

I had a coach I adored when I was ten and then he left to pursue a graduate degree. I kept two of his letters as his words were inspiring to me even then.

9 Oct 1978 - Sent to me on letterhead reading THE (ex) COACH SAYS: Happy Birthday Kirsten! How are you now that you're an ol' lady? Also congratulations on winning those PSA titles. Too bad about the 200 IM – but I'll bet you don't make that mistake again. You know, now things can get really challenging. It's great that you did so well in the 10 & under but you'll find the 11-12's a little tougher. I know that if you accept the challenge and work hard that you can do just as well as before. You have the potential to do well in swimming just stay with it. Set yourself realistic goals and go after them...How's B.? I guess by now he's eleven too...Take care of yourself! Roy

27 Feb 1979: Howdy Kirsten! Sure was nice of you to write. I realized that this was the JO time of year and I was really curious about how people were doing. You sure are doing great! I remember that I didn't hit some of those times until I was about 15 years old. If you maintain your good attitude and work hard you will probably go a long way in swimming...Take care of yourself. Roy

Seventh Grade: The year that does not get written about

Of all the years I can look back on in my life, seventh grade had to have been one of the hardest. But I did not write about it. I am not sure why. So, I must rely on my memory. I was really successful in the pool and enjoyed my team, San Luis Rey. Swimming was my everything. I also recall that my elementary school friends all went to a different junior high and my best friend Dana had a different lunch period than I did. I went to the library at lunch so I would not feel like I did not have friends.

Around this time, I dislocated my shoulder on a start. I finished the swim. I got out of the water and walked over to my mom who was timing. I was crying and she says to me, "You can't win every race." And through sobs, I said, "Look at my shoulder." I think she might have felt a little bad at that point. She took me to the doctor. He moved it around a little, thought it was back in place, and told me to take it easy for a couple of days. I was literally back in the water within days. My shoulder would plague me the rest of my swimming days.

In March 1980, I had an accident. While waiting for our ride to practice, I was being a total bitch to my brother and his friend, Al. My parents had this rule that we were not allowed to have friends over when they were not there and I decided it was my place to enforce that (even though Al was just waiting for a ride to practice, too). I took some crackers from Al and decided I was throwing them out the door. I went outside and the two of them slammed the door shut on me. I reacted by

14

pushing the door open. But the door had a stained-glass window, which went straight through my arm. I looked up and saw my brother's face covered in blood. It was mine. From there, everything felt like slow motion. We ran across the street to our neighbor who called 911. My brother ran to get my mom who was teaching tennis nearby. I ended up with over a hundred stitches in my arm. I had completely severed my radial artery and cut everything around the nerve, but not the nerve, which the doctor said was a miracle. It left an ugly scar, which has only slightly faded with time. It looks like a giant scorpion on the inside of my left wrist. I was in a cast for six weeks. I remember Reagan was shot during this time. While I did not write in a journal about it at the time, I did write an essay for my eighth-grade English class a year later.

(Essay from March 16, 1981:)
"What A Bloody Mess!"

What a bloody mess that accident was.

Just about a year ago exactly, I had this little accident. This accident was almost a death situation, but it helped me to decide how I chose what I wanted to be when I was older and it helped me overcome blood.

This is how it happened and how I overcame the fear of blood.

Exactly one year ago I accidentally put my left and right arms through a stained-glass window. Luckily, it was my left arm that got the worst of things.

My left arm was gushing blood, there were little things popping out from all over my wrist. I ran across the street to a neighbor who called the ambulance. She and her 3-1/2 year old daughter tried to administer first aid, unsuccessfully. But before she knew it my mom was there. And shortly thereafter the ambulance, fire department, and at least half the neighborhood.

I arrived at Tri-City Hospital around 5:30pm. They took a few pictures, bandaged me up, and made me wait two and a half hours before I went into emergency surgery. The so-called emergency surgery lasted about an hour and a half. I slept the whole time and the three days I was in the hospital.

I came back to school five days later with a cast the size of King Kong.

Two months later I was out of that and out of my two braces, doing the same things millions of kids do, except I had a hundred stitches a couple of days before. That's why I say what a bloody mess. And it's true. I overcame the fear for blood. Now I can become a doctor. Could you imagine being a doctor scared of blood? It'd be a little strange, hah?

(There is also a letter to Lisa that I wrote during this time. Of course, it was about a boy. The letter is dated May 8, 1980.)

Hi Lisa,   ①   May 8

I got your letter today. Thank you. To answer your questions:
yes—my arm is fine.
Yes—I'm fine.
Yes—There is a space for you on my arm. Guys around are pretty cute, but the guy I like is the cutest. He's got reddish-brown hair and big brown eyes. He's pretty tall (5'6"). He has braces and freckles—the freckles make him very cute. I'm not going with him, but his friends keep, or did, ask me for him because he's shy. I didn't say yes, I said I'd say yes if he would ask me himself. Then yesterday his friend asked me to the dance for him. I didn't answer. I guess he likes me but I'm not sure. His best friend

says he likes me. But I neve
know. Hes very, very, shy. But
such a Babe. People don't think
he is but I do. Hes not "surfed-
out" like most guys are. Oh,
I haven't even told you his
name: are you ready its, its
DAT ██████████ !!!!!!
TOTAL BABE OF 1980!
Hes in 8th grade. He never
talks to me, unless were around
his Best Friend. Anough
about me and my romance,
so howz' yours? How are you
doing? Great I hope. If you
invite me to your party please
send me an invitation.
You know about almonzo,
whoever. I like that about

all the kissing? I never
watch Little House. Tommor-
ous our Last dance for 7th
graders Hopefully Pat will
ask me to dance. I pray he
will. I'll screem if he doesn't!
I think I've told you about
Pat before. Or maybe it was
always Jim ███████, who knows,
I HATE JIM ███████ ! ! !
I get my cast off in 3 to 2½
weeks Hooray ...
see you!!
Kirsten

P.S.
write Back!

After the cast came off, I would get back in the pool as soon as I could. But I no longer swam for San Luis Rey. I hated the new program and was such a bitch to our coach. I remember him slamming his hand against a wall once because he was so frustrated with me during practice. In the fall, I would make the switch to SDA. I did not know anyone on that team. I did not feel like I belonged at first. I remember one of the first things someone said to me was I was not as fast as everyone said I would be. I liked the coach, though. Johnny pushed me harder than any coach ever did and was a good fit for me. Weight would become a major center point leading to distorted perceptions of myself that were dictated by numbers on the scale. (We had pool deck weigh-ins in front of the boys and a fat lane). Throughout the course of my years there, I would make some good friends. And the boys were a motivating reason to practice.

Fall of 1980 and a boy named Ian

I neglected the red diary for the better part of a year. I came back to it when I started "going with" a boy named Ian in 8th grade. I sounded happy to start that year. I know I had made some friends in Betty, Tammy, and Connie. That same year, I had an eighth-grade English teacher named Mr. Byer. I think we saw him as this curmudgeonly old man who was too hard on us to spell correctly and demanded we write an essay every week. I kept all those essays. And when I reflect on a single person prior to high school who most influenced me it would be him. He encouraged me to enter the school talent fair for writing at the end of 8th grade. I would win first prize in two of the three categories and get second in the other. I was awarded the writer of the year honor and had my name displayed as part of a giant plaque in the front office. That award meant as much to me as any I had received in swimming up until that point in time.

(*First place essay written on September 29, 1980:*)

"A Tribute to Mr. Two"

This is a tribute to Mr. Two, the one who never can push himself that much more to beat number one.

It's Mr. Two who has to push number one those extra yards for the winning touchdown. It's Mr. Two who throws the winning pitch to number one for the final run. Mr. Two, it's you who makes the track star stride for his endurance so much more. It's you who pushes the swimmer to pull so much harder at the end. It's you who pushes that person so far that he breaks a world record.

Mr. Two, you know it's you who makes number one excel to the breaking point. You, who deserves the credit for the winning touchdown, homerun, and world record. You're the one who strived so hard to push number one to receive no recognition.

This is for you, Mr. Two. The most important of all battles between man, woman, and child is your push for the Superbowl title, world series, or the gold, which fails to succeed. You push number one to that world record. This is in recognition of you, dear Mr. Two.

(*I sent Lisa this letter on October 20, 1980:*)

Hi Lisa,

What's up with you? Not much here, Haven't had much to do lately. All I usually do is think about the guy I like. Speaking of liking someone who or do you like anyone? The guy I likes is Ian ████, absolute Babe. Some of my frinds were talking to him about me and then they asked him if he liked me and he said yes but I didn't Believe them so they asked him to tell me what he told them and he just said it. I hardly beleived it when he told me himself. Our first dance is on Friday the 23. I hope he asked me to it. It will be a blast because he'sgot such a great personality about him which will make it fun., I hope. But then again he may not even ask me to the dance, if he even goes to the dance he probably WON't ask me to dance.

So what have you been up to? Howare your parents and Kal/ Kan, just kidding, I mean Kelli? My family is doing pretty good themselves.

So what's going on in school, not to much here in school, even though it's fun with my friends and the things that we do at lunch and stuff. I'll try and call you, as soon as I possibly am aloud to. Do you Know what I mean.

Sorry so Sloppy!

Love,

Kirsten

Bye.........,...............................

October 31, 1980: 1st day Me-n-Ian

November 2, 1980: I haven't written since before 7th grade. I just figured I'm in 8th grade now. Totally having fun, too. I'm going with this guy named Ian. He's 14. Blue eyed, taller than me, and a Babe. His B'day is on October 15, just like mine. He asked me on Halloween. We've been together 2 days now. Right now I'm a rock (music) freak. I love rock. Soft rock, mainly. I like the beach totally. I'm gonna try and write in this thing more often, but no promises will be made. What I really need is a new one of these. At Xmas, I hope I get a new one!

Today Ian called me and asked me to the movies. He had to work until 7, and I need my sleep and had to be back by 8 so we didn't go. It would have been a total make-out session. I hope we go next weekend. Mom thinks he's cute. I didn't think they'd say I could go. I think mom is sick of me saying she's old fashioned. Dad was gonna let me stay until 9, but then decided not because of mom. I'm kind of glad. If I can keep writing up until 1981 I'll be ok, if not, tough shit.

November 3, 1980: Today nothing much went on between me and Ian. He was mad at me for going to the library at lunch instead of staying around him. I talked to him and he said he wasn't mad. One of his friends said he really likes me, a lot. I think he does. For some reason I really think he does. I love him so much. I probably like him more than he likes me. He walked me to my locker and asked me to come over on Sun. I said I don't know where he lives. I'll probably go. I'm totally in love with Ian. I don't really think I've felt for someone the way I have feelings for him.

(*Essay dated November 3, 1980:*)

THE LIFE OF A SWIMMER

Competitive swimming is one of the most agonizing sports anyone could be involved with.

It takes the strength to get up at 4:30am to go lift weights, then put your wet swimsuit from the night before on and jump into a 78 degree pool for one and a half to two hours.

After morning workout, it's eat, get dressed, and off to school. In school, it's six and a half hours of nagging from teachers about the fact you should be listening, not sleeping.

Then the bell rings (by 3:30 you don't ever think it's going to ring) and you're off to the corner to wait for your mom or dad to pick you up so you can make evening workout by 4:00. When you finally reach the pool you're not really in the mood for swimming, but you do it anyway.

At 4:00 it's dryland exercises for fifteen minutes. Then you get your wet suit from the morning on and swim for two to two and a half hours.

By the time you finish all this you aren't even able to put your dry clothes on. After you do it feels great.

Great until you get home and realize you have homework to do from five periods. Before starting on homework, it's dinner and dishes time. After that's done, it's homework until 8:30. At 8:30 you finally decide it's time to hit the sack for 8 wonderful hours of sleep. Wonderful until the alarm wakes you up.

The only time I ever get to sleep in is on weekends, if I'm lucky. If I'm not lucky I usually end up down in San Diego or Los Angeles somewhere for a swim meet.

Being a swimmer takes lots of work. To be the best in the end makes you want to keep on. The best part is, if you succeed well, that morning the coach gives you off.

November 4, 1980: It went a little better at school. Ian walked with me to my locker a couple times. He walked me to math. At lunch we sat across from each other. Then we sat on the bleachers. NOTHING HAPPENED. My friends and his friends were there. He's so super sweet. I was tardy to English because we walked from lunch together. During PE he seemed really sad. After I got dressed, I went and sat by him. I hope he calls me tonight. I'd feel better. I almost started crying because he seemed so down. It seems like we're sharing our feelings, or I am. I go into a trance when we look eye to eye.

November 5, 1980: Things between me and Ian are going pretty good. I didn't get to see him until 4th period. We both flunked our math test. During lunch we sat on the bleachers. I wrote 'Ian is a Babe' and he wrote 'Kirsten is a fox'. Then the next time I saw him was 8th period PE. We played football, not against each other, though. After PE, I got dressed and talked to him. He asked me to the football game. I doubt I'll go. Then the bell rang, we walked to my locker. We left, he put his arm around me. We go to where we go our different ways and kissed good-bye. The game tomorrow will probably mean he won't kiss me then.

November 6, 1980: The day went pretty good. I didn't get to see Ian until 4th per. And he was tardy then so he didn't walk me to class. At lunch it seemed like he was mad at me. He wasn't though. He had a football game today, so I didn't see him. He walked me to my locker then typing. Then he had to leave. And that ended that day with Ian. A week ago he asked me, I mean a week ago from tomorrow. I hope so badly that he will ask me to go to the movies then his house. I'll most definitely go, if I can. I'm so much in love with him.

November 7, 1980: 1 Week; Me-n-Ian. The day went good. Saw Ian most of the day. In math the teacher decided she'd let me pass the test even though I didn't. Me and a friend, and Ian and his friends sat around on the bleachers. No action. During PE, we had free play. Just sat around with a friend and Ian. No action, again. Then the bell rang and I got dressed. Just sat around until the bell rang. Ian and me walked to my locker, then to where we depart. A quick kiss good-bye (this time the kiss was good). We decided to go see the LOVE story "Somewhere In Time" on Sunday. That is if dad will let me. He probably will.

November 9, 1980: Went to the movies with Ian and his friend. His friend didn't stick around long. We saw "Somewhere In Time", a good movie. Ian sure wanders with his hands. All over, almost. We didn't make out. We were holding hands, and he put his arm around me. Ian likes me lots (I think he slightly wanted to kiss me). The only thing is I don't like him that much anymore. I kind of like this other guy. I like Ian a lot. I don't want to hurt him. And things are going good for each other now. I'll see how it goes for a while.

(Second place poem written on November 10, 1980.)

FOREVER...

Within a fantasy somewhere,
Somewhere within me,
there stands a place.
This place is for all good,
the good of love and feeling for another.
For us,
this place stands all alone.
The place for two hearts to meet,
and stay forever bound and tied.
Within a fantasy,
somewhere in time,
we shall meet.
Somewhere in time,
perhaps anywhere time wishes to send our hearts,
our feelings of love.
Those feelings of love,
shared by two hearts,
reaching and touching for each other.
The hearts wanting to feel,
to touch the new experience.
The experience from the joy of love.
My fantasy waits in open arms,
the arms which will hold the dreams
which will appear later in life.
Life is the key word,
for I have forever to fulfill my dreams.

And with forever...
I shall.

November 10, 1980: I broke up with Ian after 2 weeks. It was fun while it lasted and I hurt him bad. My friend told me at the end of the year that he liked me so much. I guess he still did at the end of the year. I didn't even sign his yearbook. I'm still curious. (*Written on the page dated November 10, 1980, but this was likely written at the end of 1981 because of the yearbook reference.*)

[*Ian was the first boy I French kissed. I cannot believe I would not write about that in detail. I remember it vividly, though. The first time he tried it, I had no idea what to do. I was startled and likely overwhelmed by a tongue in my mouth. He had apparently told his friends that I did not know how to kiss, and it got back to me. I was so motivated to prove to him that I was a good kisser once I heard that. I am pretty sure he had no problems Frenching me subsequently! I remember I loved kissing him. I also remember it being more like three weeks, but maybe I want to believe that I could have lasted longer than two weeks! I do not think the poem was about him.*]

The Diary I called Jennifer
(1981-1983)

Somewhere between ending my last diary and starting this new one in 1981, my whole attitude about myself changed. I still loved boys endlessly, but I was also really hard on myself. I wish I could pinpoint the one thing that changed that. This diary has served as a painful reminder of what it was like to be me as a young teenager. For the sake of avoiding too much repetition, the parts that don't add much value to the story have been abbreviated.

Eighth Grade, cont.

1/1/1981: Happy New Year!! Jennifer. Yes, that's what I think I'll call you. That's what I want to name my first (hopefully only) daughter.* This is the second diary I have had. The one was more a soap opera (boring), you know, I never wrote in it. Well, I'm going to change it with this one. Now I really think I'm old enough to remember to write. So this will be an interesting 'soap'. More tomorrow.

[*I had two; neither of them is named Jennifer.]

1/4/1981: The time went by so slowly today. Even when we went shopping. I bought myself a pair of jeans. It's nine o'clock and I'm dead beat. I got into an argument with mom and dad on how a 13 year old should be able to stay up past 9:00, but I'm sure glad (sometimes) that I can't.

1/5/1981: School started back again today. Was it ever boring. Swimming wasn't much better, either. Johnny gave us this speech on the hard workers. I doubt I was included in that. But I have been working out pretty hard lately. He says I'll qualify for the Arizona (*All-Stars*) dual meet. Hope he's right.

1/7/1981: I conned mom into letting me stay home from school on Fri. Johnny made me get out of practice early because I don't sound healthy (I'm not). If Vicks 44 is right I should be over this in, at the most, 3 days.

1/11/1981: The meet's over. Thank god. I did so terrible. For being sick and having the flu I guess I did alright. I'm not sure yet if I qualified for the dual meet...it would mean so much to me to qualify.

1/14/1981: I stayed home from school today. Lucky me. I made cake. Without frosting. I didn't swim but I went because Johnny needed me to fill out some papers...for the Arizona dual meet. I qualified! I'm so happy. Now Thor (*my brother*) doesn't have to go by himself...Mom and I went by the Van's place and I ordered a pair of customs. They're dark blue, turquoise, and light green. They're going to be so neat looking.

1/15/1981: Stayed home again. But today I went swimming. I think I have my first crush of 1981. With Tim. He's 15, tall, blue eyed, blondish-brown hair, and a surfer. The only people who I've admitted it to are Rhoda and Mary. Tim swims on the same team as me. He never in the world would go for me. I'm just too fat and ugly. And everyone knows it. Usually when people are slow, they're pretty, I'm not. And when they're fast, they're ugly, but I'm not fast but slow but still ugly. Get the picture?

1/16/1981: Well, in one week I'll be in Arizona with some family and wondering how my hair will look. Probably gross and yucky. I better bring my curling iron or tons of bobby pins.

1/17/1981: Went to the movies with Betty today. We almost didn't get in, but I knew this guy that worked there so he let us in for free and it ended up a better deal. We didn't meet any guys like she dreamed we would. We followed these totally gorgeous guys for a while but decided they were a bit too old for our <u>extravagant</u> taste.

1/18/1981: ...I ate quite a bit. I feel fat. I hope I didn't gain anything. Mom and I bought a scale. Ha, ha.

1/27/1981: Haven't written because I've been very tired and not home lately. I don't think I ever really liked Tim. Because now I am madly in love with Jimmy. I found that out on the way home from Arizona. I think he kind of likes me – details later. Next week I get to start morning workouts. I want to be good to prove something to dad.

1/29/1981: ...In the past 2 days I flunked 2 math tests. Stuff I don't understand. I've missed 2 workouts in 4 days this week...I really like Jimmy a lot...I want to see him again so bad. I love him.

1/31/1981: Yesterday dad and I went to play racquetball, then mom and I went shopping at the mall. I have eaten so much since yesterday. I hope it doesn't show on the scale when we weigh in on Monday but it shows on our scale. Tough luck for me. But I have until March or April to get down to 130 pounds*. I can hardly wait for Culver City meet. I have got to prove to dad that the $300 gas bills are worth paying for.

[* *The girls had Monday morning weigh-in on the pool deck in front of everyone. Punishment for not making weight was having to swim the workout butterfly in the "fat lane". I never did, though, since my shoulder was already becoming a chronic problem. My saving grace, I suppose; I would have been in that lane every week. Weight was documented in Johnny's green journal together with our workouts, practice times, and meet results. 130 pounds for a strong, athletic girl standing 5'7" is a mind-boggling number to me and something I never quite obtained.*

This was the beginning of a self-destructive compulsion with the scale. My self-value and warped sense of self often dictated by what I weighed. I remember writing my friends notes in eighth grade and giving them updates in bubble letters (sometimes even colored in) of my newly achieved weight. These friends weren't swimmers and probably thought it silly to be so focused on something when I looked just fine to them. Weight is a constant theme throughout these next few years.

Johnny's determination to have us with the lowest possible body fat also meant that we endured the occasional caliper fat test and, even once, a water tank was brought in to more accurately measure our body fat using hydrostatic water weighing. The only bright side for me there was I might have weighed more than most of the other girls, but my body fat percent was not as high as most either. All of this to determine who might be the fittest or fattest without any thought of the psychological repercussions.

Years later when I swam masters for Johnny, we would talk about the impact those weigh-ins had on so many of us. In hindsight, he admitted he was fully aware that the focus on weight was detrimental to many of us. Until writing this memoir, I think I believed I walked away unscathed. But looking back, those weigh-ins and the constant struggle to be the perfect weight so I could swim the perfect swim permeated throughout those years after I walked away, undoubtedly making the struggle to be okay with who I was so much harder. The image in the mirror so often distorted, admittedly, sometimes even to this day. Thankfully, I did not succumb to eating disorders, just mental self-torture.]

2/3/1981: This one kid whose friend I kind of liked called me a few times to talk. But I found when I talked about Scott (the guy I liked) I didn't feel right about it because of Jimmy. I guess I really must like him. But I already know I do.

2/4/1981: Same old routine. Wake up, school, swimming, dinner, sleeping, and what I do most of all, think about Jimmy. I swear when I'm finally beginning to understand something he pops into my head and that's all I do then is think about him. I really must like him a lot if it goes as far as to destroy my concentration.

2/5/1981: Report card day. I got two B's and 5 A's. I should have gotten 6 A's but in Outdoor Living Mr. Brown wouldn't give me an A. I hate brothers! Especially mine. I mean it. Mom and Dad baby him so much. He's their little baby, and I'm the tin soldier who's only thought about when there's time to think about it, and then one day the soldier's gone and they won't really realize how it really was.

2/9/1981: Swimming was ok, even though I didn't feel too hot (still don't). I worked super hard on a 1000 timer. I averaged 1:09s, not too shabby. I felt like puking after I was done. 4 more days until Culver City. I'm supposed to get my period by then. Yuck.

2/13/1981: Today's the day of the Culver City meet. And guess who may be going...Jimmy. When I heard his team was going I totally went hyper. Ask anyone at workout. And what makes it even better is they're supposed to be staying in the same hotel as us...I bought him a Valentine's Day card. It's soooo neat.

2/16/1981: Well, Jenni, he was there! And I love him even more than before. I get to see him in 10 or 11 days. And when that comes he's going to give me his picture. Saturday night I asked Jimmy for his picture and he said he'd give it to me at the next meet. Then on Sunday at the end of the meet we talked for a few minutes about everything (swimming). His coach said Jimmy asked for my phone number. So I gave it to his coach, because his coach asked. Then today he said he charged Jimmy 50 cents for the number. I hope he really wanted my number. I doubt his coach would come up with something like that if he really didn't want it. It seems like everyone finds things out so quickly, like before I knew it everyone knew that I liked him. I sure hope he likes me.

2/18/1981: 8-1/2 more days until I see Jimmy again. And get his picture to show to everyone. They'll all agree he's a total. Even if they don't, I do. I love him…Well in six weeks I have to lose 6 pounds so tomorrow I get serious and stop eating and run more.

2/20/1981: Today is mom's 39th birthday. We plan on going to dinner and having cake. This weekend I have to totally starve myself. I have to lose 6 lbs. in 5 weeks.

2/21/1981: Today we sold our boat and got another one plus $2700. The boat is a ski boat. And this family loves to ski. Mom says as soon as we get use to the boat we can start to invite friends to go with us. She wants to go to the lagoon in 2 weekends. It should be fun if dad doesn't lose his temper too much.

2/22/1981: Just another day. But it didn't go by without at least 100,000 thoughts of Jimmy. I really like him, a lot. He's different from most (all) of the guys I've liked. He's smart, gorgeous, has a great personality, and loves to swim, he's also super sweet.

(*Essay dated February 23, 1981.*)

"It's All For the Best, I Guess"

When I work hard in swimming and my coach finds out that someone beats my best time for an event, it's all nagging. It really can be a pain, especially in the shoulders (which so far I've gone from spasm to pull). My coach thinks now that the ole shoulder is better so whenever I don't make a certain interval, he threatens to make me start the set over.

I think the things that are really hard for me to accept is the fact that I'm the youngest in the senior group (the top group). The oldest and fastest kids are 17 and 18. I just turned 13 in October. Just last week I was voted to be put in the second fastest lane. The intervals in that lane are five to thirty seconds faster than the lane I used to be in.

I really am beginning to finally realize that my coach really thinks I can go far. If I'm willing to work. Now he's beginning not to take my non-sense about not being able to do something. And even though I don't think so right now, I'll remember back when I'm older and have made it that it was the right thing.

What I miss, though, is staying up late, watching TV, having weekends free to be with friends who don't like the things I do, and living a normal life like most other 13-year-olds. But it's all for the best, or will be someday.

2/25/1981: ...You know if he ever read my diary, he'd probably think I was strange or something writing all that I do about him. Last night was the second night in a row that I had dreams about me and him. What's even better is that they were good dreams with things happening between us. Maybe it's a premonition.

2/27/1981: Welp, today was the swim meet. It was a pretty good success. I bettered my times. Jimmy was there. I talked to him. Personally, I think I'm beginning to bug, I think he knows it too. He asked me which picture of him I wanted.

3/1/1981: ...Yesterday at the swim meet Jimmy's coach said something to me: He asked if Jimmy had called me yet. I said no, and Jimmy was right there. Then his coach said, "Jimmy, I gave you her phone #. How come you haven't called her?" Jimmy looked back at me and then he started smiling and started squirting his coach with water. Today went something like this: He couldn't find his picture so he asked for my address and said he would send it to me. He'll probably lose it. I won't be able to see him until JO's in one month. He isn't going to So Cal's. So I'll have to wait until then...It's hard not seeing the guy I love.

3/2/1981: I am really looking forward to going to Germany in the summer. I'll live those couple of weeks without Jimmy. I'll just enjoy it more when I see him. I love him and will forever or until I marry (maybe I'll marry him!).

3/9/1981: I'm thinking of how on Thursday Jimmy is getting pictures back. He probably lost my address and probably won't send it and then he'll probably forget to bring it to JO's. Maybe the kid doesn't like me. Not that he ever did. Everything was probably just a put on before. We'll just have to see in 3 more weeks.

3/12/1981: Tonight we didn't go swimming. I ate. I've got to learn to lose my urges for food. It really is beginning to bug me. I wish I could just stop eating and get down to my expected weight.

3/30/1981: Haven't had much to say. Last weekend was JO's. I did awful. I saw Jimmy a lot. I asked him how come he never talks to me. I took a close-up shot of him. He posed for the picture. I was utterly shocked. He still has my address and said he'll send me his picture as soon as possible. I still love him – more than before.

4/6/1981: …I have Jimmy's picture (not school). I swear I still love him. I love him soooooo much more than any other guy I've ever liked.

4/9/1981: Today was report card day. I got straight A's. All my classes are too easy. I've got to lose 10 lbs. Johnny said I've got to slim down and make 500's consistently on 5:30 before he thinks I'll really and truly be ready for Juniors (Nationals). Well we'll just have to do something about that. "You've got to be slim to win." I wonder if Jimmy is French. I want to marry a Frenchman. I'll be happy if I even marry. If he's not French, I'll marry him anyway.

4/20/1981: I did it! I called Jimmy! I couldn't believe it. But I did it. We talked for about 10 min. At first I didn't think we'd have anything to talk about. But we do. A lot! He likes to water ski. We talked a couple of minutes alone on water skiing. I found out he was born in Taiwan, lived in South Carolina, and has lived here for 7 years. Gosh, it was great! I love him, forever.

4/21/1981: All I thought about was how I called Jimmy. When I tried to explain to someone about our conversation, they just kind of acted bored about it. But I loved it and that's all that matters to me. He sent his picture today so I should be getting it tomorrow.

(*First place short story written on April 27, 1981:*)

"The Sky's Falling Straight On Me"

One day I was just walking along, and I noticed this cat up in a tree. This old lady kept calling, "Louis, Louis, come down from there," but every time she would call "Louis" the cat would snarl and scratch.

Being the dummy I am, I thought I'd be the cute, little, friendly neighborhood boy scout. What a mistake that was. She immediately had mistaken me as your normal New York mugger.

She started screaming and yelling, "Police, police, I'm being mugged. Help, help." I started reaching into my jacket to show her my boy scout badge and she mistakenly thought I was pulling a knife on her. So, then she started hitting me with her purse. I kept trying to tell her I was only thirteen, but she had this crazy idea that I said flirting. She said some words I never even knew grannies knew.

By now Louis was getting antsy that granny was being, so called, harassed. So, Louis made a leap for me and landed smack-dab on top of my head. I instantly fell down and surrendered. But granny was nowhere in sight.

The next thing I knew the cat had scratched me. I saw the blood and fainted. When I was awoken by two police officers, they started asking

31

me all these questions. I tried to explain but granny kept disagreeing. She kept saying, "The guy's got a knife, check him, you'll see." All they found was my identification.

I was soon bandaged up and released. Boy, see if I ever help an old lady with a purse again. On those kinds of days, it just feels like the sky is falling down on you!

4/28/1981: In a month we'll be water skiing for 5 whole days. Alright! I hope nothing goes on in school. I wish Jimmy could go. That would be so hot. He's not going to the meet this weekend. The meet will be fun anyway. Lany and I are going to have a total blast. If no other teams go, we'll probably be seeded super high. Stud, Radical, Love it.

5/10/1981: I realize it's been an eternity since I last wrote. El Centro was really fun. I found out Jimmy was totally going for another, but she's moving. I guess that's lucky, but I want to get him back for that one. Ignore him like I don't like him but admit to other people that I do like him. On Sunday, I'll put my revenge into action.

5/25/1981: Sorry! It's been more than eternity since I last wrote. A lot has been going on. At Pentathlon I saw Jimmy. I tried to ignore him. It was tough, but I did, until the end when I asked him for his picture. I really do still like him. This past weekend was trophy meet. I saw him again. We didn't say anything to each other. It was like we didn't even know each other. I kind of regret it 'cause I want to know him. I won't see him again until August. Tomorrow we leave for 5 days of skiing.

6/6/1981: I've been sooooo busy. We just got back from skiing, then it's been a very hectic week at school. Last night was grad dance. It was ok. I had to dance with this guy I do not like at all but he likes me. I saw this guy I think is cute there with this girl I hate. I could've barfed. Other than that one yucky dance and Erik there with a bitch it was pretty fun. I've been having a lot of dreams about Jimmy lately...We have tests all week, dad's birthday is on Fri. and we leave for Germany Sat.

6/14/1981: We made it (to Germany)...Please help me to watch my weight. 63kg (139 lbs).

6/21/1981: The 1st week. I almost died but made it. It's been so cold here. Been playing quite a bit of tennis. There's this one guy who I played tennis with. Ina (my cousin) says he likes me. I don't like him! Then today there was this 21 yr old who was such a total babe. Then there was this other guy about 17 who's so cute, but dumb me, still stuck on hopeless case, Jimmy. Oh, well, 5 weeks left here then SUN.

6/22/1981: I feel like CRAP. I look it, too. If Jimmy were to see me as I look now he'd probably fall dead in his tracks. I'm so fat and ugly it's no wonder nobody cute likes me, especially Jimmy. If I only had a bit of self-control, instead of 'see a piece of cake, eat it', I wish it could be 'see a piece of cake, SKIP it', then life wouldn't be as it seems.

7/20/1981: Today was the real first day in a week and a half that I worked out. It felt awful. Johnny's going to be so mad at me that I didn't work out that much while I was here. I'd say Lany and Katie and everyone else will be "creaming my ass" when I get back. I plan on working hard until PSA's and after PSA's so that I can make Jrs next year. (*PSA's was the big end of summer long course championship meet.*)

7/21/1981: Today was better with swimming. I think I'll do alright at PSA's. I plan on working hard. I just don't know if I'll be able to keep on interval. Hopefully, I'll be able to. I plan on concentrating more on swimming when we get back. I'm looking forward to swimming hard again. But I'll miss it here.

7/22/1981: Why do I feel so fat? I look it, too. I don't eat breakfast. I must be eating too much in the afternoon. I'll have to watch that. Like just now I had 5 cookies. At least a pound there.

7/29/1981: We've been home since Monday. Boy, it feels good. Even swimming feels pretty good. There's a new guy on our team. I see such a resemblance between Jimmy and him. This guy is older and bigger than Jimmy. I still luv Jimmy (I guess). I'm so confused about who I like.

7/31/1981: Tomorrow I can see Jimmy again. I keep wondering if he's grown those couple of inches from the last time.

8/1/1981: Why isn't anything working out for me? It's so depressing. I used to be such a good swimmer. I used to be cute. What happened? I had the chance to be good, but no matter how hard I try, I die. And I'm not even cute. Jimmy doesn't even look at me anymore (he never did). I wish he'd like me and swimming would go better.

8/16/1981: Sorry I haven't written, but lately I've been so busy but haven't had much to say. I (sort of) met this guy at the CSA meet last weekend. His name is Kirk. I think he's sort of cute. I never noticed him before. Maybe it's because he's "B" in most everything. I hope he's at PSAs. Maybe I could get to know him better. Him or Jimmy. Oh well!

8/19/1981: Today we had HS physicals. Boring. I didn't really meet any people. But I saw a lot of really cute guys (about 5). This year, though, I think I'm gonna concentrate more on school and swimming. I think I may drop guys for a while. I mean I'll still have them as friends but I don't really think that I want to go out with anyone. Not that any guys would want to go out with me anyway. I just really want to concentrate on school and swimming. My goal for swimming is to make Jrs while I'm 14. But in order to do that I have to work really hard. Which I think by now I'm really ready to do just that. I'm really gonna get serious. I think I've just given up Jimmy and all the guys. It's gonna be really hard. But I'm gonna keep it in my head. I hope people won't think of me as unsocial. Maybe I will go to a couple of dances or football games. If someone asks me to go with them. I'M REALLY GONNA GET SERIOUS & NOT FALL IN LOVE OR THINK ABOUT GUYS TOO MUCH.

8/20/1981: I wish there was something I could do around here, other than sit on my fat ass. I hate it. I totally don't have anything to do and I don't have a tan. You think for not having a tan I could at least be earning some money. Well, today we started our taper. I'm glad. But now I've really got to be cautious about my eating. So far I haven't been doing too well. All the scales are so mixed up. One says this, the other says that. Crazy world.

8/21/1981: Today we finally did something that wasn't so boring. First I went swimming and then we went to the beach. I think that was probably the last time for a while. I don't want to get too tired for PSAs.

9/3/1981: I guess I've been pretty busy. PSAs went really great. I bettered every time except 50 free. But Johnny said I'm not a sprinter so I guess that's OK. I think I sort of like someone. But I don't want to like anyone so I won't like him...I don't know about me and guys. Oh well, I guess I'll just see when school starts.

High School – 9th Grade

9/16/1981: I guess it's been a while. Either I've been too lazy or too tired. But I thought I'd get to it this morning before school starts. It's been going really well. Lots of homework, though. There are so many cute guys. But one especially. I doubt he knows I exist. I think he's a junior or senior. I'm swimming high school. It's really a lot of fun. Even though our team isn't too big or good. I'm really enjoying it. The teachers kill you with homework. It's just been the third day. I'm gonna die if PE is always like it was yesterday. We ran a mile. Killer.

[In an ironic twist, I would develop my lifelong love of running from this PE class. I ended up the fastest girl in my PE class and was recruited to

run cross country based on my 6:20 mile time. Contrary to popular belief, swimmers can run! My geography teacher was the cross-country coach. He called me up during the middle of class to talk to me about it. I was so embarrassed!

9/20/1981: All the guys in our school are so cute. Joe (sr) and Chris (soph) are the totalist. I don't like anyone, though. The reason is probably because I'm in love with every cute guy. I saw this guy who I liked in 6th grade. I guess he's gotten a little cuter. I went to a dance last night. It was really a lot of fun. I just danced by myself most of the time.

9/23/1981: ...School getting sort of fun. There are so many cute guys. We have a backward dance coming up. I hope to find someone to ask. Who will say yes.

10/23/1981: ...There's something to Chris that really attracts me. Maybe it's because he's got a really shy personality to him. I love shy guys...we were introduced to each other, but it was a quick thing because he didn't seem too interested. But he smiled and I've hardly ever seen him smile so that made me happy.

11/12/1981: Time sure does fly...Lately, life's been pretty good...we won our second HS swim meet...freshmen football is League champs. They beat Oceanside...Chris just faded out of my mind. I mean I still think he's cute, and his brother is the best looking guy in school...I've been realizing how much I like this guy James. He's a senior. But I really think I like him...I don't think he knows I exist. And we've never met each other. I wish I could meet him and find out what kind of guy he is. He seems like a real passionate guy. But he probably already has a girlfriend. Even if he doesn't he probably likes someone. I'm so negative. I wish I were more positive. Besides who believes in Freshman Senior romances? Me!

11/15/1981: Why is life so, so full of depressing things? But then it's nice another time? I wish I knew. I just wish: (*I would write about my fantasy of Kirsten-n-James forever. He would understand my commitment to my sport. When we kissed it was fireworks like the 4th of July. He did not care that I was only 14, he respected me and did not have any thoughts of sex with me. We went to the movie "Endless Love" and then went back to his house and danced to Journey and Loverboy).* ...wake up from this dream! Well, I guess I can't help myself for dreaming like I do. Maybe at my age, when you want something so bad, like James, you just can't help yourself.

11/17/1981: "Time endears, but cannot fade, the memories that love has made." I don't really quite know what it means by that. I really wish I'd know...I think when I saw it I was thinking about James...I'm really confused by him. I don't know why, because it's not like he talks to me or anything...I kept seeing him sitting next to and talking to this girl...I was totally depressed about it during PE so I was being a total bitch. I don't know I guess whenever I get depressed I have to be alone. It really worries me...Am I just so immature? I don't really think I'm too ugly. Maybe I'm just not what he likes.

"The shadows over me,
the abundant thoughts of you.
I keep wishing they'd be true.
I really think I love you."

11/20/1981: ...I really like (love) him, a lot. But he's different. He's what a lot of people call a stoner. Maybe that's why his eyes are so weird.

11/21/1981: Well today was a swim meet day. CIF Championships. I got a 6th and 8th. I guess I did pretty good. I tried to keep my mind off James, but I found it hard. I really must like him, lots. Actually I know I love him. I just wish he weren't a total stoner - or acts like one. Hopefully he just acts it. Tomorrow I'll get to see good old Jimmy. I really must like Jims' and James'.

12/3/1981: Last week we had a dance. Of course, no one asked me to dance. Like usual. James wasn't there. A lot of people from Oceanside went. There were a few babes there. This guy named Steve was who I wanted to dance with. Someone told him, but this small, chubby chick kept asking him to dance. But I guess she must have been better than me. Personally, I don't know what's wrong with me. Do you?

12/7/1981: I keep wanting to write that I love James. But I wonder, why? I wish he would notice me.

1/1/1982: Happy New Year! Well, it's been a year since I started you. I sure haven't written too much, though. This year I'm writing my resolutions in you. It's private. My secret ambitions. First, I'll start out with reasonable goals and work up to my way-outest dream. OK. First, I'm really going to really watch my weight. I'm gonna try and keep it low so Johnny will be proud of me. I also want my parents and Johnny to be really proud of me with swimming and school. If I do get surgery on my shoulder, which I probably will, I'm really going to push myself to the MAX. I think my SC season isn't gonna be much, but if I work super hard and keep my weight down, I really think I'll have a great LC season. I also want to stop being so depressed about myself. I always feel that I'm really ugly and that nobody likes me. I feel I have no chance with anyone. I'm really going to try and change that. My next to the toughest goal is to write in you more often. I've really been lazy. I've got to get up and do some things. My craziest dream, this dream is forever, is that I could meet Timothy Hutton. I've daydreamed that I wrote him a letter for my 16th birthday and asked him down; he came. But anyway, I hope I have a SUPER GREAT year.

1/5/1982: I found a picture (black/white) of Timothy Hutton in the paper...I'm writing a song for him. The words come easy but to think of how the tune can go is weird. It's about dreaming...I'm so bummed. There's a dance on the 15th or 16th but I can't go because on the 15th I have to get this type of surgery done and I'm supposed to be in pain for a while. Tomorrow we get to start swimming at Carlsbad. It'll be the first time I've been in the water for almost 4 weeks. I need it though. I'm driving myself insane by not swimming.

1/6/1982: We went back to swimming tonight. It felt weird. I talked to Johnny. I may not be swimming SC season. Mom's thinking of taking me to LA to get surgery, which I will probably need.

1/7/1982: Timothy got nominated for some kind of award...Whatever it is he deserves to win...I feel like getting a nose job. I want to get that bump out of there. Maybe if I ever meet Timothy he'll like me as I am.

1/9/1982: ...Today at the mall I had so much fun. We were following these four guys. We followed them for a while, then the guys split into twos. They knew we were following them. So Patty and I followed the two cuties while Sue and Christy followed a cutie and an uggo. The guy we were both attracted to only smiled and looked back. The other guy waved a lot to me and smiled and said hi.

1/11/1982: Tonight at swimming I got a body fat analysis. I have so much fat on me. I have almost more body fat than anyone, only one person had more. But I guess for being out of the water for at least four weeks I was OK. Over NORMAL. Oh well, I guess I've got to work on my bod a BIT more...I had fun when I spent the night at Linda's. Jeff and Chris were there. They're both such cuties. I was about the only one talking to them though.

1/14/1982: Tomorrow I get "opened-up". It's a day off and I get to spend the day in a stupid hospital. Yuck. I found out though that I should be fine after the anesthesia wears off. So hopefully I can go to the dance on Saturday. The dance should be fun. Maybe if I'm able I'll dance with someone...In actuality, I don't like anyone which is hard for anyone to believe, but not me.

1/17/1982: Today I went to the mall with Sue. It was fun. Hardly any cute guys were there. I saw Lany for the first time in a while. She might be coming back to swimming again. Well, my shoulder is doing good on the outside but inside it's all messed up! My shoulder is semi-dislocated with all this tissue pulled off of it. I have to make a decision if I want surgery or not. I don't know.

[I decided not to get surgery. I was told there was no guarantee I would be able to swim again after that since they had to open up the shoulder to perform the surgery. The thought of not swimming again scared me more than the hope a pain free shoulder brought. Flash forward fifteen years and they were able to completely reconstruct my shoulder arthroscopically and it literally changed my life. Swimming without pain was something I had not known since I was twelve.]

1/31/1982: ...I'm really depressed about how I look. I'm embarrassed to be seen at swimming or PE because my legs are really fat and ugly. I wish I could be like I was this summer in Germany. It felt so good for a while when we were there. And now my face has totally broken out so I'm eating a lot to get my frustrations out but that doesn't help. I just keep getting fatter and fatter. I've got to do something about it. I started off by finding a picture of a beautiful girl and putting my head in place of hers. The next weekend I'm going to LA for a day and then to Knott's Berry Farm. It's with the team. Lany's going so it should be fun. In school I sent these three guys a flower. Two of the guys don't know I'm alive so I signed your secret admirer. The other one is a pretty good friend. All three are cuties. I guess in time everything will work out for me. I hope it works out well. Afterall, I do want my daughter to be able to read about all my problems. Hopefully, she won't be like me. I'll feel sorry for her if she is.

2/3/1982: ...This week's been confusing. Some guy named Mike wants to go out with me, but he's not my type. I'm beginning to fall for this guy, I have fallen, that's a pretty good friend. I don't want to ruin our friendship by liking him (Paul) because I like him too much to do that. I just wish we could be really close.

(Letter to Lisa on Holly Hobby stationary dated March 15, 1982:)...I just got over a cold. I only stayed home one day. I couldn't handle staying home. I missed two days of swimming which is worse than school. So I guess you're still alive. We survived the Jupiter effect!...Friday night we

had a dance. Incognito played. They're so bitchen. I have the tape. Have you ever heard of them?...I have another bitchen tape. By the Innocents. They're my favorite group...We probably have different tastes in music though. As soon as I save enough money I'm going to buy Joan Jett's album...We have a backwards dance coming up and I was kind of planning on going. There is only one guy I'd ask. His name is Paul. We're pretty good friends...My friends say he'd say yes. But I don't know. I guess it also depends on who's going and playing. If it's a punk or rock group, I'll go. If it's one of those Boogie Machines or a soul group, I'm not going...So, how old do you have to be to be able to date? I'm suppose to be 16, but I'm trying to talk them into 15, like all my friends, which most of them can date anyway. I'm kind of hoping they'll let me do it this summer too. They already let me go the movies. I bet if I had a boyfriend they would let me go...PS Stoked means happy or glad. Like: I'm so stoked.

7/16/1982: I guess it's been a while. I guess I should inform you on the past and present situations. This thing with Mike turned out weird. He ended up liking Sue and then Bobbie. Bobbie and he are going out. We're friends. Paul and I are friends. Pretty close. Or were. The year finished up pretty good. I got to know this guy that me and my friends were in love with all year long. He's a sweetie. I guess I also made it through finals. My report card read: 4xA and 2xB. They were mostly minuses but that's ok. This summer's been pretty busy. Omi and Maria stayed for six weeks up until July 1. Then we (Thor and I) started Jr. Lifeguards. It's so much fun. There are so many cute lifeguards. Except for the guy that's in charge of my group. But that's ok, I can look at the other guys. I've become pretty good friends with this girl named Jennifer. She's nice. I met this guy at Disneyland. I think I'm forever in love. He was the first guy who ever talked to me first. He's from Canberra, Australia. I'm so bummed that we didn't see each other more. His name is Ernie. I'd say he was about 6 feet, brown hair, brown eyes, and a hot smile. I wish I could go see him, but all I know is his name and where he's from and that he plays on the Australian baseball team. That's why he was here. If I ever see him, who knows what I'll do. I guess I've changed on what kind of guys I like. Blondes aren't as attracting to me as darker heads. Who knows? I've also changed a little on priorities. It seems swimming isn't #1 to me anymore. I could care less. After PSAs I'm taking an extended break to play tennis for school and take more time to learn about myself. Swimming just doesn't matter. I won't quit for good. I need a scholarship. I just think too much is expected of me. Maybe it's me, but

I want time. I kind of want to take a modeling course. Sometimes I really don't think I'm that ugly. Maybe it would help with my confidence.

7/17/1982: Hi! I want to write something, but I don't know how to express myself. I keep trying to forget about Ernie, but Thor keeps bringing it up. He tells everyone, "Can you believe he talked to her first?" The guy just doesn't give me any credit. Doesn't make me feel too good sometimes. I don't know why I'm so hung up on Ernie. I know I'll never see him again in my life. And if he would have thought I was cute or something he probably would have asked for my address or asked me to go on the ride with him. He was probably just being nice. I probably am so hung up because he's the first guy who's ever noticed me or talked to me first. I'm probably just infatuated with him that there will always be a remembrance for him in my heart. I was thinking if I get so attached to someone like Ernie so fast, what's going to happen when I have a boyfriend? I mean am I going to be forever in love and never break-up and never see anyone else, and be hurt when he breaks up? I really hope not. I'm trying hard to forget about Ernie. I never will, though. I'm old enough now to understand my emotions. He took a picture in the Haunted Mansion, maybe I got in it. Then maybe he'll remember me. And how happy he made me, but if he doesn't that's ok, 'cause I'll always remember him for talking to me. [*I have never forgotten that encounter.*] If I ever travel to Australia I'll have to make it an effort to look him up. I'm sure the baseball team of Canberra will know who he is and where he is. "Ernie, you made my life more of a pleasure knowing you exist. And guys do notice me. I hope I see you again. Or marry someone as sweet as you. Forever in love."...It seems lately I've been feeling better about myself. Mom even thinks so. She says I'm not as anti-social anymore. And I don't hide my personality as much anymore. I let my real personality hang out. It gets a little crazy sometimes. But it's me. I'm even beginning to be me on the swim team. I think people like me better that way. Sometimes I'll dislike myself for eating a lot and not caring until I try my pants on. People say I've lost weight. Especially my thighs and legs. I really don't think so. I still weigh quite a lot. But only I know that. I'm even beginning to like my hair. I'm letting it grow out. When I blow dry or let it dry naturally it looks really good. I usually put it back in barrettes. When I go to the beach, though, and it dries it gets frizzy. But that's ok. Sometimes my eyes will even be pretty when I wear the right colors. I'm gonna have the greatest year this next school year. I won't have to take any slack from the seniors because I'm a sophomore. I'm going to try harder in school. I began not to care the end of my frosh year. I cut Algebra once and homeroom a couple of times. This break I'm taking from swimming may do me some good because I'll have more time to study. Mom wants to get me a tutor before school starts so that I can refresh my brain on Algebra and get a head start on Geometry. I don't mind. I want to learn. This school year I'm gonna relax and open up. I want people to know me. The real me. People think I'm super shy. Maybe sometimes, but if you really know me I'm (I think) a pretty fun person. There are only a few people who really know me, though. Sue probably knows me the best. Bobbie probably does, too. But not like Sue. She's such a good friend. Sometimes I think she'd love to get rid of me. Maybe I get too self-conscious. I remember when she was messing around with this guy, Todd, and Bobbie was going out with Mike how much I felt left out. I'd ask if they hated having me around. They always said "no", so did the guys. I never liked Todd from the start, and I knew all he wanted to do is lay her. She didn't think so. Then he told her. She was hurt. I can't really say I felt sorry for her. She called me after he told her. She was crying. I didn't know what to do. We both agreed that she knew it would happen. Todd dropped out of school and went back to his old girlfriend. Now she moved back to Virginia and he called Sue. Says he wants to see her. He's moving to Montana the 20th (she's on restriction then). He says she's the only one who could keep him from moving. She came to her senses, though, and is going to let him move. She's been hurt so many times this year. But she's always been there to help me with my problems and sometimes I really feel bad when I don't call back. I don't want to lose her as a friend. Bobbie is another story. She's a good friend, but she doesn't care about her life. She smokes pot and takes drugs whenever they're available. She used to disappear and come back stoned. She's a character. She's a good friend, though. Mike is a pretty good friend now, too. Sue, Bobbie, and I used to hang around this group of guys. They were cowboys [FFA]. At first they didn't like me. They said I was a surfer chick. I guess they didn't like that. Especially Todd. I guess they got used to me, and then they got sick of Sue being over there. They said she was a hoser (*slut; hooker*). She'd only been on her third guy in that group. Next year I'm going to try and be more open and try not to be too offended by what people think or say of me. That's their problem. Mom said I could even go out to a movie or somewhere with a guy until 10:00 or a dance until it's over. I could always lie and say there was a dance. Who knows? They may change my dating age to 15. I hope so. I'm feeling better about myself, maybe guys will ask me out. I hope so. I've updated enough.

July 17, 1982: "MY DREAM GUY" [*written in highlighter as if it were stamped across the page*]

"Physical Stature"
Two types
Hair – Light brown: dark brown
Eyes- dark brown: dark blue
Natural complexion – med. dark: med. dark
height – 6'-6'3": 6-6'3"
Body – muscles: muscles
Chest – hairy: hairy
Teeth – white: white
Smile – "hot": "hot"
Physique – excellent: excellent

"Personal Stature"
About 3 to 7 years older
Not too protective
fun, smart, SEXY
above average income (eventually)
likes kids and adventure
and most of all LOVES me!
(PS I love English and Australian accents.)

"SECRET AMBITIONS" [*written in highlighter as if it were stamped across the page*]

I guess while I'm at it I might as well also write some of my personal ambitions. 1. I guess that's pretty obvious: I want to marry a gorgeous guy. 2. I've often dreamed of being a model. No one, but no one, knows that I'd love to do that.* 3. Everyone wants me to go to a university**. All I want to do is go to a school of fashion. I'm not beautiful, or pretty, but I'd love to work in fashion. 4. I also have this ambition to live in a big house on the beach or Texas (no one knows that), 5. I want 3 kids: 2 boys and 1 girl. I've even picked names. I'm a dreamer... I love different names. *** 6. My biggest ambition is for me to lead a very happy and successful life, however true or not true my dreams and ambitions are.

[*I cannot read that and think I must have really wanted people to see me as beautiful on the outside; pretty enough to be considered worth photographing;*
**I went to college and got a practical degree in business, which was definitely the right move;*
***I had one boy and two girls. I almost predicted that one right!*]

7/18/1982: Hi! I guess there are certain things that life won't let you forget, or maybe it's me that doesn't want to forget. I'm talking about Ernie. It's like I want myself to remember him. I do. But I don't want to be in love with him. I want to be in love with his memory because he gave me some confidence in myself. It seems I want to hang on like a lover. It comes to my mind again that am I going to try to hang on to someone, if I ever find someone? Eventually, I want someone forever, but now I'd be happy with a summer romance or having a boyfriend, but I don't want him forever. I'll probably be scared to lose that someone, like I'm probably scared to lose the memory of Ernie. I make myself remember him. I'm only in love with the memory. I just wish maybe the memory would take its place somewhere in a warm, meaningful place in my heart. The memory is precious, but how could I be in love? I wish I could be hypnotized and have my "real" feeling investigated into – or meet someone who'll put Ernie in his place.

7/27/1982: I've been pretty busy lately. It's been so much fun. Jennifer is spending the night tomorrow because we're going waterskiing. Yeah! Thursday we're going to Sea World for Jr. Guards and Fri we're going windsurfing with guards. Last Wednesday we had competition in San Clemente. A couple of cuties. That Friday we had Nationals. Oh my God, I've never seen so many cute guys and nice bodies. I'm infatuated with some babe from Carpinteria. Don't know his name, though. No big. It's just a face and bod! Next Fri we have competition here. The "face" won't be there, but Bobby P. will be. He's a cutie. I was thinking about how I want my "first-time" to be. Lately, I've been thinking a lot about sex. I must be at that age, but anyway this is how I want it to be: I want it to be very romantic, passionate, sexy, adventurous, exciting. I don't care if it's love. As long as it's passionate and I feel it's a like-love. I don't want the first time to be sex, maybe unless it's Mr. America, or someone I've admired. To me love, him sex.

(*Included with this entry is a Dear Abby column:*)

Anyone Can 'Have Sex'; 'Making Love is Special'

DEAR ABBY: What is the difference between "having sex" and "making love"? NEEDS TO KNOW

DEAR NEEDS: In "having sex," the name of the game is sexual gratification. It's a selfish exercise, a physical release in which the partner is a faceless object. (Anyone will do.)

In "making love," one is motivated by an overwhelming desire to give pleasure, express affection, communicate one's feelings of caring. It's the ultimate in sharing. In making love, the partner is a very special person. (No one else will do.)

Love is a metropolis. Sex is a whistlestop. Love is an eternal torch. Sex is a sputnik!

8/6/1982: I want to win again so badly. I'm so damn fast, why don't I do anything about it? I was looking at some old medals from almost 3 years ago. I went a 1:06 low in the 100 m (free). Today I do a 1:03 high. When I was 11, I placed better at PSAs than when I was 12, but that's understandable (wrist). I have so many first places and seconds from when I was 10-12. It can't all be from my wrist or shoulder. They hurt me, but I should have been making Jrs last summer. And I don't want to hear that when you're a kid it comes without work. I've worked to be good all my life. I want to prove I can do it AGAIN. I will. I have to lose 15 lbs. or be 130 lbs. whatever first.

8/25/1982: I've been really busy. I've been having fun lately. Competition at Moonlight was a blast. I met a lot of people there. Industry Hills was fun, too. There were so many cute guys there. Momma, was I in heaven! I did so good at PSAs! I have so much confidence about swimming again. I bettered every time by about 3 seconds each. I came pretty close to Jrs. I'm going to make Jrs for sure next year. Right now I'm taking a long, long break. Almost 2 months. It feels good. Sunday night after PSAs we went to a party. I got so wasted. I couldn't believe that  it only took 4 beers. That's never happened before. I made a pretty good fool of myself. But I'm forgetting about that now. I had 3 days of bumming around and shopping before I went camping with Jennifer. I stayed from Thursday morning until this morning (Wednesday). I had so much fun. Jennifer and I had a couple of quarrels, but we worked them out. We were camping with another family. They were so nice. They had 3 boys. David and Paul B. and Steve O. David is 16 and Paul's 12. They're both cuties and funny. Steve is 14, 15 days younger than me. I really started to like him at the end of the trip. I think he sort of liked me. David told Jenn that he talked about me a lot. He didn't try anything, but yesterday he kept rubbing my calves (lucky I shaved) and then on the beach he was sitting super close to me (I think something would have happened then except Jenn was there). Tuesday we all went to the movies. All that happened was our shoulders were touching. That night was weird. We got back around 9 and everyone was around the fire (except adults) talking. Around 11:30 everyone was asleep except Steve and me. We talked until about 12:30 and then I fell asleep. (He said I looked cold so he put his jacket and towel on me). Then he fell asleep. I woke up and asked Jenn if she was coming. She didn't wake up (she fell asleep on Steve's cot). So I went back. And a little later Steve came in. He slept on Jenn's cot that night. You should have seen the look on his dad's face. I'm scared of what everyone thought. He said that when he woke up he couldn't find me so he looked for me. He went to the girl's bathroom and then our tent. He's so sweet. Last night his dad got him really upset. I thought something would happen because of that afternoon. He didn't even look at me. Today all we said was good-bye. I like him. But I'll never see him.

8/26/1982: ...I thought about Steve a lot today. I guess I really do like him. I talked to Jenn today. Steve asked her for my phone #. I bet he doesn't call. She asked him if he likes me. He said what do you think? I really hope the answer is yes. But he didn't call me today. I don't expect him to call me at all. I'll be bummed for a while, maybe I'll get over it. Maybe he'll call me tomorrow. With my luck he'll call when I'm gone...I'll be bummed. Mom leaves 6th for New York (*to play senior US Open*). PS Talked to Lany. All the rumors are lies. She's living in Del Mar. She's still a good friend.

8/30/1982: Hey, how ya doin'? I'm doing great. Steve called me – twice. Once he called me Saturday, before we went to the movies. He said he'd call me back later, but he didn't. I was bummed. But he made it up by calling me last night and saying he was sorry. We talked for about an hour. He said that whenever the song "Vacation" (The GoGo's) comes on the radio or he hears it, it reminds him of me. I told him that the song "Jack and Diane" (John Mellencamp) makes me think of him. He said he'd talk to me later. One of these days I'll find out if he likes me or not. Hopefully he does...I really like him, a lot. But the question is: does he like me?

9/2/1982: Life's been great. Steve calls me every day at least once. And we usually talk at least 2 hours, at the most 4 (usually 2 different times) We went to the movies last night. We saw "Poltergeist". I was so scared. Nothing happened. In a way I'm glad. Today we were both in a good mood. We were kidding around about how we were gonna get married and have kids and stuff. And then he said when we turn 16 we're gonna elope and live on our own island. He's funny. He's leaving tomorrow for Mexico. PS I weigh 135.

High School – 10th Grade

9/21/1982: It's been a while. But, I guess I was pretty depressed about Steve. I guess we kind of don't like each other anymore. When he got back from Mexico, he didn't call me, so I called him. Finally, he called me back. I asked him if he liked me; he said he did. I asked him if he still did. Didn't answer. Today Rhoda (*they went to the same HS*) told him I said hi. The dick didn't even answer. Guess whom I'm in love with again? Paul. I asked him to the backwards dance. Said maybe. Bet he says no. Oh well. Saturday I get to go to a concert. The Motels, plus some. From 10am to 10pm. Bitchin or what? I think mom and dad are changing. I love it. There is this guy at school who looks just like Miles from swim. I think Miles has gotten so good looking. School is such a cruise. Physiology and Geometry? Ouch. The other day I talked to Chris E. I love him like a brother.

9/23/1982: My world is falling down around my head. My friends don't seem to think I matter anymore. Paul said a for pretty sure no. And I'm not going to the concert and I'm fighting with my parents again. I hate life. I wish I could square things away with my so-called friends. They've changed so much. I know I'm the same. Sue's too mature and good for someone like me, and Bobbie has so many other friends. Today they all just left me. The world's a bitch. (*Knife drawing*)

11/19/1982: I guess it's been a while. I've been pretty busy. I've been in and out of love about 20 times this year. Of course, none were in love with me. Their loss. School's been somewhat of a pain. Geometry is killing me. That's my only hard class. I'm still gritting it out with friends. I just don't have that many this year. I hang around Mickey and Becky. Mickey and Becky seem to be better friends than me and Mickey. I really wish that Sue and I were still as good of friends as we used to be. I think we would be if she didn't have guys as the number one thing on her mind. My better friends are in swimming, like Mary. I got Chris K. and Mary together. I guess they're going out. Swimming was tough there for a while. I had a big discussion with Johnny about it. I almost quit because of things people were saying. Now everyone is so nice to me. Not that I mind. Miles got his braces off. He looks so good. I've always had this kind of feeling for him. Only Mary knows. In school I'm so attracted to this guy who kind of looks like Steve from swim, glasses and all. But I don't know his name. I'll find it out. (-Brent)

11/28/1982: So what's new? Not too much here. My life is pretty straightened out again. I'm feeling better. Why can't movie stars be real? Last night we went to see "An Officer and a Gentleman". Best movie I've almost ever seen. Richard Gere is so damn good lookin. Nice body. I really just fell in love with the way he kisses. Just the way I would want someone to kiss me. Exotically and passionately...I would so much love it to be an actress or model and be in my own screenplay. Except for a few extra pounds and a few zits, I really don't think I'm that disgraceful. Up in LA guys noticed me a lot. I've never gotten so many compliments before. The guys were pretty cute, too. I know one day the guys will be running to me. And they're gonna kiss like Richard Gere. Mary said that maybe a reason I don't like guys in HS or they don't like me is different maturity types...When school starts after Xmas I'm changing my image. Hopefully for the better. Let it be known that I'm only doing this for myself. I'm gonna become an all-around better person so I can be more beautiful – to me. That's all that counts. Not to bring a negative subject into a positive convo, but I'm really going to work hard in school and swimming. I've got to get over negative and become me. POSITIVE and POWERFUL. People'll still love me. The inside won't change. If it does, it's for the better.

11/29/1982: Two whole days in a row boring you with my never ending lonely life. Tuff. ...I'm a little overweight right now. Must be because of Thanksgiving. Lord, help me. Today I wasn't thinking about any of the guys there except maybe Paul...Speaking of Paul. What is it I have with him? Ever since the first day of ninth grade I've been so infatuated with that dude. He's really changed, though. He has to impress all his friends by playing stoner. I don't think he's that way. I think I'm giving up on high school dudes. Maybe I should give up all together. No, that wouldn't be too smart. Maybe some college guy will notice me. Maybe he'll act on an impulse and say, "Hey, I'd love to meet that chick." And wallah it would be love. Mary doesn't like the way Richard Gere kisses. She's got Chris to kiss so I doubt it matters to her how RG kisses. I ~~like~~ love it!

12/7/1982: Paul really upsets me. Maybe it's because I still like him. Even though he's changed so much. He's on his 3rd girl this year...This Friday and Saturday I have a swim meet in East LA. All the teams from San Diego are staying in the same hotel. Fun! Too bad our team is the only group of partiers. Oh, well, their loss. The guys from LA have the nicest bodies. The swimmers aren't as nice as the non-swimmers I've met. The swimmers are all on ego trips. Last night I was thinking about Ernie. I fantasized that we meet again in Hawaii. What a fantasy. Me, hah! Miles got a haircut. Damn good lookin'. I was thinking about Tim the other night. I wonder how he is. I heard he has a girlfriend. He was so cute. Penny used to like him. Penny and I are becoming better friends.

12/8/1982: Tomorrow I'm wearing this really neat outfit to school. It's different. I'm looking forward to the meet in LA this weekend. Seven of us are riding up in Katie's Cadillac. Could be quite interesting. Miles will be among that batch, so will Jeff, Mel, Sadie, Katie, Mary, and me. Could be very rowdy. I can't keep this to myself anymore. You're the only one I can tell without having to worry about someone telling. I kind of have a crush on someone. But I can't because he's with my friend. I'd never hurt her and I think they both really like each other, a lot. Well, there's at least a 1,000 fish in the ocean. Hopefully, there's one for me.

12/19/1982: I did pretty good at the meet last weekend. Came close to some best times. I don't know if I'll make that SC cut this year. I hope I do. I think Patrick* is a babe. At the PSA party I told his brother to tell him I loved him…Speaking of parties, I got kind of got wasted off my ass on Friday night. I went to this party in Fallbrook with Mary and Chris. I was drinking rum and coke, wine, beer, and smoking cloves. Buzz city. I scammed (*made out with*) on this guy. I was so numb from the cloves though. On the way home I threw up on Chris's driveway. As Mary says, I "ralphed." She told everyone at the meet. Now they all call me "Ralph". I swam a best time in the 400 IM, though.

[*I lifeguarded with Patrick for several years. I do not remember liking him.]

12/29/1982: It's Christmas vacation and I'm still too lazy to write. So this morning I figured I'd better do something since I didn't go swimming. That blew my 100%. Boy, do I ever have feelings of guilt. My shoulder keeps getting worse with every practice. Only four left in "Hell Week", then it should loosen up. That's why I stayed home this morning. This summer we're going to Germany. Time unknown. I'd love to stay a long time, but with swimming… I'd like to clear some things up about last time we went. I had one of the greatest times. We were almost always busy. I didn't argue much with anyone. And while we were there I lost so much weight, and my face had at the most one zit anywhere. Maybe my skin reacts better to not being in the sun. And their chlorine is probably different in their pools. My face is pretty bad right now, though. I think my weight may be going down just a tad too. My face is bad probably because it's Christmas and my period is just around the corner.

January 1, 1983: Happy New Year! I can't believe another year has gone by. It was a pretty good year. One of my best. But 1983 is going to be even better. Just think I'm getting my driver's license, I'll be an upper classman, I'm gonna be making my Jr. National cut. I'm really looking forward to this year. I'm gonna have a damn good year. I've been thinking about some of my resolutions. First, and probably one of the more important, school. Starting Monday I'm gonna bust my ass in school, especially Physiology and Geometry. Another important one is swimming. Now that "Hell Week" is over and my shoulder is recuperating I'm really looking forward to an excellent season. Jr's short course and a possible Jr's placing long course. My most, most important resolution is to have a great year with my family. I'm really gonna work hard at being part of the family. I want everything to work out with dad and his jobs. I want our whole family to be happy. And as usual, everybody's typical resolutions of losing weight, stopping fingernail biting, overeating, and knuckle cracking (which I do only on occasion). One sad note, Opa died 9 years ago today. I remember when he died. I faked crying. A few months ago I started thinking about him and just cried. I cried myself to sleep that night. I hope Oma lives a long time longer. She's really sick, though. Her heart is bad. I hope doctors put their modern medicine to work and help her pull through. Oma's strong. Enough sad things. I've been thinking about college a lot lately. My first choice is SMU. Maybe because it's a swimming powerhouse. I want to go to school in Texas – or here. Some other schools I'm interested in now are UCLA, Texas Tech, Alabama, or Indiana. Hey, you know what? I feel so much better about myself even though I'm eating a little more than normal. But in a way I think I'm starting to turn into a pretty good looking gal. I'm not saying when guys see me now they're gonna ask me out every second, but there is hope. Hey, have a great new year. I think I will.

1/2/1983: I must be going insane. I want to be an ACTRESS. I do! Very seriously. I think it would be sooooo fun! ...Sometimes I dream about being famous, rich, and sleeping with the best of Hollywood's men, and then marrying one...I want to be beautiful, on the pages of calendars, seducing the minds of men with my physical appearance. I am a dreamer, but hell when you want something, why not dream about it if it's too impoooible to go for it, right?

1/3/1983: First day back at school. Could have been better. Paul looked "hot". Swimming went good. I had a really good set of 400s. I went my best workout time by 6 seconds tonight. We're resting, must be why...Thor is getting damn fast. Beating me... I dream of them writing an article about us being the top brother/sister swimmers ever produced in San Diego...I've also dreamed of me on the front cover. I'd be giving a cute smile with sparkling eyes and wet hair. Everyone would fall in love with me.

1/5/1983: ...My life isn't too interesting right now. I guess my dreams are the only things keeping me going. I swear, I'm such a loner. I hardly have any friends. All I have is Becky and Mickey. You know what I do when they're not there? I go to the library. One thing that I wish would change, is that I would have more than two friends. But other than that life's pretty great...(*I proceed to write a story about me and John Moffet, the future Olympian. He motivated me to swim well, saw I was nervous, made me laugh, watched me make my cuts, fell in love with my personality, kissed me.*)

1/6/1983: Next Friday is our winter formal. Incognito is playing. I want to go so bad. Maybe I should ask someone, not at school, to take me. Maybe Miles will want to. Ha. He'll think I like him. Just as a friend. Honest...(*I then write in great detail about the fantasy I had during practice that day of how I get my scholarship to SMU and about the 280ZX my parents buy me because I got a full-ride.*).

1/11/1983: I've been very, very busy lately. We had a meet Friday, Saturday, and Sunday. I did really good. I went all my best times. I didn't make the Arizona team. I was first alternate twice, and second alternate once. Not too bad. I took off 6 seconds in the 400 IM. Now I'm only 12 seconds off the cut. Last night I was upset at myself. Sometimes I think I let myself down. Today I didn't go to school. I was tired. I'm lagging in school. Physiology and Geometry are getting pretty tough. I had to make cheat notes for this test in Physiology because I didn't feel much like studying. Bad girl. It probably has something to do with me not making the team. My mind is all boggled up. What's really freaking me out is lately I've been having all sorts of dreams about this guy. In all of them he likes me but is going out with my friend. I'm really confused because I don't think I like him for more than a friend. My friend is totally in love with him, but I don't know if he is with her. She doesn't always treat him nice. He's the nicest guy I know. He deserves to be treated only the best. Anyway. Lately I've been trying to come up with some sort of dream to write about. My mind must be really confused right now. I know things I want to dream, like boyfriends...(*I then write about having my boyfriend who runs track at UCLA come to a swim meet and watch me*

50

swim. My teammates are all shocked at how attractive he is when they meet him and they're all jealous. He only had eyes for me.)

1/12/1983: Hi! How ya' doin? I'd be doin great if school wasn't killing me with worry. I think my grade is slipping fast in Physiology. I know NOTHIN'! Tomorrow we have a quiz in Geometry. I haven't been to class in a couple. I don't even understand what is going on. If we don't do anything this weekend I'm going to study. Finals in two weeks. I'd better start studying. Tonight in practice we went one hard set. I went a 400 IM broken at the 50s. I went 13 seconds under the cut. Johnny said that if I could get that down 4 more seconds in practice that I should make my cut. I really want it. Tonight Mary and I went to weights. There were some cute guys there. They're always so nice and talk to you. Friday we don't have school. Mickey, Becky, and I are going to do something. Lisa might come down. I don't have any money. What to do, what to do. And then I've got to try and get studying in. Today Mickey was being weird. She pushed me in the mud twice. Once my leg got grossed out, and the other Chris saw. Mary says she really likes him, but the way she always talks about "jumping (another boy's) bones" makes me wonder how much she really likes him. The winter formal is this weekend. Chris and Mary are going. Of course, I'm not. But what'd I expect? Hey, but I look at it this way: I'm a whole hell of a lot better looking this year than last year. Another thing I've come to the conclusion that Paul used to like me. Just by the way he used to treat me, and how he does now. Sometimes I catch him staring at me. It's nice, I guess. It's sure not the same as when the old Paul used to look at me. But, then again, I'm not the old me, either… We're going back to Germany this summer for 3 weeks…Some German guys are pretty good looking. I wonder if any German guys will notice me this summer…I'm looking forward to being with Oma and Tante Maria. The song from "An Officer and A Gentleman" was just on. I love that song. Every once in a while I think of Richard Gere and the way he kisses. Found out the other day John Moffett is already a freshman at Stanford. We might be going up to LA this weekend, too. I wonder if the guys up there will notice me like they did last time*. (At LA meets the guys don't even take notice.) Lisa asked me once what I had that attracted these guys. She wished she had it. So do I!

[*I'm pretty sure this was in reference to when I went to visit Lisa in Orange County and we went to Knott's Berry Farm. It was weird because boys were paying attention to me that night. I also stole her Levi's jeans because they fit me perfect. I confessed this to her years later.]

1/13/1982: School went better today. The quiz in Geometry wasn't too tough. Lisa isn't coming this weekend. So I'll have time to study...In less than a month we have a big swim meet. Last year it was at Belmont. We stayed at this fully disgusting hotel. I hope this year we stay in a nice hotel like we did the year before in Culver. I kind of hope this meet is in east LA. I like that pool. Besides, I want to have a chance to swim close to some cuts. My shoulder gave me some problems tonight. I was bummin' about it and so was Johnny. The other night when I was crying he told me I was damn good, sometimes I wonder if he ever regrets it. I mean just by the way I swim in practice and stuff. I try to work out hard like Sadie, Katie, and Mary, but all the time they still beat me in practice. Even in IM. But in meets no girls on our team can touch me. The first time since I've been on this team that I've been better than someone. I like it. I'll like it even more when I make my cut and can really be the best one. I would love one year for Johnny to be telling someone like Allie (*younger swimmer who was very fast*) how the fastest IM that came out of his program was me. I've got to push myself if I expect to make it. I've put on a little weight again. This time on my legs. I think I should start running again. Maybe that would help. Couldn't hurt to try. I wish my face would clear up. Make-up usually helps to hide the blemishes. I wish they'd come up with some new kind of drug.* I want to be a model. Last night, during practice, Mary W., out of nowhere, comes out and says that my eyes looked so pretty...On General Hospital there's this total mega babe guy. I keep waiting for the cast to come on afterwards but they never do anymore. This guy is the guy I've always dreamed of. If you looked back at my perfect guy page, his description fits perfectly. Except he's got green eyes, dark brown hair, and an accent. He's what I want to marry. (*The actor was Rick Springfield*.)...There's this coach at school. His name is Jason. He's so cute. He's about 22 or 23. He looks kind of like Superman. He is super though.**

[* *They did. Accutane. I took it my senior year of college.*]
[** *He would stay at that high school long enough to become two of my kids' favorite science teacher.*]

1/17/1983: ...You know that Superman guy I was talking about, Jason? Well, I'm totally in love with him. (*I then write about a fantasy where he picks me up in his RX7, asks me out, kisses me, then I get into some love triangle with a senior, but he was the one and he didn't care if other teachers knew.*)

1/18/1983: Guess who I had for a sub today in Geometry? Jason. I was so shocked and stoked. He's such a cutie. He can be a dick, though...I'm beginning to get bummed about not making Arizona. Especially since they're going to have a western dance one night. I would have had the perfect outfit: my white mini, my boots, and a cute top, plus my bandana. I'd be so cute. I wore it to school Monday. It looked good. A lot of people thought so.

1/23/1983: We had Jason for 3 days as a sub. He's cute, but a dick. To get my mind off Arizona, mom and I went to the movies. We saw "The Man From Snowy River". It was so good. The guy is Tom Burlinson. He was Australian. He talked just like Ernie. I'm going to try and be a foreign exchange student in Australia for next year. I've been wanting to do it for a while, but Sue and Mickey said I shouldn't. But Sue and I are hardly friends, and Mick is moving soon. I'm bummed about that. But I really want to go. I hope it's not too late to sign up. If I go, I just hope that it's in a city where I can swim. Tom Burlinson kisses really gently. His hands are so manly. The way he kisses this girl. Oh, he's just so soft and gentle. I think the movie should have starred me. I still have this dream of being a model or actress. Last night I had this bandana over my nose and a hat on. All you could see was my eyes. I think they're pretty. I had make-up on them, but it still looked good. My face is really breaking out though. I hate it. In three weeks we have Belmont. I'm doing a little better in swimming. Sadie said it looks like I've lost some weight. Not after the way I've been eating this weekend.

1/24/1983: Today was a really good day. I was in such a good mood – until I got home from practice. Mom's been bitchin' at me about my grades. She's always comparing me to her friends' kids, worst off is she's comparing me to Linda. I'm trying so hard in school. I have 2 C's and she's having a shit. Maybe if I didn't swim and have other things on my mind maybe I'd stay home and be the full-on schoolgirl. If I had a boyfriend she'd probably tell me not to see him. My grade dropped in Physiology. That class is damn hard. I have no clue what is going on. I wish I did. Linda is getting a B so mom expects that from me. Linda is a junior and taking the same class as me. A "B" average is pretty good I think. I forgot to check into going to Australia. I really want to go, but someone was saying that I could end up in Brazil. If I go there, I'd tell them I changed my mind...Dad just came in and bitched at me, too. She always runs to him and it's getting me damn pissed. I just want to get away from here. I wish I could go to Australia now, or anywhere to get away from all these damn pressures I have. (*A story about me being an exchange student in Australia follows. I sat next to Tom Burlinson on the plane but didn't know it was him. We had a connection. And then we started dating.)*

[There is a huge gap in writing from this point until May. It's strange to me looking back that I would not have written in detail about this time. The Belmont meet happened, and I was part of an 800 freestyle relay that made the Junior National cut. I PR'd by swimming a 1:54 in the 200 free. We were a fast relay and likely would have made finals at Juniors. I missed making the 400 IM cut by a second. I was pretty crushed. It is the only time I can remember crying in swimming because I was disappointed. I made the decision not to go to Wisconsin for the meet even though I could have done time trials. I did not want my parents to spend that kind of money just for a relay because I knew they did not have it. Johnny was not happy with my decision. I have a nice postcard one of my teammate's sent:

Kirsten, We are having a good time. Mary did super 1000-10:19. Mel did good too. Katie – well she was a little too rested 2:14 200 fly. I swam 200 back 2:16. The pool is so bitchen. I feel good in the water. I hope I do good. I'm going to swim 400 IM today. 800 relay is today. I really wish you were here. We would shred. Too much to say and not enough time. Have to tell ya all about it when I get back. Wish you were here. Thanks for the note. It was inspiring. Oh well. Thanks. See ya later. Miss you. Love, Penny]

(Excerpt from letter to Lisa dated April 11, 1983:) ...Hey gal, how ya doin? I'm starting to feel better. I was down for a while because my best friend down here moved this past weekend. I was bummed. And I'm not a loner, but I don't have many close friends down here. I know a lot but so many of them are on some kick that they belong on the cover of Vogue or Cosmopolitan. I need to get away from this place for a couple of days...We should get together soon. I need to have a laugh and a half again. Maybe my spirits would be lifted up again...We don't have but one semi-cutie here. Oh, Oceanside needs so much help...Lately me and my mom have been talking a lot more than usual about guys and, you guessed it, sex. Me and my friend always were trying to figure out why guys couldn't ask us out. So my mom got into the conversation. Then we always talk, not in depth, about sex and stuff. I always tease her about some stuff. We're getting along really well. We kind of came to the conclusion that high school guys are just too much of an ego trip to look at the finer qualities (ha) in a person. I asked if I could ever go out with someone over 18. She didn't disagree but she thought guys that age might know too much for me. I just can't figure out what my problem is.

I actually think I've gotten better looking. But cie le vie...School is a sore subject right now...I ended the swimming season really good. Actually, I did almost great. I just missed qualifying for Junior Nationals in the 400 IM. I was so bummed. I could be in Milwaukee this week, but no I had to miss it. We're talking bummed but there's always this summer...I think we should get together soon...Luv ya! Luv and friendship, Kissten

5/1/1983: Bet you thought they killed me. Well, they didn't. I've been so busy lately. I didn't think it'd been that long since I last wrote. A lot has been happening in my life since I last wrote. I've had a few swim meets. One I fell in love with this guy named Bill. He's from Arizona. He had dark hair and blue eyes. There was something about him. But I guess the feeling wasn't mutual because he kept looking at Sadie. I just missed making Jrs in the 400 IM. I was so bummed...Dad got a new job. He doesn't live with us during the week. I used to want to move but now things are going pretty good with school and friends. Mickey moved almost a month ago, but I'm still having a lot of fun. Becky and I are getting along really good. And Sue and I are better friends again. And Debbie has sort of taken the place of Mickey when it comes to talking about why guys don't like us. I'm even keeping a B in Geometry. We start cat dissections tomorrow. I hate cats. Mr. Johnson hates me. He's caught me for cheating and separated me and Debbie. Mr. Smith is still good looking. And I don't think he likes Liza either. I feel like starting an "I hate Liza and friends" club. She forced herself on Blake now. Poor guy. At my ten year high school reunion I hope she's there in rags after a divorce and I'm happily married with money and a couple kiddies.* Driver's Ed is so boring. Me and this guy Steve have a good time in there. We always rag on the guy sitting next to me, Vince. I thought I was gonna wet my pants the other day I was laughing so hard. Next year I'm going to have the hardest classes. Pooh. I saw "The Outsiders" with Mickey. I fell in love with two of the guys: C. Thomas Howell and Rob Lowe. The movie was really good. We're going to Germany for 3 weeks on 20th of June.

[* *We both showed up happily married at our ten-year high school reunion.*]

5/24/1983: Maybe I've run into a few things that have kept me from being Miss Writer. Actually, I've just been lazy and busy. Well, I've got a lot to tell you. Especially about this week. But first. I'm so sick of school. There's only 15 more days left. Then we go to Germany. I can hardly wait. The rest is all boring, EXCEPT for this past weekend. Let's just say I learned a lot this weekend. The teacher was Mike D. He knows so much.

I think it was a pretty big scam job. I met him at a party on Saturday night. First, me and Tim (Jr. Guards) were talking because I was going to scam on this guy, Scott. Tim and Scott are best friends and Tim likes Colleen. Me and Tim spied on Colleen and Scott because they magically got together. One time I had to run to the potty with Tim and I saw this guy, Mike, and said hi to him, but ran off. Then I saw him again and said, "Hey, didn't I see you before?" and we ended up talking until around 11:30 when the police cleared the beach. So he walked me to the car and we talked and he kissed me good-bye. He owns an apartment on the beach with his parents. He's from Arcadia and lives up there during the week and down here on weekends and the summer. He's 17, blue eyed, blonde-brown hair, as tall as me, and really nice. At first I thought it was just a major scam job. Then I saw him at the beach Sunday for an hour. We went swimming at his apartment. Then in the jacuzzi things got hot! We kissed an awful lot, but that wasn't the hot part. We'll condense this: his hand went down my suit a couple times. When he kissed me he never stopped grabbing my ass. Then his hand went down the bottom front of my suit. Then he started touching me down there. It felt really nice. Every once in a while I'd explore. I freaked out when he tried to put my hand on his...you know. I did so many stupid things and said so many stupid things, it's been taunting me. But, hey, I know it was a scam job because I think if he was interested he'd of asked me for my phone number, but he said he'd probably see me next weekend, if I went to the harbor beach. I kind of don't want to see him again because of some of the things I said and how I acted. He probably thinks I'm a sleaze, and a total novice, but I tried not to look like a novice. Maybe. Today I was walking home from school and I met these two guys from San Dieguito HS. They weren't too cute but they were funny and pretty nice. One was Walt and I think the other was Mike. He said he'd see me again if I was lucky. I was laughing. I rubbed shoulders with Paul today. No comment from either, though.

5/26/1983: Hi Dearie! I'm mellowing out very quickly and I won't feel like doing that stupid term paper until I'm super mellow. I don't even know how to do one. I'm listening to a totally mellow station because I can't cope with 91X. I've been thinking that I wouldn't even be bummed if I didn't see Mike again. Lori said last summer he was a big scammer. I was another of probably a long string. Well Sunday I'm going to harbor beach and we'll see what happens. On Saturday, I have CIF finals. I only made consolations because I swam like ca-ca. No big. I'm hurting, though. I guess I've kind of had an attitude problem. But the way I'm swimming, who could help it?...Guess who I've been thinking about and looking at a lot lately. Paul. I'm determined by the time I graduate to go out with him or just kiss him*. He's nothing especially good looking but there's something which keeps on attracting me back to him. He drives now. Sue saw him in his black truck. I should say something to him again. But it's been so long. When I go to CIF Saturday there's this guy named Travis going for diving. He is damn good looking. He's got really dark hair and these hot blue eyes. His coach, Jim, whose also an ultra mega hot babe, said he's a spoiled rich delinquent. He goes to Army-Navy. I've been thinking about that a lot lately. Mary knows Jim from when they were younger. He's 23. I think she has a crush on him. He's so lustful. I'm definitely in lust with him. I think of things about him. I have some dreams about him. (*This is a very graphic dream where I actually push him off me when we're down to no clothes. He asks me why I won't "fuck him" and I said "I would only fuck someone I love or really, really like." Then Paul swoops in and rescues me and we finally have that kiss. Then I write about Travis (who I refer to as Connie) who misjudged me for being perceived as too easy, but in reality he really liked me "because I have respect for myself. And a feeling of control over him which keeps him calmed down." But on the side his coach had a thing for me and we were sneaking around. We agreed to part because we didn't want to hurt other people.)*

[*Spoiler Alert: This would not happen.]

5/31/1983: I'm so glad there's only ten days of school left. I have finished my term paper. So all I have left is to study for finals, especially physiology and geometry. I have to get my GPA up or else I can't get my car insurance paid for by dad. You'll never guess who called me today. I never thought he'd ever call me. But Mike called. I was in awe for the five minutes we talked. He asked me if I was going to Erica's party on Friday. As far as I know I am. He said he'd probably be going. I told him to call me Friday night. I really hope Tara goes and maybe I can get a ride with her...On Saturday, I had CIFs. I did pretty good in the 200IM. I was glad. My shoulder's giving me problems again. Sunday night we went to a party. It was really fun. Parents were invited too. I danced with dad once. He dances goofy. Mom leaves for Germany Saturday. I hope she has a safe trip. I can't wait until me and Thor go, too. I'll miss dad and Heiko (*our dog*) a lot. I wonder how things will be with Mike by then. At least when he called today I know he must have been thinking about me...Today I was thinking, if I have a serious boyfriend this summer, I may be ready to lose "it". I was talking to Tara the other day and she said she felt so old doing it at 17. I'm in no rush. Believe me, but I think I can handle it. I'd make sure the guy had protection first, though.

6/5/1983: Hi! This weekend's just been real fun, hah! Saturday we took mom to LAX. She made it to Germany alright. Today I went to the beach with Sue. I saw Mike for about two minutes. The first time I saw him he was halfway down the beach and he didn't see me. Then Sue and I went to get a drink and Mike was walking toward his apartment. He saw me and said hi. We talked for a couple minutes. Sue said more than I did. But, in a way, it seemed kind of like he wasn't interested in talking to her. Now I feel kind of bad because I was rude to him. We didn't even kiss. He wrote me this note saying that he was sorry he missed me and he'd see me on Sunday. I have to go. I'd even come home early as long as I can see him. Because now I've decided I'd like to have a relationship with him. If he'd like to have one with me. In a way it kind of seems like he does because I think he would have kissed me if all he wanted was sex. And I don't think he would have written me that note (on Fish-n-Chips paper). Well, we'll see. We get our yearbooks this week. Then next week we have finals. I have to see Mike these next couple of weekends. I decided that I would start liking guys not just for their looks. Sue agreed.

6/12/1983: Today's dad's 51st birthday. He looks pretty good for a guy his age. He still loves to embarrass me and Thor. Today he took us to the beach. He drove up, honked his horn, got out of the car, and acted all crazy. There were a few people from school there. Mike was there. I stayed with him. At first we just sat on the beach and did nothing. Then we walked down to the jetty. He sat on a rock and I stood up. He kissed me. During one time his cock was out of his shorts. I accidentally hit it but pretended I didn't know what was going on. We kind of just sat there and talked and kissed. I tried to kiss him with some passion, but I couldn't. Then he asked me what I was thinking. I didn't tell him. I told him he'd think I was dumb if I did. I ended up telling him. I told him that he knew so much more than me. He asked with school. Then I said no and you know. We got up, walked on the jetty, and sat down. Kissed and talked. He wasn't roaming as much today. I was pretty thankful. Toward the end though he started going down inside my suit. Then he kissed me and my hand was on his hand so that if he decided to go places I didn't want him to, I could just pull his hand out. He was kissing me all over my chest. And sort of biting and nibbling me. Things went on like that for a bit and then we walked back and he gave me a quickie kiss goodbye and said he'd see me when I get back from Germany. Somehow I could not get very excited about that. I don't think I really like him. Maybe what I said about liking a guy for him and not his looks is going to be a lot harder than I thought. When I was with Mike a few times I was looking at the cute guys with nice bodies all around me. Sometimes I even began wishing I was with one of them instead. When I got home Dad asked me to tell him about Mike. I did. I also told him that I didn't really know if I liked Mike. He said he'll do until I find someone better. I almost fell off my chair. Scott was at the beach today. I'm still kind of bummed I didn't get to scam on him that night. Bobby and Chris were there today, too. I think Bobby is so good looking. I hope I meet some really cute/nice guys this summer who'll ask me out. I'd love it...I'm looking forward to Germany. Finals all week.

6/13/1983: I think I'm going crazy. It seems as though I can't keep my mind off of Bobby. It's strange because sometimes just thinking about Bobby kissing and holding me excites me more than actually doing that with Mike. Mike does it with no feeling. Or maybe he does and I don't. That's probably it, or we both don't mean it, which is probably the best answer. But with Bobby I can see a relationship where we can talk. It's crazy that I all of a sudden start thinking about Bobby that way. I've known him since we were really young. I really like him as a person and his body and looks help. There's something really special about him, but to tell you the truth (not to cut me down), but I don't think I really have a chance with him. Everyone is in love with him and I'm just another admirer. I hope I see him a lot this summer without swarms of girls. And when I get back from Germany I'll get rid of Mike. Today I tried to study for finals. I have like 5 pages of cheat notes. Oh, well, school's almost out and it's kind of sad about the seniors. I think I'll miss Chris to say "hey" to next year.

6/14/1983: Let's just say finals were not very successful today. They probably won't be tomorrow either because I haven't started studying yet. Anyway, Steve has a hot body. Today during that ever so boring practice I just gazed at his body. It's so hot! I want to go out with him. But it wouldn't ever happen because of us seeing each other every day at practice. And we may end up being disappointed in each other...I told Sue that it will never work for me to like a guy without him having looks or me knowing him first...Maybe when I'm older I'll fall in love with someone for them, because I'm not the most desirable person. It's weird because I have such exotic tastes and love good looking men. Mary said I was bizarre. I guess that's a compliment...Tonight at practice, as usual, Johnny and I got into a fight. This was a pretty serious one. He always ends up kissing up to me. We fought about my attitude and the way I'm swimming and my shoulder and it was a very dumb and retarded conversation. If I stay with swimming, like I probably will, I'm going to get Bill. I think there's something really cute about him...I really and truly should go study. I feel bad that I always use cheat notes, but I need good grades. I can't wait to go to Germany.

6/15/1983: I want to go out a lot this summer. I really want to go out with Paul. I don't even know why. It's not because he's super gorgeous or even gorgeous but there's something about him. And I want to find out what it is. We leave for Germany Monday...Maybe the guys in Germany will start being interested in me this year. I'm going to act really relaxed and open so that people will talk to me. Lisa called me today. She is so against drinking. I don't know if I can even talk to her anymore. It seems like the only people I can talk to are Debbie and Sue. I can talk to each one of them for different things. Debbie's good to talk to about why guys don't like us and she's a really super fun person. Sue is good to talk to about sex and stuff. We always have fun little conversations about that. Debbie and Sue are my best friends. I hope this summer we can become better and closer friends...I can't even get into swimming anymore. All I think about is how fun my summer's going to be. It'll be fun with swimming too. And I guess if I think about it, making Jrs would make this summer complete.

6/16/1983: I am now officially a junior. The school year as a sophomore is over. It's been such an excellent year. I made a lot of new friends and I think I've gotten kind of cute. I want to cry because the seniors are going/gone. Blake. He looked so excellent tonight. Would I ever love to go out with him. Even if he wanted to take me to bed I'd probably let him. There's something about him. Maybe I could change him...I have this feeling that by the time I graduate me and Paul will have gone out (at least on a date). But you'll never know about it. There's this song by The Innocents called "Wild at Fifteen". I've decided to use that as this summer's theme song. I'm going to have such an awesome summer. Of course, guys are going to be a major part. Or so I hope. I hope I can start it off by scamming on someone in Germany. I hope guys there won't think I'm too bad looking. I hope guys here won't think badly of me and that they'll ask me out. I have to find out where Blake goes to the beach and take it from there. I'm coming to the conclusion of my first real diary. I know it wasn't too interesting, but I'm hoping my next one will have more "love" in it. I love you. Love, Kirsten

The Horse Diary
(1983-1985)

The summer before Junior year

6/18/1983: Today's the second day of summer vacation. I slept most of today. Too tired from swimming. The stupid sport! I don't even know why I do it. Must be the scholarship. Last night I kissed up to Johnny. The jerk. Oh well. I don't need to see his face for three weeks. I'll miss Steve's ultra mega body, but I can cope. I keep thinking about him. Maybe I like him. But swimmer-swimmer, on the same team relationships never work it seems. But I don't really think Steve will ever like me. But actually I do think guys are noticing me more. Which makes me feel a little better about myself. Lisa came over today for a little while. It seems like she's changed. She seems kind of stuck up lately. She acts like she's the 'cool cat' and Oceanside's not the place to be. I admit I am not one of those people to wear 'I love Oceanside' shirts or stickers but I don't cut it down even if I don't like it either. Monday we leave for Germany. I'm really excited. This is bad, but what I really want is to meet some guy that I can mess around with. I think I'll play dumb/seductive/flirt Kirsten but whatever it takes. I like to mess around but I don't know much about it.

6/23/1983: Our first couple of days in Germany have been pretty hectic. The sun's been shining for us. Maybe I'll want to live here when I'm older.* My German is terrible right now. This trip is going to go by too fast. Oma isn't doing too well, but I think she'll be alright. This weekend Thor and I are going windsurfing with the swim team and this other swim team. I hope we don't feel too out of place. I guess I'm kind of shy toward those things. Today we went to Hannover to watch the German Nationals (I didn't get to swim after all). There were a lot of good looking (extremely white) guys there. Personally, I think the guys here are better looking than our guys. None of the guys here are noticing me. I've gotten the 'once over' a couple of times, but I don't know what it means here. Probably get away. And all of the cute guys from tennis are on vacation. So there's no one especially cute to see…So far Thor and I have been terrible with swimming. I really want to get serious again. After watching Nationals today it kind of made me realize how I felt about swimming again. I wish I could swim under Mr. Faltus (*German coach*). Their swim team is more fun. Ours is just too serious.

[*I did for two years after I graduated from college.*]

6/24/1983: I finished my first swim workout in a while. An  accomplishment. I can't come back out of shape or else I will really be bummed. Today we went to the Bagger See (*a local lake*). It was fun. We just got back from ice cream. I saw a lot of cute clothes and shoes. I wish I could just ask for money, but I don't. And mom limits what I get. I want to come home with some new types of clothes that aren't so common by us…We're going to Berlin. I'm less afraid of travelling through East Germany than most Germans. When I'm older I kind of want to marry a German. Do the opposite of mom. I haven't seen Stephen from tennis yet. I'm still in love with him from those three times I saw him two years ago. He's who I want to marry. If he's only about 23 then there's only 8 or 9 years between us. If he can wait. I have a sort of fantasy. (*I write about having graduated high school and going to Germany that summer after having had a successful nationals back at home. I meet Stephen at the tennis courts where he takes an interest in me. We go on a date. Didn't go great because I wasn't easy. He apologizes. We go out again and become inseparable. He asked me to marry him at 19 and said he'd wait until I was done with college.*) Tomorrow we're going windsurfing. Fun!

6/28/1983: Camping was more fun than I expected it to be. Of course, I ended up in love with someone. It's weird because I ended up liking Knut first – I thought he was pretty excellent looking, especially his eyes. He was really shy and didn't say much to me. Then last night we all were drinking pretty much. I was very buzzed. I scammed on this guy named

Ulf. He was really cute, but acted like he knew everything. But he didn't use his hands as much as I thought he would. He did kiss really good, though. I hate myself for doing that because the whole time I was thinking about Lutz. Out of Knut and Ulf he was the lesser attractive but I wanted to be with him. Not especially kissing him but just talking to him like I did most of the afternoon. He had a really excellent body. His eyes were hazel. He had an overbite, but he was the nicest guy there. During the day yesterday I told him what scam was. And Thor called me a scammer. I got really mad. Then I went and really scammed on Ulf. In front of everyone. Thor got really sick and was puking up everywhere. I was worried so I stood outside and waited for Thor to come back with Kai. Lutz was outside. I asked him what example meant or was in German. He told me and asked me why. I told him that an excellent example of a scam job was that night. I didn't want him to think of me that way, but I didn't want him to think that I liked Ulf. I didn't want to go today. I just wanted to sit and talk to him. I cried good-bye. I think they thought I was doing it because I was leaving Britta. Little did they know those tears came when I looked in Lutz's eyes. His birthday is September 4. I'm supposed to write his sister. I'll make sure that I say something about him. He taught me this word – geil. It's an extreme like for someone. Ich geil Lutz! In two years, if I get to see him again, he'll probably be in the German army. I told Britta that I really liked him. Maybe he'll say something to her, but then again I'll probably end up never seeing him again. But I won't forget him even though I only saw him a couple of days. We laughed so much on that trip. Erni (*Britta's brother*) is so funny. We camped with the swimmers from Oldenburg. I don't want to go swimming tonight or ever. Ich habe keine Lust dazu (I have no desire to). But I have to. Inside I do want to make Jrs so bad. I wish I could swim here in Germany. It's not all so damn serious. I want to live here when I'm older. So many guys looked at me (my bathing suit) this weekend. But Britta said guys here just don't look at you for your looks and body. A change from us. I like that! Thursday we're leaving for Manon's (*my cousin*). Wednesday we're going to Berlin for two days. Then we're going home with many thoughts of Lutz and how stupid I was to scam on Ulf and not talk to Lutz instead. In two weeks, we'll be back home. I miss dad (and Heike) but I don't want to go back even though it's about 85 degrees instead of 60 degrees. Well, now I have to go workout with Mr. Faltus.

6/29/1983: We're back to typical German weather, but I'm not complaining this time because I like it. I seriously do want to live here when I'm older. I think I would really like it. I could marry Lutz and we could have cute little kids. Sounds good, but I'm never going to see him again anyways, so I don't know why I'm even thinking that. Maybe next summer he'll want to come out to California and he can stay at our house and I'll drive us all around. Who knows if I'll still be swimming at the rate I'm going. My shoulder is giving me mega problems. It hurts so bad. I hope Johnny entered me in the Irvine meet then I can swim very rested. And if I happen to make Jrs I'll probably fall on my face. I might just take the summer off anyway. I wonder if Johnny would take me back in the fall. Probably not. I think mom and dad could probably pay for college for me. Then I could work on improving myself so that I'm happy with it…We go home two weeks from today.

7/3/1983: Manon's was really boring, except for the first day. Me and Manon hit it off right away. They had their cousin Jo (Joachim) there. He was so good looking. In lust. That night we all went to a disco. I sweat so much. I supposedly danced with him all night, but he moved all around so much. We got back and Marc, Jo, and I looked at cars. I sat between them. My and Jo's legs were very together. Then we were all laughing because I tried to tell those two what scammer meant. Jo said he's never done it. He acts like a playboy. Oh well I'm still in love with Lutz. Manon is supposed to be coming to us in October for three months. Yesterday, I shaved all the hair off my legs.* I seriously think I'm going to take a mega long break from swimming. My shoulder's giving me too many problems. I can't cope with it anymore, either. And I promise myself not to get fat. Today I saw Stephen. He's gotten skinny and butt ugly. I was totally disappointed. I also saw Thomas today. He looked pretty hot! He speaks really good English.

[*As swimmers, we weren't supposed to shave our legs because it created extra resistance in the water. We only shaved a few times a year for big meets. Doing this was a huge statement on my part.]

7/5/1983: We were at Britta's all day long. It was pretty fun. I saw pictures of Lutz from two years ago. He looked so young. I guess he didn't say anything to Britta about liking me because she didn't say anything. I really like him. Tonight I'll make up some kind of dream with him. Seems like dreamers never get what they dream about. I don't know why I'm so verliebt (in love) with Lutz. There's nothing special about him except his body. BUT his personality and he's so nice. I don't want to leave Germany (not just because of Lutz). I'd like to swim for a year under Mr. Faltus. Tomorrow we're going to Berlin. I hope it's fun.

7/9/1983: Berlin was pretty fun! There are so
many different kinds of people there. I've never
seen so many punkers in my life. Some looked
cool and some looked questionable. We did a lot of
sightseeing. It was cool when we went to the wall.
The wall's so terrible. Seeing it makes you want
to cry. The East German guards were cool. We
waved to them and they waved back. They looked
at girls through their binoculars. They almost
fought over the binoculars. It was so cute. Then

we saw these two Russian soldiers who were guarding this thing. We
waved to them. They couldn't move around like the East, but they'd lift
their hand up a little and then they saluted us. Then I waved goodbye
and they saluted us again. It's so sad that all the countries have to be
separated. All the people over there seem like they're so nice. They can't
all be happy over there. So many people have tried to escape from there.
Some of the ways they tried to escape, some were weird and some didn't
work. They showed that and that was so sad. When I'm married and have
kids, when they're old enough, I'm going there again and going to show
them. It's too fascinating to ever let anyone pass up. I wish everyone in
the world could be together. I wish we could have gone into East
Germany. I'm going to have to tell Mr. Smith that those "no good stinko
commies" aren't really that way. That they're cool and super friendly.
Some of their ways may be cruel, but they seem so neat. We did so much
walking around. Berlin is a really neat place. It's such a fascinating and
interesting city. I want to go back in two years. For my graduation
present I want a trip to New York, London, Paris, Rome, Berlin, and
Nienburg (*my mom's hometown*). Just a couple of days with each, except
Nienburg. I'm so confused with swimming right now. I don't want to
swim the rest of this summer. I want to have a summer that I can look
back on when I'm older. The teens are supposed to be the important
years. And I do want mine to be more than swimming. I know I can make
a comeback with swimming if I break now. I'll be more determined and
motivated. My shoulder isn't a cop-out. It really hurts and sometimes the
pain is unbearable. I'm going to make something out of my life. Bis
nächstes Mal (*until next time*).

[*I would be living in Germany in 1989 when the wall fell. I was in Berlin
with friends celebrating a few days after it happened. So surreal. I have
been several times since. It's hard to even imagine anymore that it was
divided and so many lives impacted.*]

9/1/1983: I realize nächstes Mal has been a long while. I wish I could tell you that I've had such a busy summer, that I haven't had time to write, but I'd be lying if I did. I wanted to be able to look back on this summer. The only part I even want to remember is Germany. I don't want to ever forget that. I had the best time I have ever had over there. I didn't want to leave. I really felt like I had friends (boys and girls) over there. Unlike here. I want to go back soon. I wonder if I can wait two more years. Maybe once I get over Lutz and Jo I'll be able to get over the craving of wanting to go back so bad. But it wasn't just them, it was how all the guys over there treated me: with respect. I miss Germany. Lately, I have been so negative about myself. I chopped my hair and I sort of regret it. My face is complete acne. It was so clear in Germany. Sue has forgotten me as a friend. I don't have many friends at all. I'm worried that when school starts I won't have anyone to hang around. I want to hang around Becky and Debbie, but I don't think the feeling is mutual. I want to hang out with Sue, too. I wish she wasn't a friend. I hate what she does to me, but I still want her to be my friend. We have fun together. We really do. But she's too interested in guys and getting laid. Why do I get all the friends who screw me over? The only friends I've had who haven't really screwed me over are Lisa and Mickey. Both who live far away. Mickey is coming back to California. Supposedly this weekend. I hope so much that she goes to school at EC. That's doubtful. Tomorrow I'm going to try and change my self-image. Tonight I start exercising. Oh, I hope I have the best school year ever. I especially hope I have friends. Real friends and lots.

High School – Junior Year

[9/22/1983: *While I do not write for almost two months in my diary, I did write a couple of poems that might give some perspective on my mindset at that time:*]

WHY DO I LIKE THEE?

Why do I like thee, Paul E?
You know and hate me.
I often wonder why
I never have enough nerve to say hi.
Why? Why?
You seem like such a fun loving guy.
The kind of guy I'd want to get to know.
To be your friend, and more, as the
relationship would grow.

66

We could have such fun
Go to weird places,
be ourselves,
laugh at the world,
and grow together as one.
Why do I like thee, Paul E?
It seems to me that you were made PERFECTLY!

INSIDE

Look inside,
do not be afraid of what you might find.
Look inside,
and turn the key.
Open the door and set yourself free.
Turn on the light switch,
see the light.
Daylight is now lit as well as night.
Do not hide behind this door
Keep it open and explore
Look for what's right and wrong
Look for the things that move life along.
If one must hide he has not set
himself free.
If one is not free,
he cannot be what he wants to be!

10/30/1983: It has been quite a while. This time I can honestly say I have been having a pretty good time. My summer ended pretty fun. Lisa came down for a few days and we had a really good time. Mickey didn't show. She won't for another year. We still write all the time. The first six weeks of school went really well. But I can already feel my grades beginning to slip. My classes are hard! And as for friends, I'm really content. I do have a lot more people that I'm close to. Especially Debbie. We're practically best friends. Sue is even around sometimes. But now it's not that I'm the tagalong, she is. Her boyfriend is 24. We'll see how long this is going to last. I got my license a couple of weeks ago. It makes it so much easier to call someone up and say let's go somewhere. Last night Debbie and I went to her friend Sue's in Vista. We went out drinking. I wasn't even buzzed because I had to drive. But Debbie got so wasted. She was really bummed over this guy. So she had to drink out her depression. I would have, too, but driving and all. I was pretty depressed last week. You know

I don't think I'll ever get over Lutz. I've never ever (not even Paul) felt this way about anyone. It's pretty crazy and stupid because I'll probably never see him again. I wrote him a letter yesterday. The first love letter I've ever written. I want to be with him so bad. I'm seriously thinking of going back to Germany next year. Not just because of Lutz but because I like it there so much better. I wrote Tante Ruth (*my aunt*) and asked her how much she'd charge for me to come live with them the first semester of my senior year. And go to school there. I'd work all summer before and then fly back. The way I feel is that I want to spend the rest of my life there. I'll miss my family a lot but I love Germany. I guess I'd have to find something (Lutz) that I really loved to keep me there. I have another fantasy to tell. But first let me tell you about sports. Tennis has gone really good and ends next week.* I've started to sort of get back in the water. I'm glad I am because I really am longing for it. I guess once a swimmer always a swimmer. (*So the fantasy is an excerpt on how I thought I wanted my life to look: Lutz and I are in love. We married when I was 20 and I went to some fashion school there and then started my own business. We had a beautiful German wedding followed by a honeymoon that involved me doing the Ironman and winning it. Finish line caption was "Happy Bride". Grew my business even bigger through franchising. Kids not in the picture for a few years.*)

[*My mom was a tennis pro, so we played tennis whether we wanted to or not. I was actually pretty decent, so it was easy for me to jump in and play that fall in high school. And I had a ton of fun doing it.*]

10/31/1983 (Halloween): Two days in a row – must be a miracle. I have gained so much weight these past few days. Must be Halloween. I was feeling good for a while. It's weird that with not swimming I haven't lost any weight. I haven't been eating as much and I don't look as big but maybe getting back in the water will help me. My face looks bad. When I see my derm next week I hope she finally agrees to put me on Accutane. I hate having acne! I wrote a really pretty poem today. About love and oceans and stars. I like it.

OF LOVE AND OCEANS

Love is deeper than any ocean
and brighter than any shining star
It tranquilizes you like a crashing wave
and enhances you like the shimmering moon
It entices you to go farther than the flowing current
and moves you like the setting sun

It can give you a chill like the water's breeze
and warms you like a powerful ray
It can pull you under and take you away,
leave you stranded, or show the way
It can pull you to the heaven's for a night,
take your hand, and show you that all is alright
It can be like a tidal wave, hitting so strong,
but often so unright
It can hurt you and leave you damaged for life
It may give you the feeling you may never come back
But it may be a bad dream teaching you a thing or two
you may need to know
Love can also be an eclipse
Leaving you lonely, but longing for more
Leaving you desperate,
and then feeling you don't care
It can make you feel so secure
and yet empty for reasons unknown
Like the waves and the heavens above
Love is but a mystery known only to a unique few
Unlike me and you
We wait for our first to share
Love is perfect,
but unlike Aphrodite, not all can possess its
power and passion
Love is like a calm ocean wave crashing on the rock,
sincere yet powerful
Love is like the farthest star
Suspended by gravity, never knowing when it will end
Love is a beauty possessed by all
It's a fact that all must see,
even me.

(Dedicated to Lutz. Because I know things will work out for us, because I think I love him. I know our love will work.)

I never told you, I started writing a book. So far it's 6 chapters. I haven't written in over a month. I go through stages. Well, I'm tired. See you in hopefully a short time. I love Lutz.

11/1/1983: Three days in a row – must be a record. One of my favorite songs on the radio is "Promises, Promises" by Naked Eyes. One of the only mellow songs I like. It sounds like my life story though. I want to get away from Oceanside so bad. Dad thinks I don't love him. The tension in this house is strong. If it were based on a rubber band it would have snapped by now. Sometimes I want to see a psychiatrist just to know that I'm alright. I do wonder. Not as much now as I used to. Maybe it's just that time of year to feel the pressures. Dad's been with his new job a while and hasn't made a sale yet. You know he's so damn concerned with changing our lives from how his was, but I can't help but think he kind of wants us to have it that way. So our kids will feel sorry for us, too. I don't know about this family. I love them all so much. Just sometimes I need to be alone to think and cry and I'm not a lovey-dovey daughter so I wish that would stop them thinking I don't love them just because I can't give them a kiss or hug every five seconds. Like Thor. He's the affectionate one. Dad would never have an idea of Thor even disliking him. He doesn't and neither do I. I just don't understand how he can feel like he does. I've been losing my concentration for the past couple of weeks. They came up so fast – the pressures. I wish they'd go away. I like life, I wish it would be normal again. Love (if you believe me), K.

THE RABBIT

The rabbit, it spins in his cage
My mind, it follows in rage
The poor rabbit he does not know
of the freedoms life can show
For he is caged and lonely
Locked inside and looking homely
Man can be cruel, to say the least
Look at the rabbit, the poor little beast
But when the rabbit is free, he runs from destruction
Man stalks his path for his abduction
On the roadside we can see the result of man's technology
In the mountains they are taken from their hibernation
And used by man in his quest for damnation
The rabbit, though small he may be
Is a valuable creature to society
He shows what man is doing
Killing the world without our knowing
I see the rabbit spinning
I open the cage and send him running

My mind it follows him, now he's free
Even if it's just a short eternity.

11/2/1983: Yes, I do need help. My head hurts and my life is spinning! Why can't it be perfect or maybe even the life of a plain Jane, but no it can't be, because Kirsten Hegberg's life was not meant to be full of daisies or roses. You know how I'm feeling right now? I feel like taking Accutane, going on a pretty strict diet, exercising my cellulite off, and just caring about myself and getting good (great) grades in school. I don't even care about impressing anyone, just myself. I know it sounds ignorant and pretty damn stuck up, but I don't care. I want to work on me. I don't want to have my head spinning from worries/pressures. I want to know I'm worth something to myself. I don't care if anyone tells me I am. I have to believe it myself first, and then, maybe just then, I'll believe others. I just want my life to be a little different. No competitive sports, no user friends (I only have one), no family quarrels. I just want to live my life my way. I really don't want to quit swimming because I love to do it. And I probably do now more than I have in a while. I just have to get back into it. This is how I would start to change my life. Seriously. My diet would consist of mostly fruits and vegetables plus diet drinks. I'd cut out sugar completely and rarely ever eat meat. I'd eat less than 1500 calories a day going down to 1000. And I'd exercise my butt off because I love to work out. I'd run at least two miles almost every day. I'd go to the gym every day and ride the bike, plus do at least an hour of aerobics. I'd totally take care of my skin and hair. And I'd work on having almost perfect measurements. This all probably could happen, except mom and dad would be awfully heartbroken if I quit swimming. Unless I got 4.0s and I can only prove that twice a year. So there goes that idea. I'd love to do aerobics. And I like to run, and love to cycle. And of course, swim. You know I'd really like to be a triathlete. And I'm such a competitive person that it would be a challenge to me to be good at something besides swimming and sometimes even tennis. Maybe I should be a body builder. Except sometimes I like my body and don't want to make it any bigger or bulkier. I wish I could just come out and tell mom and dad how I feel. But I know they'd be disappointed in me. Lutz should be getting my letter soon. Oh, no! Last night I had a dream about him. About the letter. He kissed me. A kiss you could feel. I hope I work out these problems.

11/4/1983: I'm so tired but thought maybe I should keep up the good writing habits. Today Lutz should have gotten my letter. I feel like calling him and telling him not to hate me, but not much good that would do. Well, tennis is over for the year. I'd be playing league except I have a doctor's appointment Monday that I don't want to miss. It'll probably be another disappointing doctor's visit.* I wish she'd just see my face and see what I'm going through. I'm not an ugly girl and I don't think I deserve to be going through what I am. I know, sounds pretty ignorant. Oh, well. I'm going to try and cut down the calories this weekend and jack up the exercise. I do need it. This dead person needs her sleep. So I'll be seeing you soon. Maybe there's hope.

(*It was very disappointing. She put a giant needle in a zit and gave me an antibiotic for the acne. No dream Accutane.)

11/6/1983: Let all be warned Kirsten is back. I think she's finally out of her state of depression. Since yesterday she feels good again. Inside that is. She feels like her old self, outside she looks the same, except she wears a smile again. She still has severe acne and is still a few pounds overweight. But maybe those things will start to deteriorate too. You know what also popped into my head today? Sex. I went to play tennis with Debbie and the guy she likes. It was fun(ny). He made me begin to think about sex again. I don't have any clue as to why, but he did. And I was just thinking, yes I do love Lutz, but if he's going to be my first I do think I have quite a long wait. So I don't think I'm going to wait. It may just happen that an opportunity may not come up until I'm with Lutz, if he doesn't hate me, but if it comes up before then and I like the guy I may just take the opportunity. I wrote Mickey tonight. It was five pages. More or less a story of how my first time would be. It was pretty good. I thought. This weekend was pretty good. I think I'm finally coming out to the old me again and I'm glad. You know what is mean or selfish, I'd like for a guy who's seeing a friend of mine, to make a pass at me. It would make me feel good even though it's mean to my friends. I guess sometimes you've got to think what you want. Tomorrow I start to swim serious again. It's hard to believe that I've been out of the water since the middle of June. That's exactly five months. It doesn't seem that long. I'm kind of glad I'm going back. Maybe I'll shed a few pounds. I have this feeling things are going to get better. I really do. I'm even getting along better with dad. Mom leaves on Tuesday for Arizona for a week. We'll see just how well we get along. Well tomorrow we have morning workout so I'd better get to sleep. I'm feeling so much better.

11/7/1983: [I can remember writing this poem imagining what it would have been like to have someone who checked all the boxes, didn't judge me, and loved me for me. But I also knew I couldn't pretend forever even back then.]

DAVID

I have a friend who does not exist
He takes me places when I wish
He's perfect in every aspect
and treats me with much respect
His experience shows in his touch
His eyes show that he cares so much
The power in his hands,
it intrigues me
Leaving me weary,
and my world is seen unclearly
You have a name I like to call you
It's so plain but it will have to do
David...That's the name
but you're not as plain as the name may claim
You're gorgeous,
quite handsome in fact
Your eyes show me that you're not an act
You're the first who's ever cared,
said you loved me, and always shared
But David you do not exist
for you're too perfect for all of this
My imagination it always works, but my David is
all mine to keep, to love forever and is
there when I need to speak
I feel sorry for the rest,
they've never seen me at my best
Unlike you David,
I keep it all for you
And if you never come to me
I must find someone else to spend eternity
My mind it plays with my friend,
but in time I must grow up,
and only then will my friend David ever end.

11/12/1983: I'm trying to think of what I did all week so that I'll have an excuse for not writing. I guess over all I was just pretty tired. Lutz's letter hasn't come yet, if at all. I have this feeling he's going to write back even if it's to tell me he hates me. I think that would be pretty cool if we did get married...I've started swimming seriously again. Am I ever tired....I'm bailing in school right now. I'm trying to do better again, but it's so hard. My "A" in chemistry is already down to a B⁻. I just haven't been too enthused about doing homework or studying for tests. Mom gets home from Arizona tonight. We all got along here pretty good with the exception of the first night. Dad and I got into a gnarly fight over stupid things like usual. I wonder if I'll be going to Germany next year. I really would love to go, except that I'd miss it here. I really would.

11/13/1983: ...I think mom feels sorry for me because I don't have a lot of friends. And I don't have many. Really just Debbie and Sue that I can hang around. I wish I had more. I'm really a friendly and outgoing person. I even talk to a lot of people, but it's like I don't know them enough to hang around them. I like the few friends that I have now. Sue's even getting better. But I guess I do wish I had more friends to mess around with on weekends and stuff. Manon comes next Sunday. Maybe I won't be so bored on weekends. You know what I really want to do is triathlons. I think if I practiced enough for them that I would be pretty damn good. I like being in shape.

11/14/1983: Just a quick 'hi' before I go and try to write a speech on older women-younger men relationships. I'm all for it. I didn't go to practice tonight. But I ran two miles. I wish I had a perfect body. But I don't and there's not much I can do about that...Tomorrow night is our tennis banquet. It's free food. I hope it doesn't last too late...I'm beginning to doubt that Lutz is going to write. I'm beginning to get this idea of how he may really feel about me, but what can I do?

11/27/1983: To tell you the truth I don't know what I've been doing since I last wrote this. Let's see: I got most inspirational in tennis. Manon came. Thor had a birthday. I lost 2 pounds, and I quit swimming. I guess that sums it up pretty good. I quit swimming forever (except high school) last Wednesday. I think it was for the best. I want to work, but dad won't let me. So for now I guess I'll just do homework and workout. Manon and I are going to start on an exercise routine. Actually we already have and my body is feeling it. But if that's what it takes to have a perfect body then I guess it's worth it. Tomorrow Manon and I are going to see "All the Right Moves" with Tom Cruise. I told Debbie I think he is the perfect one. He fits my description of the perfect male in every way.

11/28/1983: I'm so tired. School's exhausting. Like I figured I bailed almost all of those tests we took last week. Out of the 5 A's I had I now only have 2. If I had my choice I'd drop chemistry and just write. I would love to be an accomplished writer.

[*On November 28, 1983, Debbie and I would begin a 'friendship journal' that consisted of a binder and a string of topics we would write to each other about during the school day. We would hand off the binder to the other and respond to a topic or start a new one. We called it "Dee and Deb" (My brother always called me Dee and it just flowed better with Deb.). Those conversations were so relevant to that time period. Because this is my story and for the sake of Deb's privacy, I will keep our conversations relevant to how I was feeling. There are, however, some conversations that just deserve to be recorded. Labelled DD. I am K. She is D.*]

K: How do you mean good – in bed or as a person? I bet (boy's name) is wild in bed. I want mine to be older, too. You know this sounds bad, but I'd go right to bed with Tom Cruise or someone famous or incredibly good looking. God, Debbie, I'm ready. I want to laugh out loud.

D: I think he would be wild too! Doesn't he look like he would be radically awesome in bed? It's like some climatic org_ _ _! I just want to totally attack him next time I see him. Yes, that's what I am going to do. I am going to jump his bones.

DD 11/29/1983-
K: OK, OK, let's pretend that you royally jump his bones, without preparation (i.e. safety) and you kind of like skip <u>something</u> and you kind of gain <u>some</u> weight. To put it bluntly, you get pregnant. What are you going to do?

D: Have his baby, what do you think I would do about it? I would make him face the responsibility (which, deep down, I know he wouldn't). No, seriously, you know I would never do that (jump him) without seriously thinking about it or maybe discussing it with someone, probably you. But the desire for him is so strong. I don't know what to do!

K: Skip him (if you want!). There are so many guys out there who would probably love to go out with you. And if they did get you pregnant (because something failed) they'd stay with you. Sometimes I wish I had a baby. Someone just for me to love. If I had a kid now I'd name the girl Tierra Milan and boy Zachary Lee (after my dad, even though he'd kill me if I got pregnant). Sometimes I wish I didn't have to go to college... How do you feel?

D: I want to go to college...The ultimate dream (right now in my life) is for me to go away to college and he goes with me...I really like this guy. Why is he such a nobody? He has no ambition. So why?

K: ...As for him having no ambition, who cares if he does, as long as you love him and are happy?

D: Sorry dude, it matters a lot if he has no ambition. I can't have some immature, insecure asshole in my life. Someone who doesn't want to achieve anything in life.

DD 11/30/1983-

K: ...I haven't felt strongly about anyone in about a year, probably longer (no, about a year). That time I said I love Lutz, I lust for Lutz. I could probably love, but that time I was in the I love Lutz craze, I was so upset with my life in general, that knowing I love someone far away helped. Pretty stupid reason, hah? I know. But I haven't liked, really, anyone since then. I've messed around, but that's okay. I can't wait forever. But, Deb, I'm really ready to devote myself to one special guy and love him, be his friend, and make passionate and suspenseful love to him. I always think about the perfect traits for a guy: Personality, caring, friendship. If a guy isn't the best looking thing in the world, if he has those characteristics almost nothing will keep me from falling in love with him...I think I've done a lot of growing and a lot of my values have changed. I think I've developed a more caring and understanding personality. And now I think I can go into any kind of relationship without always being so self-conscious of what other people think. If a person opts to be around me, then I opt to share with them things about me. Like I'm doing now. I hate to say this because I am still a little reluctant of a super closeness with someone, but you're the person I open up to most. Maybe it's because I think we're so much alike, although we're so different.

D: ...I totally understand what you said about "getting too close." We have a very cool friendship. I don't think either of us feels obligated to hang around each other or call the other. It's hard to try to hold back in a friendship when the closeness, the caring, the trusting (and all the other things that makes up a friendship) is so strong. I know that sounds kind of "weird" but when there is a good friendship you shouldn't deny it...In other words, just because we have both been burned by people we shouldn't just stop having friends.

K: I don't know what got me on the friendship bit. I know I don't owe anyone anything in return. But I'm sure glad that I have the friends that I do, even though I don't have tons.

D: ...I know I have some very close friends who will always be there. You see I would rather have a lot of friends that I share different parts of me with...I used to expect to know people 'like a book' but not anymore. I just accept them for what they are while also accepting that they will share what they want with me.

K: You talk about no one knowing you. No one knows me. There are certain new things I always learn about myself. Things I don't share with anyone, not even my diary (and that's my best friend). Some things I'm too proud of or ashamed to tell even my diary. I tell it about sex, my feelings, my friends...As for having a lot of friends, it's not important to me, because the friends I have now understand me in all the ways I think I need to be understood.

DD 12/1/1983-

K: In Nov. issue of Cosmo there is an article on casual sex. So, Debbie, how do you feel about it? I don't think I could cope with someone not knowing your name while he's _ _ _ _ _ _ _ you.

D: Actually I wouldn't mind having casual sex just my first time...

K: So you want to be broken in by means of casual sex? I didn't laugh, because that's how a lot of people feel. As for me, well I want someone who cares for me to be the first time. Someone who knows my name and respects me for being what I am. And won't hate me because I'm terrible in bed the first time...My mom has been commenting on how bitchy I can be and how sensitive I've been lately. I don't know what it is. Sometimes I wish I could go to a psychiatrist and be put under and find out what this emotion is that will block me from being affectionate. I should ask her again.

12/5/1983: I didn't know growing up would have to be so hard. I didn't know that by quitting swimming my parents would take it out on me for the rest of my life. I can't handle them anymore, or anything they do. All they do is accuse me of things and it hurts me. All I am now is an object. A look-alike of something they used to love when she was something, when she did more with her life. Well, fuck them. I hate what they're doing. It's not fair. It's not fair that I have to be ugly. This whole life isn't fair. The only things keeping me sane anymore are my friends. And my parents could never believe that because they think I'm an unsensitive, uncaring little beast. That's the last thing I am. My God I love them, but why do they have to do this to me? I want so much to share my love with someone. Someone who understands every part of me. Someone who doesn't love me for what I was or should have been but for what I really am. They'll never understand that. And I know for the rest of my life I'm never going to hear the end of the first real decision I ever made on my own. I know what I want from my life. I see it more perfectly than anything else. Even loving someone. Sometimes I'm beginning to doubt that anyone one is going to be able to love and respect me for what I am and want to be. Especially them. But my life won't mean much without their support. It's almost hard to believe I said that. They've hurt me so bad. They probably look at it as repaying me for the hurt I've caused them. They'll never know how sorry I am, because it probably ruined any chance for this abnormal child to have any normal relationship with her parents. But she did it on her own. When I turned this page, I saw how lonely and blank these pages look. But they get filled with my words, unlike my heart which is probably never going to know the true meaning of love because it's been scarred by the things she cares most about and I don't know if I'll be able to mend that scar because scars don't mend, do they? I'm gushing tears right now. I can't help it. I'm so sad. I'm so glad that I have Debbie and Sue as friends. The two people in this whole world who even vaguely understand this mistake. I don't want to kill myself. I want to prove to those who think I'm a failure/disaster that I can do it with or without them. Scars are lifelong. I hope mine go away. They hurt.

DD 12/6/1983-

K: Last night I cried myself to sleep. I couldn't handle it anymore. I wrote about five pages in my diary and there are tear drops or should I say tear stains. Debbie, my parents are treating me like an object, not a daughter. I swear I'm going to have scars because of the hurt. They're taking everything out on me because I did something on my own. The first real big decision I made on my own and they're going to blame me for it for the rest of my life. Everything I say to my parents is, "I don't care." And most of the time, I don't. Sometimes I think the only people keeping me sane are my friends...Maybe the reason I'm becoming "weird" as you put it is because everything else outside of my school life is so mixed up and hard for me to understand...I'm so glad we have a minimum day. I was going to cut and go to the beach and watch the ocean and its freedom and right to live its own life and make its decisions...I think I need a psychiatrist.

D:...I can relate to what you are going through with your parents or maybe I should say "understand." Maybe it will go on for a while. Maybe it will stop tomorrow. It's not good to hold it in though.

DD 12/8/1983-

K:...As for my virginity, I'm mixed on it. I'm proud that I haven't just jumped into bed with a guy. But I'm not too proud of the fact that I haven't really had the opportunity, or should we say I haven't been seriously propositioned. Maybe you don't understand but I do. It's personal, I guess.

D: I do understand because I feel exactly the same way. It's cool that we agree on things like that.

K: I think I'm fooling myself by saying that I don't care if I have a boyfriend because I think I would really like to have one. You know, I want to work so hard on having the perfect body. Not necessarily some skinny-winny body. I could never have that. But I've been caught in the body beautiful trap. And I would love to have a beautifully built body...The doctor told me to take aspirin for my feet and knees to help stop the pain. Maybe I should just avoid the pain aspect and kill myself physically until I'm happy with my body...I wish the scars left on my face from that really bad acne that stuck out would go away. In the summer it's not so bad because people look more at the body and not so much the face...I feel like getting totally drunk and then puking. I always feel good the next day after I've puked...I have this obsession about wanting and dreaming about things I'll never have. I need to know that a lot of what I'm feeling is normal.

DD 12/9/1983-

D: Kirst, what is your "honest" opinion on o_ _ _ s_ _? (*oral sex*)

K: It sounds gross! BUT after reading some of those eroticas I feel different. I know this sounds kind of rude but it seems like it would be very, very stimulating! Even reading some of those it was. Personally, I think the guy's got the grossest part, but the girl's wouldn't be so bad. How do you feel?

D: Well it sounds gross and "dirty". BUT I agree it does sound stimulating and penetrating. But I think the girl has the grossest part. Think about it. The girl has the big thing in her mouth and all of a sudden he starts to (you know what). And you swallow it! But the guy doesn't have to swallow it. In actuality I don't think it is that gross. I really think I would rather be the stimulatee instead of the stimulator. What about you?

K: So you tell the guy to 'get out' if he starts to cum in your mouth. Anyway you could just spit it out.

D: Well I really don't know about what we talk about sometimes. I am ashamed. I guess it's just natural though. I mean we are curious. We are 16. (Oh my gosh almost women).

DD 12/13/1983-

K: I practically have a one track mind. But what's the world without a few of those? I think it would be pretty unpopulated! Anyway...I have this feeling that our turn will be coming soon for having boyfriends and sex. I seriously doubt they'd go to our school, but we'd meet them somehow. And I think by the end of next summer I won't be a virgin.

(*several exchanges on test we failed, teachers irritating us, Christmas presents,...*)

K: "Let me be your stranger, hold you to the light. Don't even change if you try. Everybody runnin' round loose in the world. Let me take a piece of your life. Somethin' in everyone, everyone everywhere...nothing like they say, here comes the night...Everybody talkin' in the pale moonlight wouldn't change if you tried. You light the sky with your standin' there. See all the clouds roll by...It's nothin' but heaven here. Here comes the night..." I LOVE that song. It's by The Innocents. They also sing this song "Hold My Hand." I get in this almost tranquilized mood every time I hear it...91X is driving me crazy...Now they play a cool song – "Girls, they wanna have fun." Yeah, I can totally relate to that.

DD 12/14/1983-
D: You look so intense with those eroticas. Have fun!

K: Those eroticas kill me – so does March. He was very incredible looking. We should make-up some totally erotic erotica and send it to Playgirl.

DD 12/15/1983-
K:...All I can really say is that I don't have a part in me that I haven't shared (except my virginity) in total intimacy with a person. Mike and I got pretty intimate. As far as you could go without losing "something". So as far as sharing something locked-up the only part I've never given out is my virginity.

12/15/1983: Ten days have gone by since the ordeal with mom and dad. It's not even really that clear to me anymore, but I guess it's better for me not to remember. But things are going better (knock on wood) now than they were before. I'm even trying now not to get so upset about things. But every day now when I come home my mood changes from good to bad pronto. I don't know what it is. I've been so moody. Must be something wrong with me mentally. One of the prettiest songs is on now. Mellow, but it's beautiful. It's called "Born Again." "Come show me your kindness, in your arms I know I'll find it. Don't you know with you I'm born again?" It's beautiful! I can't wait for the day I'm lying safe within his arms. I long for the security of a boyfriend. But I guess I have to keep longing until I shape-up. I'm going to work on it during vacation. Just to break even with all the calories I take in. Tomorrow's the last day of school. I don't think anyone knows how happy I am about that. Two weeks won't even be enough time! I guess I just have to make the best of it...I hope/plan to go out and get wasted a couple of times. Just for fun. I want to take my pressures out in the bottle. I sound like an alcoholic. I'm not.

12/19/1983: Well after last night's "bawl" session, I finally got mom and dad to see that maybe I really do need a psychiatrist. So they're looking into it. I poured tears and sobbed for about an hour last night. Something is really disturbing me and I don't know what it is. I want to find out so bad. It's when I walk in this house or am near it, the slightest little thing and I blow up. At nothing even. Just so I can yell. I don't know what's making me act the way I am. I don't! It's not an excuse for my actions. By no means. And I am definitely not possessed. I honestly don't know what it is...All my friends have boyfriends or guys to like. I don't. I don't fit in. All I do is dream and write poems about Tom Cruise.

"MR. CRUISE"

The cloud it has been said
Has a silver lining to which it is wed
And the actor, it is known
Works hard so he'll become renown
As for me, it has been seen
I write it on paper to say what I mean
So for you I write what I wish to say
Knowing our paths will never cross the same way
You are constantly moving
Having your own life and doing the choosing
I stay at home and do what they say
Wishing at times to run away
You do not have to dream
Unlike me who would cease to exist by any other means
Now, I have these feelings I'd like to express
Not knowing where they're coming from I should regress
But something special does exist
Some feelings that have no real reason to persist
But persist they do
And if I didn't know better I'd say I was falling in love with you
But it's hard to be in love
When all you have is a picture above
My favorite words I like to say are "Incredibly intriguing"
And they describe you perfectly, up to this very day
Your smile, it destroys me
melts my heart, and leaves me lonely
I wish I could see
what you were like in actuality
To see your eyes close up
Would leave me flying up
But wish to see you I do not
To disappoint you I want not
For myself I think not highly
A man's idea of perfect I am very unlikely
Let it be said my thoughts flow freely
For when I think of you my eyes do glee
My spirit is opened up, and set free
Just thinking of you makes me me
And if one day we shall meet
I ask thee not to weep

Feelings I have, too
Though our meeting is very unlikely,
I ask not to be hurt by you
Good luck in the future with your dreams
My thoughts will not cease to exist,
for happiness for all I do wish
Good-bye to you, Mr. Cruise
For in my eyes you will never lose.

I'm obsessed. I don't want to be. Not even. It's stupid for me to dream about someone I can never have, let alone know. Maybe he's my way out. Sometimes I wish he wasn't a person. Someone who didn't exist. Then I could be obsessed and not feel guilty about my dreams and poems. I want so much to have someone real to dream about. Someone real to hold me. I'm sick of always fantasizing. Always hearing about other people's love lives. They come to me for advice. But what do I now? The other night at Debbie's we talked for three hours about sex. Pretty pathetic, hah? Sex starved teenagers...Maybe if I accomplished something I was really proud of I would feel better about myself in general. But I don't even know if it's myself that's destroying me. One day I'll find an answer.

12/21/1983: I miss Mickey. I talked with her tonight. Mom and Dad will probably kill me when they see the bill, but it won't be the first time. Mickey said she's been having depression problems. And that she's seen a psychiatrist. But I'm not depressed. And I haven't been for a while. I just can't explain what's going on. I really don't know. I want so bad to have someone unlock the mystery. The one I wrote about in mom and dad's poem that I'm giving them for Christmas.

ODE TO MOM AND DAD

It's hard for me to express
When it comes to sentimental stuff I tend to regress
Not your faults, not by any means
No matter what it seems
You raised an individual
Something out of the everyday visual
I love the freedom I have
And ask of you to respect it, too
But this is not an apology for my faults
But a Christmas present, for of material things
I have emptied my vaults
"The daughter with the champagne taste"

I know it should go to better things, I shouldn't waste
But I love to spend and spend I tend
But to write I love even more
And maybe someday this daughter of yours will score
She'll hit the big times and ring the crystal chimes
You say I owe you nothing, it's all because you care
but one day, I promise you, I'll learn to share
My emotions, I tend to hide
Nothing against you, I don't like to confide
To the world I remain a mystery
But through your eyes they'll be able to write the unabridged history
Still I share not all with you
I lock up a lot and throw out the key
From inside my window, I see you search in vain for the key to the
hidden mystery
I express myself best on paper
No emotions (not that many), my life to you remains but a caper
Through acne and blemished skin
There exists almost no possible way to win
If it's a consolation for you to know
The love I feel I really cannot show
The picture-perfect daughter I will never be
Not even if given an eternity
You thought the terrible two's ended at two
Quite the contrary, bet you found this to be true
The only true way I know to express myself is on white lined sheets
Not eye to eye or with a hug
So for Christmas Nineteen Hundred and Eighty Three
I express my gift by what God has given me naturally
Dad, Mom sorry to have caused such a fuss
But I know I must be special, or you would have sent me out long ago
on a Greyhound bus
Merry Christmas and a Happy New Year, too
Love you both, I surely do!

It doesn't seem like Christmas to me. Not this year. I want it to be special. But it doesn't seem the same. Maybe because of me. Maybe because of Manon. I never want to have a sister. I could never have handled having a sister. I'm too selfish. I know it! There's something else bothering me, too. I don't think that it has anything to do with how I'm feeling/acting. But anyway…This obsession with Tom Cruise is becoming such an obsession. It's very unexplainable. There should be no reason for it. But I see him as the perfect male. His personality. His eyes. He's not gorgeous – but something really intrigues me. I get jealous when someone mentions him being cute. Jealousy over someone I don't know – imagine that. But now it's more than just him. Now it's the idea of knowing someone famous. Someone well-known. I wonder if it's normal for sex-starve teenaged girls to dream about what they never can have. But you see inside of me I believe that maybe someday I really will be making love to someone renown and he'll love me, too. Oh what I dream and what will happen in reality are going to be so different. But I don't want them to be. Why can't they happen that way? Why can't I make it happen? Just one of my fantasies – just once. Maybe if I were more beautiful. One day. Maybe? If only you could talk. Only you could know me. But what could you do?

12/22/1983: There really isn't much for me to say. Sure I could go on about Tom Cruise, my feelings and emotions. But I don't really want to. Today I went shopping with mom for a couple of hours. The whole time I just felt like crying. On the way home I just started to cry. I really don't know why. Maybe it's because this year Christmas just doesn't seem like X-Mas. Like I said I'm pretty melodramatic today, so until next time. Love and kisses.

12/24/1983: 'Twas the night before Christmas, and all the through the house not a creature was stirring not even a mouse..." And so the story goes on. And we all know what happens. Anyway it is the night before Christmas and everyone is awake and well. We just got back from the annual open house. It just doesn't seem like it this year. Oh, me no know! We went to the gym (again) today. There's this guy there (named Stacy). He's a marine and instructs aerobics on certain days. I'm falling for him. His body is perfect. He's incredibly intriguing, too. I wish I were older and knew how to flirt. I'm terrible at it! But I would love so much to get to know him. He seems nice, but in a sense 'I know I have a hot body' type. I've never talked to him so I don't know. I hope we have a GREAT Christmas.

12/25/1983: I don't like Christmas. I mean I'm glad Jesus was born, but I wish there wasn't a holiday like it. Or maybe just this year. With how my life has been and all. It took me five minutes to tear the wrapping paper off all the presents and then stack them neatly. I knew every single thing I was getting. I was more surprised with the stuff in my stocking.

Howdy All!

I can hardly believe that it's already Christmas again!
Alot has happened in my life sice last Christmas. It is so
amazing where all the time goes!

Anyway...let me begin by seeing if I can fill you all in
on what has been happening in my life lately.

As of little more than two months ago I got my driver's
liscence. The world hasn't been the same in a long while.
Anyway I haven't had any accidents as of yet and don't plan
on having any in the near future.

Now that I'm driving it means I go anywhere utterly possible.
Mom and Dad don't like the idea of me being so independent too
much. But,hey,what can they do?

School is an entirely different story. I can hardly wait
until June 1985! Graduation! Then it's off to college. I'll
probably be going to UC Los Angeles or UC San Diego. But anyway that's a long ways away. And until then I have to suffer
through Algebra and Chemistry. But I guess in order for me to
have any hope of making it as a writer/director/producer I have
to know how to balance chemical equations and such. Yuck!!!!
As long as I can pretend to know the subjects good enough.

You're all probably wondering about my swimming. Well
there isn't much to wonder about, because I quit the world of
competitive swimming forever. Alot had to do with personal
reasons and then the other reasons were because of bodily injury.
I think the doctor's are going to classify me as a teenage
cripple. I want to do triathons.Yes, I know I'm crippled.
But until they stick me in a wheel chair nothing, except swimming,
will stop me.

Well, I guess I've filled you all in on
just about everything(except on my love life,
but that does not exist). Now I'll wish you
all a Merry Christmas and an EXCELLENT New Year!
Hope to hear from you all soon.

Love and Friendship,

Kirsten

MERRY CHRISTMAS!
HAPPY NEW YEAR!!!!

*[I was definitely ahead of my time back then. I wrote a Christmas letter
to my friends with an update on my life. Note: I still write Christmas
letters.]*

It took me twice as long to open that than it did for me to look at everything else. Even then I knew half of the stuff in my stocking. I got one piece of school clothing. A turtleneck. Oh, yea, I got two pairs of underwear and a pair of gloves that might count. I got two pairs of nice shoes and a pair of tennies for tennis, too. Other than that I got little things. And $25 from Grandma and Grandpa. Mom cried when she read my present. I know I shouldn't have given it to them. Neither of them said it was a good poem until I asked them. I <u>was</u> so proud of that poem. But I guess not. I'm crying right now. I hope no one walks into my room. I don't feel like talking. And if mom or dad walks in they're going to ask me what I expected. I expected nothing this year. I didn't even want a Christmas this year. Mom will start to cry if she sees me. Why can't I be happy or even content? I hate being so damn selfish.

1/1/1984: Happy New Year! I do truly hope that this year goes better than last. Although last year wasn't that bad. I just hope that this year things will work out between me and my parents. I want so much to have a close family. They don't believe it and I can't show it. Today dad confirmed that I am going to go see a shrink. I'm glad. I need it. These past few days have been better. Except today there was some tension. I just hope that this will be an excellent year. My secret resolution is to lose some weight. Actually that's basically it. Except doing well in school.

1/2/1984: Tomorrow is yucky school. Oh, how I dread going back. I want to see my friends again, though. And my classes aren't so bad, except chemistry. I loathe that class. I can honestly say chemistry is a major reason I can't cope with school. I simply hate it. I wish mom and dad would understand that. I don't see what good it will do me. Pointless. Simply pointless. Today was the first day that I looked in the mirror and said, "Hey, you look good." That is the face. I'm really pretty happy with how I've been looking. Except that I've gained a lot of weight. I've already said that I'd like to lose 20 pounds. That's a lot, I know. But I think if I cut down and did a serious exercise program, I might just come close. I think things may all work out. Maybe seeing a podiatrist, nutritionist, and psycho may help me. Today we saw Stacy more than just at the gym, but McD's too. He's so incredible. I could fall for him, except his rolled up Levi's have to go. I told Manon that he didn't seem super stuck-up (seem because neither of us have ever talked to him). She thought he was probably not shy when you get to know him. That he was like any other guy, sex first, relationship second. I told her I'd write when I found out. I really want to. Maybe I should make a resolution not to dream about relationships with guys I've never spoken to or have a chance with. No more Tom Cruise. No Stacy to start the year off. Just looking and wanting, but no dreaming. I wish I were confident enough to flirt. There are so many guys I could flirt with. But I'm not confident enough yet in my outward appearance to just flirt with a cute guy. Besides I don't know the first thing about it. I think I'm going to be very caring of me and my body this year. Work for perfection. How cool! But I'd also like to work things out with my family.

DD 1/3/1984 –

K: Happy New Year to you, too! I really hope that this year will be an excellent one. Looking back on last year it was a big year in learning and growing. It wasn't so bad with school and friends. Actually that was pretty cool. The biggest problems came in the family. And those were most major by the end of '83. I really want to have things work out with me and my family. I can honestly say I want that more than anything right now. Just to be able to communicate with them would be so great. My parents are looking for the psycho for me. Know of any good ones? They're asking. I'm mainly seeing one so that I can find myself. Learn to appreciate me more. And to learn how to cope with pressures a little more. Actually I don't know why I'm seeing one, but we've just all agreed that Kirsten "Dee" Hegberg needs a little bit of psychological help. It's weird, though, lately I've been feeling so much better about myself (except my weight). I think I look better, especially my hair. And my skin is starting to clear up. Debbie, maybe this year won't be so bad. By the end of January I should have started to see at least two doctors maybe three. I think I'm already on the road to feeling good. Which is my biggest resolution – to feel good about myself. I think if that happens a lot will fall into place. Last night I was writing in my diary and all of a sudden "pop" something in me said, "Hey, gal, did you ever think of making a resolution like: stop dreaming about all those guys you've never talked to or could never have?" And so that's kind of something I thought I'd try. Dreams can be harmful. Especially about the opposite sex. I should also resolve not to think about sex so much – although I feel mentally and emotionally ready. But unless it comes up, which it usually does, I'll try not to occupy too much of my time thinking about it.

DD 1/5/1984-

K: I don't understand how all of a sudden you hate your life. It seemed like everything was going really well for you. I guess we both can play the hiding our feelings part pretty well. I doubt you need a psycho. From what you tell me you haven't got half the problems I do. I wonder if psychos can make you change your view on life, or even if they can change me. It's all too complex for even me to understand. Anyway, from my point of view, neither of us are severe mental cases. We're a lot the same and, the way I see it, if we stick by each other things are bound to work out. (PS Crying helps!) I can honestly say I was shocked to hear you say that you didn't want a boyfriend. And that you didn't care about sex. Up until that statement I thought you did. I care about it. And, yes, I do think about it. Quite frequently in fact. And I, contrary to you, believe that I'm ready for sex and the responsibilities of it. I'm beginning to understand my body (I think). And I can feel that emotionally and physically I'm ready for it...Tonight was the first night I really got a close up view of Stacy (what a name). And his face doesn't fit his body. I know I changed my mind quickly. Let me further inform you that I've come to the conclusion (actually I have for a while, but haven't been able to admit it) that it'll take someone doggone attractive and with a hot personality to keep me with him. I've known for a while. I don't think I'm a one man woman (girl!). Look at what happened with Stacy. A month of "he's incredible" and then for the first time I see him smile and it's "bye-bye Stacy." I don't know if that's comprehensible. The only guy who I've ever felt that I could handle for a longer period of time is Paul. If he would have been the way he was his freshman year I would have been in love forever. But, thank God, he's a jerk now and I've noticed it. Anyway, I still have this desire to know what he kisses like. But Paul's done and gone with so...My cousin had a friend over tonight who she knew from Germany but was from here. He wasn't too incredibly good looking, but I have never met anyone with a personality as great as his. I was so attracted to him for that. And then he had this tremendously gorgeous smile. And you never would have believed his eyes. They were this hollow blue-green and absolutely fascinating. Every time I looked into them I was lost. Then this one time my mom and cousin were talking I looked over at him and we stared intently in each other's eyes and then he gave me a grin back. So did I and looked away. My stomach took a crash landing on that one. I'd even dare to venture that he might have been just a little attracted to me. It was like the vibes were strong. I wish he would have said something to my cousin about me, but no. Anyway, I've never met anyone with such an excellent personality.

1/8/1984: In the five days since I last wrote, Manon has left, I don't "feel" for Stacy anymore, and I'm in love with a personality. First, Manon left today. I'm sad. Really. I love that gal. I wish I was closer to all of my cousins...As for Stacy, he had a yucky smile. That wasn't all it. I guess it's just the way you see people sometimes. This one time was enough to change the way I feel all together. Now let me tell you about this guy, Chris, Manon's friend. Let it be known that this guy was not the most incredibly good looking guy. But he's the type of guy I want to marry. This guy had the most fascinating personality I have ever encountered. I have never been attracted to someone that quickly just by their personality. I was so attracted to him. I can't help but think he was a little to me. Maybe he looks at everyone that way.

DD 1/8/1984-

K: ...I want to get good grades this year. I may stick with Chemistry, but I don't know. It's killing me. My parents keep bringing up the quitter bit (mom) and the general education. They keep saying I'm so set on just doing one thing that they don't want me disappointed by my expectations. Personally, I don't know what to expect.

DD 1/9/1984-

K: ...Going over some of our last stuff we wrote, I'm beginning to get sick of the virginity and sex stuff. It doesn't interest me at this time of my life anymore. There are too many other things in my life that are taking my mind away from that.

DD 1/10/1984-

D: I feel like scum. Michelle bugs me. History is boring.

K: What does scum feel like? I hear ajax is good for removing it...

DD 1/13/1984-

K: I'm not going to the Distillery tonight. No one invited me, either. So I won't ask for details...I have gained 7 pounds since when my cousin first came. That is pathetic. I'm so disgusted with myself for letting it happen. I weigh as much as my mommy now. She can't believe it either. I feel royally obese. And now losing 20 lbs. seems like it will hardly get me anywhere...(A cheerleader) is a rude bitch (pardon the grammar, but it fits). She just told Darren that she bought him some Oxy5. She thinks it's cool, but it's so damn cruel.

[*Acne covered faces were an awful adolescent curse so many of us were subjected to in high school. Those who never had to deal with it were often the cruelest. I had an encounter in the bathroom once where I came out of a stall and a cheerleader was looking in the mirror, side eyes me, then looks back in the mirror and says, "Oh my god, I have A zit. I'm going to die." It was like a knife as my face was covered in them. Those moments were harsh and find a way to stay with you long after your face has cleared.*]

1/15/1984: I'd like to try and forget about Chris. He was too good to remember. I could fall in love with his memory, but I'm not going to fall in love. I don't know if I was meant for love. I guess just not now. I think a lot about college – where to go, the cost. It's so confusing...Maybe I'd even meet a man who understands me for me. That's what I really want. And maybe someday I'll find him – but in the meantime messing around might be fun. I'm embarrassed to say this but I weighed 159 lbs. on Thursday. That is so damn disgusting. I gained seven pounds in two months. I feel so fat and gross. I need to work out; hard, desperately. I guess I'm going to have to learn to suffer through my aching legs...In July we're going waterskiing/ houseboating for a week. I'm already looking forward to it.

DD 1/17/1984-

K:...Do I seem like I'm acting more mellow and different to you? I'm noticing it myself. It doesn't even seem like I can carry on a decent conversation with anybody. Even you. It doesn't seem like things have been as normal between me and my friends. Kind of like I'm putting a circle around me. This is weird, Deb. Just writing this down, from what I barely felt (or wasn't sure about), makes things seem so clear. And now it seems like I'm noticing what I'm doing. I don't know what it is and now that I've started it I wish I could finish it. I think in a sense I'm jealous. Maybe of you a little, but not of your friends. I don't like being jealous of people anymore. I guess I'm jealous of the types of relationships my friends have. It may sound like I want sympathy, but I honestly don't. It's sometimes I just wish that I could come to school after a weekend and tell you and Sue what I did in more than one sentence. My parents kind of throw the guilt on me, too. It's like "why don't you go out and do things with your friends? You're always home. We don't want you to become a hermit." I guess I don't want to throw my friendship on anyone. Maybe it's just the way I see it. Sometimes I'm scared to ask people to go places with me. I know it's weird. And you probably can't understand. Believe me I don't feel any better since I said that. And I don't want anyone's sympathy. Actually I don't think people should feel sorry for me (and I know you don't). It's all my problem. I've always been a little, no a lot, self-conscious. I worry so damn much. I think I wish I had more friends that I could call and say "hey, let's go out" instead of having a few close friends. But believe me I value the friendships I have so much more than I'd value other friendships. I guess that's why I don't try and be fake and have hundreds of friends. You know what? I really have no reason to be jealous. If anyone should be jealous, it should be the other people. It's just lately I feel a little different, less caring, less sympathetic, less me. Oh, I don't know why I just went into that totally unnecessary explanation. Why is life so damn confusing when there is no reason for it to be?

D: I understand what you're saying. I kind of noticed something seemed wrong...You have always been there for me. I appreciate that.

K: Thank you for trying to understand. It's been bugging me lately about not having a social life. Sometimes I wish I could go back to Germany. I love it there so much. I have a lot of friends there. I love to travel. I've seen more of Europe than America...Today I'm going to go do aerobics. I really, really need to lose weight –

bathing suit season is coming up. I want so much to be able to wear a two piece. I want so much to have a clear face. I want so much to have long nails. I want. I want. I sure hope I get.

1/17/1984: Exactly two weeks from today finals will be beginning. Yuck. I'm too lazy to study, but I know I have to. I need good grades. I'm so sick of worrying about it. I can't wait for this semester to end…I feel like going dancing and working up a sweat. I feel very much like scamming. Sometimes I like to know that some guys don't mind kissing me. It seems as of lately I've been thinking about Mike. In some ways I regret not seeing him again. When I think of him now he didn't seem all that bad. I'm more embarrassed for how dumb I played. Oh well that's over now and Mike has been out of my life over half a year.

DD 1/19/1984-

K: I really have this desire to go out with Jim. I don't really know why. I guess in a sense I'd like to know if he's really as "educated" as he carries himself. That sounds bad, I know. It's just lately I've been in the mood for a major scam. You know how long it's been since I scammed – since we were in Germany (he was a good kisser, though. Too bad he was so damn drunk. I blew it with Lutz right there). I like to kiss. I even liked to kiss Mike – even though there was no meaning or feeling in them. He was really forceful when he kissed, but that's all it was. Once - the last time I saw him, I made it be more passionate. It was a little, not so much force. Do you ever think what it would be like to kiss a certain guy? I used to wonder about Bobby, now I wonder about Jim. I never end up kissing the ones I wonder about. But that's irrelevant. Matter of fact my whole little story about kissing was.

D: I have never scammed on a guy, except once. I totally led him on…we started to French and all I remember is he totally thrusted that tongue in my mouth. So that made me thrust mine in his.

1/22/1984: Today was pretty cool. I had a good time with Debbie. I've been busy. Finals in a week. I'm so scared. I just can't wait for this semester to end. I'm scared to swim high school. I feel like there's going to be a lot of pressure to be as good as I did the past couple of years. I guess I just have to prove to myself that I can do it. I guess I'm scared of being beaten and upholding an image too. But physically I shouldn't be out of shape too bad because I've been working out and doing aerobics. I even think I may be beginning to lose weight. So maybe it won't kill me to swim…I saw Jim at the gym. I am so attracted to him. But from the girls he's liked I sure am not in the right zone of classification. All I want right now is a hot body and good grades.

DD 1/23/1984-

K: Do you really think you'll go to a JC first? Aren't you going to apply to any four years? You know college is just right around the corner. We have to take SATs in the spring...I am in a good mood today. I think we all are. That's cool. Let me tell you my idea for my final speech: Kids murdering their parents.

1/23/1984: Tonight I hardly have any homework. Thank you. Today I went to the gym for a couple of hours. Jim was there. I'm so attracted to him, but I know – really do – that this feeling could never be mutual. I'm not feeling good about myself right now. State of depression, except at school. I think I hide there, or I am the real me more. I haven't figured it out yet. I really don't know if I'll ever figure it out. You know what dad said to me today? Something totally contradicting to what he usually says. It totally shocked me. He said he wanted me to find a boyfriend and he understood about guys. Mom and I both simultaneously said, "How do you know?" It was funny. And then he said, "I think whoever you find is going to be lucky...you're so mature." If he only knew. That's another thing. At school I can have so much fun. I can giggle and laugh and get in trouble. People think something is wrong if Kirsten isn't shooting off her mouth. I always say what I feel at school. And I can always be my own person because so many people know me in so many different ways. I can be giggly/girlish, sophisticated, the dippy blonde, an athlete, a student. I can be whoever I want, except in a downer mood. At home it's almost expected, but they always ask if something's wrong. I'm beginning to sense a difference in Thor's and my relationship. I think he's growing up and is ashamed of me, but I'm proud of my little bro and I like to show him off, but I guess everyone does change, even brothers. I'm tired and I really want to cry – just for no reason.

DD 1/24/1984-

K: I'm sitting here watching videos. "Girls Just Want to Have Fun" is on...Be back...I love this song and band (Spandau Ballet). They're babes. They're all so good looking. I'm completely intrigued by English and Aussies...The Suburbs are on. "Love is the Law". They're pretty good looking too.... They're about to show this really cool video by a group I love..."I'll stop the world and melt with you" is on the radio right now. 91X is playing some cool songs tonight.

1/24/1984: Damn Lutz! I hate him. I just felt like saying that and getting it out. I haven't thought of him in so long. Something made me think of him tonight and I just wanted to say that. I really felt something for him, but he didn't even send me a letter back telling me he hated me...It all seems so useless and pointless falling for someone. Kirsten never gets the opposite sex when she wants it or needs it. Jim was at the gym today too. Damn him for making me like him or feel for him for no reason. We can't even say hi to each other. I sound like a total depressant. And that is exactly how I feel.

1/25/1984: I really can't hang with life right now. It seems like everything is just going blaaaa! Nothing seems right; it all seems so damn depressing. And it is. Nothing is going my way right now. I feel disgustingly fat and humongous. I think that I look totally gross. And my face is also pretty sick looking. You know it's been over six months since I've had this severe acne and all that seems to have happened is the bumpiness is gone. Now it's all blotchy and red and simply disgustingly ugly. If this ever clears up, hopefully it will soon. I don't know how long I'll be able to go without having an almost clear face. If I ever get severe acne again I'm not going to subject myself to the pain. It hurts too damn much. I've had so much hurt in my life this past year – I can't hang. It's ripping me up. Not a single guy will look at me and that stabs even more. It hurts me so much. I feel like I'm always walking around with needles in me. I'm hurting psychologically severely right now. Someone, anyone help me.

[*During this time, I would have periods where I just wanted to die. I hated everything about myself and didn't want to be part of this world. I kept the pain killers I had been given after my exploratory surgery and always had my eye on the medicine cabinet; pills would have been my out. In one fight with my mom, she actually told me to do it if I cared so little about them and the repercussions. It's sad that suicidal thoughts can be interpreted as anything more than an individual being so overwhelmed by their life, fear of disappointment, fear of the unknown, fear of just about anything, that a parent would see it as a personal affront to them. I loved my parents, hated that they didn't understand, but they were never the root cause of my unhappiness. Turning the corner to home was the trigger for me; it was where I was faced with trying to be someone or something but was not sure what that was yet. Fortunately, my calls for help, a friend to turn to, and my writing would keep me distracted enough from actually following through. But it remained an ugly monster in my head throughout this time period and the desire to disappear would toggle on and off like a light switch.*]

DD 1/26/1984-

K: ...Last night one of my favorite songs from last summer came on – Do Do by Furr...Dana was telling me about her sex life in first period. She's crazy to talk to...I'm kind of excited and scared about speech tournaments. The reason is kind of stupid. You see I hate to fail. All my life I've always succeeded and now this speech thing is something totally new and different for me. I don't want to fail. I'm a very success oriented person. I just simply hate to fail.

1/26/1984: This is what Cosmo had to say about my name. The first and last letter. K – you are secretive, self-contained, and shy. You are very sexy, sensual, and passionate, but you do not let on to this. Only in intimate privacy will this part of your nature reveal itself. When it gets down to the nitty-gritty, you are an expert. You know all the little tricks of the trade, can play any role or any game, and take your love life very seriously. You don't fool around. You have the patience to wait for the right person to come along. N – You may appear innocent, unassuming, and shy; but we know that appearances can lie. When it comes to sex, you are no novice but somewhat of a skilled technician. You can easily go to extremes, though, running the gamut from insatiability to boredom with the whole idea of sex. You can be highly critical of your mate, seeking perfection in both of you. It is not easy to find someone who can meet your standards. You have difficulty expressing emotions and drawing close to lovers. – Well, well, well.

2/4/1984: I really do feel disgusted with myself. I hate my social life, because I have none. I feel like I'm totally used by my friends. Oh, I'm fine for school hours, but good ole Kirsten doesn't exist on the weekends. Debbie will call me – to tell me about what her and Linda or Holly did that weekend. Sue doesn't bother to call me about Kevin. School's a big enough allotment for that. Those are the only friends I have. They're the only people I hang around in school. I wish I didn't. What I mean is I wish I had more friends that I could hang around with besides them. What I really want is friends to do things with on weekends. I hate sitting at home on Friday and Saturday nights with everything to do and no one to do it with. It sucks! I love going out. I want a boy friend, too. Not a boyfriend, but a boy friend. I hate it. Why can't I have a guy that I can be really close to? All I want is for someone to call me up and say, "Hey, let's go see a movie." We don't even need the side stuff. All I want is someone I can trust and turn to. Lisa has so many friends as guys. I envy her so bad. I wouldn't care about not having boyfriends if I just had some guy(s) to be close to. I really don't like how my life is right now. I want to lose weight so bad but I can't stop eating. Walk into the kitchen – eat. And my face. I can't hang much longer looking into a mirror and seeing a red blemished, polka dotted face with a white rest of the body. It looks disgusting. What did I ever do to deserve such bad acne? It's such a confidence killer. Since I've gotten acne, I've lost so much of myself. I don't feel good anymore. It's been over half a year since it's been bad. I want to cry every time I look into the mirror. It's not fair. Oh, but I forgot life wasn't supposed to be fair – not in war and acne. They're both struggles and not-to-be-won battles. In both, the survivors are left in pain. Please let my acne war end soon, no casualties and vague scars. Enough of Kirsten's depression.

THE BATTLE OF THE CANVAS

Let us draw pictures and pretend to be
Let us paint masterpieces for others to see
We draw the illusions
And think out possible conclusions
(But) they never turn out like they really should
Instead they're seen and misunderstood
Like my face-
to me it is shattered
Full of red things-
making my life feel battered
The reflection I see makes me want to cry
My parents, no one will understand why
Can't they see what's there makes me full of shame?
The face I carry fills my life with pain
An artist's touch could do me no good
How I just wish to God that it could
My life now seems empty and scarred
Scarred by those who pretend not to see
I wish they'd see that with this face
I feel like an outcast in society
To tell the truth, I don't understand why
Ask the artist to capture my cry
Ask him to and he will surely lie
This battle inside feels like there will be no end
I'm tired of fighting
My body is sore
I won't be able to handle much more
When will someone open the door?
And give me news that I will hurt no more
Please come soon, I can't hold on much longer
The hate inside is growing much stronger
My team is losing the battle fast

It seems like forever this battle will last
Someone, anyone please help me out
I can't cope with much more doubt
Help me, help me, help me out!

2/5/1984: Another day another do nothing. You know I always think of what it would be like to have a baby. My own baby. Kind of stupid to wonder, I know. But sometimes it seems like it would be nice to have someone to call my own. Well, tonight I have one of my dreams for you. (*The dream goes that I am in college on a writing scholarship. I dated Tom Cruise who happened to be in one of my film classes at USC. I made him wait to have sex but then gave in. We were together when he wasn't filming. After one long weekend, I ended up pregnant. When I told him, he got mad because he thought we were exclusive and it was another guy's baby. He was happy when he found out it was his. We moved in together and had a baby girl named Cydni Cherise Cruise. Graduated from college with a screenplay I'd written sold. I went home to visit and back to the gym and suddenly everyone was interested in me and my beautiful baby. I made him wait four years to marry me. "Miracles do happen."*) And maybe they will for me. And maybe not.

2/6/1984: Today was the first day of semester two. Well, I came away with a 3.5 GPA. I begged for an A- in algebra and got it. Now I'm kind of nervous about keeping those grades. I am going to try. I can't wait until summer. I get to work and get money. I am so damn disgusted with my life right now. I really hate it. I hate myself most. I just can't make myself feel good about myself. I see no good in making something bad into something it isn't. I'm disgusted with my fat. But I can't stop. I've been slapping myself all night to keep away from the kitchen food. I went to the mall tonight. I put a pair of pants on layaway. I wanted to cry when I went shopping because there was so much I wanted to buy but I don't have the money. I hate it. I want money so bad. It's driving me crazy. $5 a week does not suffice. I love clothes too much. All the clothes I have now remind me too much of the me that's driving me crazy. I really want someone to sit down with me and explain what's happening. I just feel like a total reject in life. And none of my friends can understand. I'm so envious of my friends' relationships with other people. Debbie and me and me and Sue have pretty good ties at school, but I hardly know them outside of the damn place. I don't like school. It is so boring. I want excitement in my life but seem to be finding none. Why? Why? Why? I know God put me here for a reason and I hope so much that it wasn't to make people look at me and be glad they're not me. When will I find the answer?

THE WALLS

Locked inside these walls
I wonder, is there a way out?
They're closing in
And now I pray to see the light
The walls, they're closer now
I must get out some way, some how
They're within arm's reach by now
I guess this is the end (there was no light)
In Heaven or Hell-
maybe then you'll see the light
What have I done wrong to deserve this plight?
I don't know
The memory of never seeing the light,
it haunts my life day and night
The walls, they've hit me now
But I'm not dead
I survived somehow
I'm hurt now and feeling the pain
Why did they not kill me?
I hate this shame
I guess they think somehow I'll survive
My life, they say, I must revive
Let the hurt go first
And then give me time to think
I am tired now-
my head is weary
I must sleep now and pretend
that someday my walls will shed some light
Until then -
Good night.

DD 2/7/1984-

K: ...My attitude on life right now is basically negative...I just feel lazy right now and not in a very productive mood. My dad told me last night that he was making me an appointment this week for a psycho. You know what I hate? My dad gets pissed at me when I can't be all lovey to my mom because she's sick. Last night he wouldn't talk to me because I was joking with my mom when she was hurting. "I'm sorry, dad, but you're asking for too much." I hope he gets me the appointment soon. It's almost beginning to be like last December. The cage is shaking inside my head. Help me, help me! Bye gal. Until later days.

2/7/1984: I really don't want to tell you about my depressing life. You know about my never getting better acne and about my pathetic weight problem. So I won't persist. So what is there to tell. Nothing really. Funny now there is nothing to say unless I'm complaining. Well, I've always got substantial reason to complain. Tonight I went out and got a job application for Baskin Robbins. I want to work so bad. I really hate this not having money when there's so much to buy. City lifeguard tryouts are in April. Somehow that seems so far away, yet in a sense it doesn't...Maybe this semester will fly when swimming starts. If I get a job I am going to be so busy. Maybe that will be great and I'll lose weight (lots, I hope).

DD 2/8/1984-

K: ...I want to get a job so bad. I just can't handle it. Get this. My mom gets so damn upset when I even mention the Accutane. She won't even give me a chance to be happy with my face. I hate it and I hate them for it. Why can't they see I'm really suffering. And I am. I feel like crying right now and have tears in my eyes. (I think JW is cute. There is something about him.) You know why I can't stop eating? Because I'm so disgusted with myself that I need to get my aggressions out somehow. Even if it is through eating, which I know is wrong. You know I have this feeling that IF I get a job and with swimming I'll hardly have time to eat. And I really don't think my schoolwork will suffer because I'll probably be a lot happier with my life in general that my happiness will reflect even in this blasted place.

2/8/1984: She (*my mom*) just does not understand what this face is doing to me. She can't or won't and I really don't feel like talking to her anyway. There is nothing to be said – so as far as I'm concerned nothing will be said. Fine and simple to me. I think the same thing that was happening in December is beginning to happen again. Except now it's just not at home, it's sort of beginning to happen at school. I only talk when necessary or asked and I kind of make myself become secluded. I even listen now. And I've been getting homework done – not that I've had much. I have so much time I don't know what to do with it. I want swimming to start (just to waste time) and I want to get a job. I want all this to happen about the same time so maybe just maybe I can shed a few pounds. I won't have any time to eat. But losing weight won't help my nearly hopeless face!

TEARS

Tears, what do they hold?
Do they show signs of not being bold?
Or do they show signs of being a child?
Does it mean you are mild?
Tears are for clowns and people who care
But why is it when I cry no one is there?
They turn their heads and say I'm to blame
It's not fair because I do feel the shame
This life of mine seems but a game
My tears are hidden, though
I still feel the pain.
The tear, it runs down my face
I can't stop it, I'll lose the race
For the tear represents my last atom of happiness
Now it is gone and I am tearless,
one year less; one me less.
But as long as I keep playing the game
Maybe people will think me sane
They don't understand what a tear can do
But do you?
No, I don't think you do.

DD 2/9/1984-

K: ...I think everything I've been saying has come out wrong, except what I said about my mom. I haven't said a decent sentence to her in two days. I haven't told either of my parents that I love them in two days either. I can't bring myself to say it to them right now. But this is what happened this morning: I walk out in the kitchen and my mom <u>attempts</u> to give me a hug. Then she asks me what's wrong because I've been cold these past couple of days. I said, "nothing," and walked away. When I came back she was by my stuff and she said it – and then this is what I said, "You want to know what's wrong with me? I'm reflecting on you what I feel about myself because you refuse to see what I'm feeling about myself!" I grabbed my stuff and started to walk out and then she throws some stuff back at me about me hating my face (acne) because I hate myself right now. What was happening in December is happening all over again. And not just at home. I think it's beginning to reflect at school, too. And I don't want it to because right now it's the only place that I have to hide. And it's crazy that I have to hide here...I really am looking forward to graduating. Not senior pictures because of my face...I hope my dad makes me an appointment soon for a damn psycho. My head is spinning again and I really don't like it.

K:...I kind of feel like going to the beach and just sitting on the jetty for a while. I love to do that. It makes me feel free. Except on the weekend there's always people there. Maybe I'll go anyway. I won't be able to stay in that house all weekend...All I know is my mom will probably (she will) be home when I get home. I know she'll probably talk to me and I don't want to talk to her. I just don't feel like communicating...I should drive somewhere. The house has unwanted tension.

2/9/1984: You know how I think I feel? What I just figured out? I think I'm feeling a lot of guilt because I want to change, be different. But I can't change myself as a person. That's the most major part, but I also think I need to change my surrounding environment. And the major place of that is my room. My room is my home. You know it was strange because when I began to rip at my wallpaper, I felt something in me rip, too. And I felt it rip in dad. I know it hurts him. He wasn't even there. I taped it up to try and mend it. I want to lose this room, the yellow and green. It all reminds me of how I really don't feel like being. Something about this room hurts me, just like when I look in my closet. I want to shed my shell, but it's hurting. Ripping the wallpaper rips me. To pull out the pins pokes me. Looking at my stuffed animals makes me think of being a child and the freedom they possess. This room makes me think of all the times I could just dream and get away, but now it almost seems as if I'm trapped inside and have to saw through the bars to get out. I am more than willing to change if only other people would realize it, too. I just feel like crying. But what good would that do? What good would any of this do? I'm still the same reflection in the mirror that doesn't make me happy.

DD 2/10/1984-

K: I didn't help my brother cheat so he got a bad grade and do I ever feel guilty. I think he hates me now. Oh well, we haven't been getting along good lately anyway. What's one more thing for him to yell at me about?

K: It's not that I'm jealous (of her friendship with someone else). It just seems like sometimes you want me to be jealous. I am jealous in the sense that you have a fun social life and I have none. So there you have it...You know how I've been lately so that has been affecting the way I've been getting along with my brother. We always debate and, even when I'm right, he has to get the last word in...You know we haven't mentioned guys for pages. It's weird because it seems like all we used to talk about was sex and boys. Do you think maybe we're growing up and maturing? Or are just bored with the whole concept? Me no know (me no know much right now).

D: I think we are bored, upset, p.o.'d and everything else that concerns boys, sex, etc. I hate even talking about it.

DD 2/12/1984-

K: ...Excited about the speech tournament next Saturday. I'm horrified about doing bad... "In the Chamber of Hellos" (*Wire Train*)....I went out with Becky last night. It was pretty fun. We had a 6-pack of Michelob and a 4-pack of California Coolers. I didn't even get buzzed. We went to four places that were supposed to have dances but none did so we went to the movies. We took our coolers in with us. It was so funny. I was laughing so hard. Anyway we didn't finish the beer so we dumped 4 full bottles on the corner. What a waste but I couldn't take that home. Anyway it felt good to go out. Today I went swimming. My back got so tan.

DD 2/13/1984-

K: ...I've been eating so much. I can hardly control it. I hate pre-OTR time. Actually, I hate OTR time, too.

DD 2/15/19984-

K: ...I think I could do a lot better away from home and away from this area and away from these people. I don't feel very good today. I feel really fat. I want swimming to start. No time to eat I hope. Debbie, we'll make it to college. And I know we're both going to be damn successful with what we do. I think we're both so strong willed. And I think we both like the word control. We will make it. I have no doubt.

D: ...So my thought for the day is that we are just too cool people.

K: We are too cool. And we can handle things a lot better than a lot of people...so maybe starting out won't be the easiest. But, heck, we can do it. I think we're both encountering the same problems. Our parents are either losing their first or last from home. And I know my parents really do want me to go. It's just letting go. One and a half years til departing time.

DD 2/16/1984-

K:...On Tuesday I'm going to the psycho. I wonder what they'll ask, and if I'll talk. My parents already had to fill out some psycho analysis form for me. I'm kind of scared about going, and I do not want my parents to be there when they talk to me. I will not talk! I refuse to be intimidated by my parents being there. I couldn't believe I almost started crying in History this morning. I just started missing the country roads and old brick houses in Germany.

2/19/1984: It doesn't seem like it's been that long since I've written, but I guess things aren't always what they seem. I think I've been kind of lazy lately. I haven't been doing anything. HS swimming starts Tuesday. Good – I get to start working out. I'm not doing too hot in school. Algebra is really bailing life. I have no comprehension for what we're doing right now. Well there goes that "A". No big (ha!), but I shouldn't let it bother me. But it's hard to do. On Tuesday, I have a psycho appointment. I don't know what I'm supposed to say. And I'm not talking if mom is in the room. Intimidation. Yesterday I had a speech tournament. I got a fifth place in finals. Now I've got a trophy to represent me academically. Oh yeah! I am really not in the greatest writing mood tonight.

DD 2/21/1984-
K: ...I do not want to take that test in algebra. I want to cry. Bring some Kleenex to class for me please. And when you hear me weep just hand me one. At least I get to get out early. And then face another disaster – the psycho. And then another after that – swimming. You know I feel like a little girl today. But you know it feels kind of "neat."...I'm ready to flunk the algebra test. Sit next to me please for moral support!

2/21/1984: Yesterday was mom's birthday. And today I went to the psycho. I didn't know what to say. I didn't feel like I said much of importance. I don't know what kind of good this is doing. It recognizes that I did see someone. But all she did was ask questions. Maybe it's a waste of money. Me needing a psycho and all. Yes, I do think I have more than your average adolescent problems and sometimes I can't cope, but...oh, I don't know. Next week mom is supposed to go in and talk to her. Maybe there isn't anything wrong with me, but it sure feels that way. Today was the first day of HS swimming. I hope it's going to be fun. I really want this time to fly before summer. Baskin Robbins called me for an interview today. I have one tomorrow. I wonder if I'll get the job. I think it'll be really neat to be making money. My own money.

DD 2/23/1984-
K: I was just listening to a "virgin" convo with those groupies. (Name) isn't. (Name) wasn't there. We knew (name) wasn't. (Name) didn't talk. I think (name) isn't. There what a summary.

3/2/1984: I've been pretty busy lately. Not too busy to eat. I hate it. I just can't seem to lose any weight. In fact, I'm gaining again and it's pretty damn disgusting. I've cut down on my face medicine load and I've started getting zits again. When will this stop? God, please let it stop soon. Swimming's okay. I'm so slow. I think I might be falling for Bobby. School sucks.

AND EL CAMINO'S Kirsten Hegberg raced each other neck-and-neck to the finish.

3/4/1984: I'm pretty disgusted with this place some call home. I hate it around here lately. Mom is especially driving me up the wall and I'm doing everything possible to make her see this. I don't say decent sentences. I love to yell and talk back to her. It gives me this sense of power and control over her. Except I get mad and upset over the most stupid things. But in a way I pat myself on the back for some of my comebacks. When I go to the psycho on Tuesday I'm going to have to tell her that my mom (and brother) have been driving me crazy. I threatened to kill myself the other day. But I wouldn't give them the pleasure. I wish I could go to Germany and just get away from this damn So California atmosphere. And I love it there. It seems so un-cliquish; so un-you-have-to-be-this-way-ish; so you don't have to be beautifulish. I'm so disgusted with the way people are here. I am especially disgusted with myself. My face is doing nothing. When I go to the dermi (so that's what he says he is), I'm going to yell at him and I'm going to get upset (I already am). I've been on this medicine for six damn months and hardly anything has happened. My face is still red as a strawberry – Same texture, too. I'm getting increasingly fatter. It's so gross but it seems almost as if I can't stop. Especially on weekends. You know "she" even weighs less than me now. Oh now I do want to leave this place. School sucks, too. I'm so bored with it. I can't wait to go to college. But the way things have been going I'll probably end up at a JC. Even though I won't go. If they make me go to a JC I'll do everything in my power to make them miserable and sorry that they did not let me go. I think I'd better go on to a lighter subject before I get too into this revenge bit. How about Bobby? You know I think I could quite possibly like him. Actually I think I already like him a little. But I don't want to because I don't need any more hurt in my life and because I'm nothing like any of the girls he's gone out with. I do wish something would happen – like a major scam. I don't like the word HURT – I just decided. Enough of my griping.

3/6/1984: Today I had a pretty upsetting psychologist's appointment. It was okay until the end when she told me that I had these negative feelings towards my parents that I try to deny or something to that effect. And then she said something to the likes that I don't like my mom for some reason or another. That shocked me. She said it was all happening subconsciously. I don't know any more exactly what she said. My mind is pretty upset by the statements. But you know I don't think I hate my parents. In fact, I love them, but then again that could be the part of me that's denying these negative feelings.* You know I don't think I really know the definition of love or am scared of it. You know after what she said to me I really felt like I needed someone to hold. Bobby was the first guy I saw, and I was tempted. God, was I tempted. He even asked me what was wrong. I was pretty quiet during workout; not my usual self. I don't know, I thought it was kind of neat that he asked. I don't know. I'm just pretty confused right now. I have a speech tournament on Friday and Saturday, and I really don't want to go. It seems almost like a waste of two days especially when I could go to a swim party Friday night and take some of my aggressions out in the bottle. I wonder if Bobby and I will ever scam. Right now I kind of doubt it.

[*Absolutely the most painful chapter of my existence. Over the years, it became so clear to me that the issue was not my parents not understanding me; I did not understand me! The issue was me trying to figure out who I was. My whole life – identity, friends, self-worth – had been predicated on my life as a swimmer. It was how I defined myself. When that went away, I had no clue who I was supposed to be. My whole existence was chlorine based. My successes. My disappointments. Even if I did not consider all my teammates my friends, they were a support group because we all had that in common. I was starting over at sixteen. And that sucked.]

3/18/1984: Gee, it has been a while. It doesn't seem like it. I guess I just wanted to wait until I was feeling better and could open up to you without negative feelings. My life as of late seems to have no meaning. Therefore, I forgot anything of the past two weeks. Anyway, that was then. Yesterday I cried on the way home from the swim meet. They just rolled out. It felt good. And it made me think. I've decided I've got to stop looking for the answers to my self-hate. They've got to find me. The pain really hurts. And I don't want any more pain. So I'm letting go. I'm going to live a life – not a search for one. I've decided that when I look in a mirror I won't look or wait for it to crack but will try to see something good. Like everyone tells me. I really hate to admit this, but maybe they are right. I'm going to have to try. I will. And I'm going to beat it. Debbie and I had a really fun day. I played tennis for the first time since November. Ages! My arm hurts!!

3/19/1984: Today was a pretty good day aside from progress reports...Today I thought I looked really pretty good. I don't know, but I am really not that bad. Heck, maybe there really is a light at the end of the tunnel. I still have to go to the psycho, but if I feel good about myself for more than a week (maybe more), I'll consider dropping the psycho. I need to go get a bathing suit or two. It's so hot. My face is tan and it looks so good. There is the guy named Jeff who totally intrigues me. Problem is he's probably over 20.

(*Excerpt from a letter I wrote to Lisa dated March 19, 1984:*)...*Leaky, Hi! How ya doin'? I'm doin' great. I really am...I got to thinking about things, mostly my life. I concluded that I must stop looking in the mirror and waiting for it to crack. I've decided to see and make do with the best I have. I hope this works. It should. Things couldn't be much worse than they were...Guys? I'm super attracted to this one guy. Except he's about 20...I do hate to be so short...history test tomorrow, but I have no clue what is going on. Teddy Roosevelt is dead and gone. Why do they insist we learn it? Love and friendship, Kissten**

[*I called Lisa Leaky based on an incident that happened in first grade; it just stuck. She called me Kissten because that's what my name sounds like when my German mom says it; it also just stuck.]

3/24/1984: This was a totally cool week. It was really cool because I didn't hate myself. In fact, I rather like me. Last night I bought a two piece. It even looks semi-decent. Deb and I went to the beach today. It was fun. These Marines kept asking us out. They just couldn't grab the clue. I hope they're not there tomorrow if we go. There was this one guy there who kept saying hi to me. He was pretty good looking. Maybe he'll be there tomorrow. Maybe he'll talk to me. I asked Bobby to go to the backwards dance. He's got a girlfriend so he's going with her. Doesn't that suck? But I love Jeff anyway. Now if I could only bring myself to talk to him.

3/25/1984: Well today I just sat around and gained back all the weight I lost. But I really did lose weight – at least my whole family thought so. You know I really hope that I get that guard job this summer. Think of all that money I'll be making. Bobby told me that last year they only had one girl guard. Imagine that amongst all those good looking guys. I think I'm going to love it if I get it even if I'm not the only girl guard....I went to the movies last night and saw "Footloose". It was really good. The guy was so good looking. His name is Kevin Bacon. Love. Anyway, my dream...(*The dream is how I manipulate Bobby into setting me up with Jeff. Jeff goes to the backwards dance with me. We went to the beach. He kissed me. We decided to see each other again.*) Now if things were only that easy.

3/26/1984: I've been kind of productive tonight. All I have to do now is my algebra and the dishes. I hate algebra. I have a "D" in there now. Doesn't that suck? It does but I'm doing pretty well in all my other classes...Actually, my life has been pretty cool lately. I lost a lot of weight; except the past two days, I've been scarfing the food down. I feel it, too. Hopefully, I can get it back down again.

(*Dee and Deb went dark until 4/4/1984. Not sure why. But it was briefly revived...*)

DD 4/4/1986-

D: The year is ¾ of the way over, and I do not have a boyfriend. I am bummed. So what's new with you?

K: Remember in the beginning of Dee and Deb when we talked so much about boys and sex? We never talk about it anymore. It's weird. Do you think that maybe we've done that much growing or do you think we just are beginning to sprout in different directions? I think in the beginning we were both pretty insecure about things. I do think we've done some serious developing. I think we've developed a super strong friendship and I don't think either of us expects much from the other except a real pal. And as far as I'm concerned you are a real pal who's been there for me whenever I need it. But now it seems neither of us needs the other as much but yet we've continued to have an excellent friendship (you know!).

D: That is interesting because it is so true. Growing and continuing to be such good friends was probably the real test for our friendship. It survived so that is really cool.

K: ...I cannot wait for this summer. I've been seriously thinking about work this summer. I guess I should discuss it with my parents first but I am beginning to think that maybe I don't want to guard. I just want a minimum wage job for four hours a day, 20 hours a week. So I'd make in a week what I could make in one day as a guard except the other way I'd have more time with my friends...I think we should party all summer. Get shit-faced every so often. We can get cloves. You'll like them. I hate smoking, but I love smoking cloves. I think we should maybe even get gutsy and attempt to pick up guys. So maybe we won't lose our virginity (we need to find out about real men) but we can still call it a summer of fun and experience. Even if my summer totally contradicts my present plans I'll still have a car and be able to go to the beach daily. Cool...My heart and soul get so excited when I think about this summer.

[The last Dee and Deb entry. That journal officially ended.]

4/15/1984: I'm 16-1/2! Isn't that neato. Yes, I think so. So what have I been doing with myself? Actually quite a lot. I got a job at Baskin Robbins last week. I don't work much yet, but it's pretty cool because now I have an income. But I'm already in debt through my first two paychecks. I've been going out so much lately. It's fun. Last night felt like a fifth grade reunion. I hadn't seen some of those people in six years. And they all remembered me. Isn't that cool? Deb and I went to the beach these past two days. I've got a combo burn/suntan. I'm getting bummed that I don't have a boyfriend. Debbie's starting to see this guy. I am so jealous. I feel so much like I'm lacking as a person when guys don't look or act semi-interested. We have this week off from school.

4/17/1984: There was this guy who came into work today who was incredible. And then tonight I went to Food Basket and he just happens to be working there. I think I'm going to have to make a few trips there. Maybe I'll be able to find out his name. Then I can dream about him and be let down like usual.

4/22/1984: ...Last night was cool This whole vacation was. It went by so fast. I cannot wait for summer, especially if this week is any indication (except for eating – gained globs). My skin's all peeling off. Last night there was a sort of party at the harbor. Actually a bunch of us just sat at this car and talked. Last weekend we went to this party at this guy Craig's house. That's when I first became intrigued by him – Craig. Last night he was there and we talked. He gave me and my bro a ride home. He's such a tagalong. Anyway. Craig is a really cool guy and I could probably get to really liking the guy, but I'm sick of talking and thinking about him because I don't want to be hurt by my feelings being rejected.

4/25/1984:

I AM ME

The drops of rain
They fall and hit my brain
Making me think of all I've gained
And all I've lost
Without any tremendous pain
To say "I'm me" is what I've learned

And now my life has turned
A lot more learning -
I still must do.
From the inside
I am finally seeing out
And looking at it
From my point of view
I see the world right now
I think I might be learning how.

5/5/1984: I sit here on a Saturday morning getting ready to go take the SAT. Yuck. A lot of weird things have been happening. Craig was confusing me. I'd call him and we'd talk. We went to the movies once and to a party once. We were never alone and he never kissed me but it seemed like at times he really wanted to and I didn't know anymore how I was supposed to be acting. Well, last night we were supposed to go bar hopping in Tijuana. Well it turns out he doesn't get the car and his back hurts. In other words he wasn't going out. Well I got really pissed because I didn't plan anything with anyone else. So I went out, bought a bottle of wine and started to get wasted by myself. When I was kind of buzzed I went to his house but he wasn't there. Now I felt royally dejected. So I went to this party and who should be there but Craig. His friends started saying stuff and I guess in a way he apologized a little. I was so damn wasted. I was hardly able to walk and Craig was pretty buzzed. We talked and then we plus two others left and went to the harbor. We hugged there but that was it. Then we left and went to some guy's house. Well, actually me and Craig stayed in the car. I don't know how it happened but we were goin' at it in the car. I guess it must have been for a while and then Tim and Scott came and opened the door and I almost flew out, but I was "sort of" on the floor. It was weird. Then we went in and sat. I was talking to people and I don't know what he was doing but then we were in the kitchen. We sat on the same chair and just sort of held hands. And then he left. He didn't even say good-bye. And then I got confused again. I don't even have a hangover. That's good because now I need to go take the SAT.

[*This night has haunted me all my life. Not because of Craig, but because I was driving shit-faced. It was a death wish that could have ended so differently on so many levels.*]

5/7/1984: [*This was not dedicated to anyone.*]

MIRROR (version 1)

We did it in front of the mirror
like two unsuspecting fools
The power, the passion
Remnants of the night past
The fight that left me in tears
The force, the strength
Memories of a haunted beginning
If you could only feel my pain
When the mirror cracked
and my illusion of you
was shattered.
A gentle breeze,
A swinging door
Then nothing.

MIRROR (version 2)

We did it in front of the mirror
like two unsuspecting fools
The power, the passion
Remnants of the night past
The fight that left me in tears
The force, the strength
Memories of a haunted beginning
If you could only feel my pain
When the mirror cracked
and my illusion of you
was shattered.
Shards of glass,
Splintered and shattered
I am swept away.

6/17/1984: I feel like writing tonight. I guess that I just haven't felt like it til now. A lot has been going on. School is finally out. For some reason it seemed like it would never end. But it did. My grades turned out so bad...I'm already sick of work. I'm tired of working period. I'm really bored of it. But it's money. It's so hard to save. Guys...really cooled down. Leslie wants to set me up with this guy. But he's out of town for three weeks. He tried to call me but I wasn't home. Tomorrow's one year for you. What a year. Happy Anniversary.

(Excerpt from letter to Lisa dated June 24, 1984:) Howdy Leak, Howz it goin? Not too spectacular here, but things are adequate. Hey, are you feeling any less depressed since the last time we talked? Sorry that I couldn't help or listen more, but time is money (according to Ma Bell). I wish we lived closer to each other. Enough of the "problem" stuff. We're at too depressing of an age. I've come to the conclusion that we do need each other more, verbally and psychologically, than when we were 10...We went water skiing today. It was great once I got up. Think I hurt my knee. Mom gave me an ace bandage and then it was easy getting up. Amazing what the mind will believe!...I'm getting so fat! It's depressing. Especially my legs. They're gross. I just feel so gross about my physical appearance right now...I have a serious question to ask you. Would you ever get married now (next year)? Don't laugh. I'm serious. I was thinking that I would. I wouldn't have kids or anything. But if I was sure of the whole situation. I don't know...Lisa, what would you do if you got pregnant? I don't know what I'd do. Face it. It's not an unrealistic question. Sometimes I wish I had a kid. Other times though I don't want any. Nuisances. I don't know about abortion though. That's a serious question...Have you thought about what college you want to go to? Or what you want to major in? I don't know anymore. It's all coming so fast...I'm being very inquisitive tonight. I'm just very tired. I never think too clearly under tired circumstances. We never see each other or talk to each other long enough to discuss those things...Leak, I miss ya. Love ya lots. Kirsten

6/29/1984: Things are so weird. Lately, I have been like a chronic depressant drug. God, I hate the feeling so much. It's as if I'm not even in control of my emotions or something. I was threatening suicide again. Mom and I got in a fight over it. The funny thing is I don't even want to die. I'm just sick of things in general. Especially my personal life. I am not getting along with Thor at all. I hardly ever see Deb. I don't know, maybe I'm jealous but it seems as if Tom is totally taking over her life. They don't even do things. They watch TV at her sister's. We never do anything anymore. It's depressing...I feel like I should have graduated this year and that I should be going on to college. And meeting new people. I think what I seriously need is a boyfriend. Someone who makes me feel like I'm worth something more. Things are just so confusing. Stupid kinds of confusing, too. To tell you the truth, I don't even know what they are. I just feel like I should get away for a while...This guy Lars is staying with us from Germany. He's funny.

8/22/1984: Man, it's been nearly two months. I can hardly believe it. I don't even know where the time has gone. Well, this summer has been the best and weirdest of my life. So much growing up has happened. New friendships. Like Leslie, and Doug and Tommy. They're these two guys we met who treat us like li'l sisters. It's neat. And then there's the part of people telling me that they think I am so cute. And you know what? I feel it. I've been feeling cute. I think I even look it. My summer of growing up. I even have a boyfriend. (*We met at the beach.*) Or for at least three weeks I do. His name is Terry. He's a Marine from Michigan. Age 19. Brown, brown, 6'2", 190 lbs., attractive and very experienced. The reason for 3 weeks is that he's leaving for NC on the 7th. I'm not letting myself become too attached. Personally, I think he's more attached than me. I guess what I like is his saying I'm beautiful and the feeling of caring he gives. I don't say anything to him to insinuate things. He says more to me. He comes off as a player. But one night I lied to mom and dad (they know now) and I went to see him. We talked about sex and all. It was a "too cool" conversation. I feel like I'm in control of the relationship even though we both want the same thing. Last night was pretty hot. We went to a movie and parking. He kisses weird. Not very passionate (to me). He drives me crazy, though, when he kisses my neck. That's enough to make me cream my pants. I'm not even horny. That surprised me. We were in the back of the Tank (*my station wagon*) last night. I finally felt a guy's dick. He'd kiss my boobs and rub my tender spots. I was on the rag so that deterred him. But I tried to rub his dick. How successful I was I don't know. He was trying to teach me how to give head, but I didn't do it. He came up on top of me and said this was a simulation of how it would be. It felt good to have him up on top of me. He said he wanted my first time to be beautiful and on a bed. He said he'd never taught a girl how to have sex, but he liked it because it made him feel like I was doing it for him. He told me that he wanted to "make love" to me so bad. He's just a lonely, horny guy. To tell you the truth, I think I'm just playing naïve. I'm sure I could just jump, but I don't want to feel like the world's greatest ass. Heck, man, if anything I'm just being selfish. I could go without doing stuff to him. I like him, but I don't and won't love him. I'm just too curious right now to let this one pass me up. I think he might be becoming attached to me. Yeah, it's a good feeling just having someone who cares. It's all gonna end. I can face that but he refuses to talk about it. Oh well. You know what's weird is that you don't even think about becoming pregnant whilst near the process. I think I'd have an abortion. Deb and I talked about that. What a summer this has been. So many memories. Terry and I are supposed to go out tonight. Still OTR.

Wednesday night/Thursday morning 12:30 am on 8/23/1984: Tonight I lost and gave my virginity. We did it on the beach. I want to say it felt great, but it hurt pretty bad. When it was first over, I hurt because I thought maybe I was just an object, but then we talked. It felt good that we could just sit there and talk. For the first time I felt a twinge of love for Terry. Something special is really happening. I'll give details later. I'm tired now.

(Letter to Lisa dated August 22, 1984:) Hey Leaky! Well, here I sit a couple hours after talking to you. Man, it was great talking to you. I love it. It feels good to know that we can talk. I can't believe that six months ago I never would have thought about telling you stuff. I thought you thought it would all be repulsive, but I am so glad I can talk to you. It makes me feel closer to you even though we're so far apart. Comprende?...So how did camp end up? Scam on any incredibly gorgeous guys? Man this whole summer has been incredible. What a summer of growing up. Can you believe it, Leak? Me, I'm almost on the brink of losing it. God, Lisa. Me. So much has happened. You know, what I like is that somebody might actually care for me. Whether his one liners are perfectly rehearsed or not is beyond me, but nonetheless they/he makes me feel good. I'm not becoming attached. I know it's just a short fling, but it trips me out when he talks about me coming to see him in NC. And then coming back here next year if I'm here. I don't regret anything we're doing and I'm sure I'll be more comfortable around any other guy I'm with. Our relationship to me is like teacher and pupil. In a sense I feel in control because I give the go ahead. Oh, I just don't know. I hope you don't think I'm being sleezy. But nonetheless I will keep you very informed. But this letter will end for now. It won't hit the mail yet, because I'm sure I'll have more to say tomorrow. Till then-

August 24, Friday

I know you wanted this by Saturday, but I have been very lazy. I guess you're probably kind of curious as to what happened Wed. night. Lisa, please don't think of me as being sleezy. I'm far from it. But yes I did go to bed with him. It wasn't great. In fact, it rather hurt. The best part was when it was over and we just sat there and talked. Man, if we would have talked first my first time would have been different. This guy is beginning to mean a lot to me. Not so much in that he was my first (we haven't done it since then). It's just that we can really talk. He needs a serious friend. That's what I feel I am more than his girlfriend or lover. He's really protective of me. Heck, man, I wait for him to beat up anyone caught looking at me. It makes me feel good. But I like for other people to look. Ever since I've been seeing him I feel like the biggest flirt. It's fun, but I do feel kind of guilty. But I thought you might want to know. I'd give you details but I don't know how you'd feel. Or if you'd be appalled. Besides, I'd probably feel better telling you in person. When are we going to get together? It's been too long. Well, I'm sorry about the delay in sending this. I'll go to the post office right now. Hope to hear from you very soon. Please don't think of me as being any less. (No, I am not feeling guilty!) Love ya lots! Kissten

8/26/1984: Man, things are trippy between Terry and me. He says that he's in love with me. Not direct "I love you", but he told me he was. Wow! He says he hasn't felt this way in a long time. He says he's never been so happy with a girl before. He's scared of what's going to happen when he leaves. Tonight was great. We talked for a long time. And then we "made love." Yes, in the car. Pathetic, or what? Actually it was great. He'd never done it before with the girl on top (sitting position). I liked it. Man, I wish I would have an orgasm. He's come close. But I think he's naturally hard-up anyway. I don't like giving head. I like being finger screwed and eaten, though. It feels damn good. He makes me feel damn good. I can't wait to do it on a bed. That'll be wonderful. Tonight was pretty great though. I'm very burnt out.

8/28/1984: At first I was like I didn't want to fall in love with Terry. But it's all so different now. I realized that tonight. We didn't make love or anything. But something else hit me. I don't want this to end. It's going to hurt so much. It hurts now to think it has to end. It's to the point where he's ready to say "I love you." He's written it. And insinuated it. The more I'm with him the more I feel for him. I hope all that he says to me about coming back is true. And that he's not just playing with my emotions. It'll hurt me to know he'll sleep with other girls. I'm going to ask him to tell me. I want him to tell me everything. I hate myself for letting myself begin to really feel like this. The thing is I have to hide so much from mom and dad. They think it's just a casual relationship with a little hanky panky. How I wish I could come out and tell mom what's been going on. I hate being bottled up, especially with mom. But they'll think I'm crazy for feeling so much in so little time. This is all crazy and hard and sad to take. I'm happy now. I hope that doesn't end.

9/2/1984: This week has been trippy. The other night, Friday, Terry and I made killer love. I didn't have an orgasm or anything, but it felt good. He came twice. Once in my mouth. It wasn't that bad tasting. Yesterday we got into a killer fight. I was very confused about what I was feeling. I told him I wasn't in love. It's so hard for me to explain what all was said. It was pretty intense from my standpoint. But the fight – temporary break-up – was short lived. We talked and then we went out to the Distillery. I wasn't the most pleasant. I couldn't bring myself to touch or kiss him, but all I wanted was for him to hold me. I needed that fight to bring out how I really felt. I guess I am probably in deep like. We just sat in the car and talked. We were both balling tears. It was kind of sad. That's when I finally saw that I cared a whole heck of a lot. Tonight he came over for dinner. It was kind of cool. Then we went to his barracks and sat. Man, I was being the biggest tease. I was being so weird. I'd laugh and totally joke around. I didn't give him head or let him down my pants. But it was cool. No sex. We were buddies tonight. It was the coolest night together. I felt closer to him. It was great. I'm going to miss him very much. Very, very much.

Monday, 12:30am, 9/3/1984: I cannot believe that she had the gall to read one of my letters. She (mom) read Lisa's letter to me about my losing my virginity.

(*Lisa's letter excerpt*) *If I was to think any differently of a friend the minute they thought anything different from me, I don't think I'd have any friends...I'm glad you've finally realized you can talk to me. If I had known that you felt you couldn't talk to me I think I would have cried and then beaten the shit out of you...Shoot, don't even think you can't talk details. I guess if I'm not doing it I might as well hear it...Just do me a favor and don't ever get to the point where it gets easy to do it with anyone...You did use protection, didn't you? Where were you? What did you talk about after that was so neat? Heck, I could have told you it wouldn't be any good your first time. Believe me, you're not alone, that's what just about everyone says...I'm glad that at least you feel a good friendship towards this guy. I was a bit worried at the beginning of the summer when you said you wanted to do it to get it over with...There's got to be another side to it other than the physical side...I know what you mean it feels good to have someone care for you. I think everyone feels that way!*

So when I got home tonight she told me. I told her I hated her. Which at this very moment I do. That's an invasion of my privacy. I lied to her and told her we were using something. Man, I would have told her had she never of pried. Never again. The trust is gone there for a long time. But anyway, Terry and I went out tonight. We went to dinner and then to SD. We were supposed to pick up Bob but didn't see him. So we came back and made love on a baseball field bench and the front seat – twice. Neither of us came because we had to concentrate too much on the things around us. But it was kind of cool anyway. He just makes me feel so good.

Things are so cool between us. We've become really close as friends. Sex is just an added extra. I don't want all this to end. It's so great right now. I want to tell him I love him because I think I really do. What a night. Do I ever feel like running away. (She had NO right!)

9/5/1984 12:00am: I don't even feel like writing, but I wouldn't want to let you down on my sex life. We went to the drive-ins tonight. We did it in the back of the car. Both naked, except our socks. He came 3 times. Me zero. I came very close a few times. I hate it. It makes me feel incompetent. I keep comparing myself to this other girl he says he loved. I know I shouldn't but I do. I told him I loved him tonight. Stupid. I swore I'd never tell a guy I loved him first. My mistake. I wish I wouldn't have. But I really feel like I love him. I am going to miss him so much when he leaves. Things are so cool. Why does it all have to end? The only two things wrong are my weight and Terry. Tonight we did 69. Trippy. We did it some weird ways. FUCK IT ALL. Man, I just can't hang. I feel like I've already lost him. Why did I let myself finally fall? It sucks. We have two more days and then it's all OVER. What an ending. I love him.

9/6/1984: Well, it all ends (in a sense) tomorrow. It's all really kind of sad. And I'm going to miss him a whole heck of a lot. I have to take him to the airport tomorrow. God, am I ever going to be shedding some tears. I hate myself for feeling what I do. I want him to tell me he loves me so much. But I don't know if he does. The only time that I don't feel like I fully love him is when I see Bob. God, does he ever send twinges through me. I hope that me and him and some of Terry's other friends will remain friends. It's almost like hanging on to a part of Terry here even though he'll be gone. It's hard to imagine him not being there. Tonight we made love in some pretty weird ways. We always do. On a car hood, a lifeguard tower, backwards, the front seat, and sitting. Wow! That's a lot. We're supposed to go to a hotel tomorrow. Maybe for once I'll have an orgasm. My last chance.

(*Excerpt from letter to Lisa dated September 6, 1984:*) *Hey Leak...Man things have been so hectic these past few weeks. I think it's finally dawned on me that school starts on Monday...My boss wants to talk to me at work. Probably because I asked for so many days off to be with Terry before he leaves me...Things are pretty cool between us. We had this one massive fight because I told him I didn't know if I loved him or not. I was so damn confused. But now I know that I do love him and care a whole hell of a lot about him. I am going to miss him so much when he's gone. He keeps saying he's going to come back for me. BS. But it's a great feeling to know someone cares a lot about you. Tomorrow I have to take him to the airport and then he's gone. POOF. Just like that. Let me tell you that hurts. I'm glad I have school to keep my mind off him. Maybe another guy will be interested. Just to keep me occupied. Believe me, sleeping with another guy will not occur for a few...My mom had the gall to read that letter you wrote me. I nearly killed her. She started getting off on it. Made me feel like crap. The cool part was she offered to go get the pill with me even though she doesn't approve. She hasn't banned me from seeing him so that's hip...This year should be a lot of fun. Seniors at last. Party time (maybe). Nonetheless I will make it fun. Sorry that this is so short. Terry's coming. Love and friendship, Kirsten*

9/7/1984: Just briefly because it hurts too much to talk about him now. All I know is he's gone and I love him a whole heck of a lot. We spent the afternoon together in a hotel. It was great. I didn't have an orgasm, but I came so close. I'm scared something may be wrong inside because I can't feel a lot of things sometimes. I miss him so much already. When I can think straight I'll give you more info.

9/8/1984: Yesterday was a beautiful day, despite Terry's leaving. We went to a hotel and made love. It was great. He's great. I regret that I never had an orgasm. I've had sex so many times you'd think my body would know. There were times though when I didn't even know he was inside of me. Which is kind of scary feeling. He came in me once, on my request, but I didn't even feel that. The airport was sad. I cried so much. God, do I love him. He finally said he loved me in "I love you" fashion. It's going to hurt so bad if he forgets me. I don't think he will but it's scary anyway. I wish it could just be our world – me and him forever. I feel so much for him. I wish I could just forget him. But I can't. Hopefully school will take my mind off of him. Even if someone else accidentally falls into my life. I will never forget Terry. He means so much to me. No one's ever been my friend and a lover, too, before. I just wish they both didn't have to come to a halt. We will see each other again. Even if it's at each other's weddings. I love him with all my heart and passion! I miss him so much.

High School – Senior Year

9/10/1984: School started back today. It wasn't bad. Paul's in my psychology class. I sometimes wish our friendship could continue on from when we were freshmen. There were so many more people at school this year. Trippy. I think about Terry a lot still. God, I really do love him. And I miss him so much. Wonder if he's thinking of me. No dwelling.

9/12/1984: Terry called me last night. He said all he does is talk about me and that everyone wants to meet me. I'll feel so much better when he's in NC away from his old Michigan girls. I miss him so very much. Tonight Deb and I went out. We had so much fun. We were laughing so hard. We went cruising everywhere. We went to see Doug, but he wasn't working. We went to see another guy from school three times. We were laughing pretty hard. Then we went to Rosarita's and ate chips and water and half of something. We were harassing the waiter, who actually goes to our school. It was pretty funny. Deb and I feel so different, but superior, to everyone else. It's like me and her against the senior class. And we're winning. Terry gave me that rose. (*saved between the pages*)

9/13/1984: Terry called again last night. The first thing he said is, "I forgot to tell you I love you." Tripped me out. Made me feel damn good. I really do love and miss him a lot. Paul sat next to me in Psychology. I was raggin on him. I can't believe how much more comfortable I am around guys now. It's so cool.

9/14/1984:

BECAUSE I LOVE YOU

This is a poem for you
Because I love you
This is to tell you how nice
you make things in life
This is to say sorry for all
I've done wrong,
Tell you I need you without the words of a song
I want you forever
However apparent this may seem
I need your love to guide me through
Show me the bright side of
darkness with your touch
I love you so much
Show me the world is bright
Give me reason to see the light
Tell me you want me both day and night
If you say that it is through
I'll trust your judgement because you're you
But my love for you will never subside
I'll love you always

And I'll hope and pray
That by my side you will stay
Until my dying day
I'll love you in each and every way
Good night, my love, I must be going
But remember my thoughts
Of you are always flowing
And when I turn out the light
Do not be afraid
My love burns bright.

[*In our Creative Writing class, we were required to keep journals. Sometimes topics were set. Other times, it was whatever we wanted. I called mine* "All of Me, Plus Some": The continuing drama, saga, feelings, and emotions of one Senior in Mr. Brooks' Creative Writing class at El Camino High School, Kirsten (no middle name) Hegberg. *I wrote in this as much if not more during that year. Journal entries are AOM from here on out. Mr. B would also occasionally provide commentary and I have included those when I felt it relevant.*]

AOM 9/14/1984: Welcome to the wonderfully zany, sometimes normal (what is normal?) world of the thought patterns, emotions, and opinions of me. For those whose names may be used as incriminating evidence, they will be spared the use of "real" names...I don't like playing games. Mind games that is. I'm a damn good liar, but to me that isn't a real mind game. What I mean is when you have to pretend to be or know less or more than what you are really capable of...I just don't like giving in to people's games. Especially since I am a great believer in the non-conformist faith. There are a lot of feelings and emotions I would like to discuss. I am full of never-ending desires, feelings, and emotions.

AOM 9/15/1984: I would like to share an aspect of my life with you that has always disturbed me. Some would say it dumb and that it'll all come my way sooner than I know. Well, it did finally come near the close of my 16th summer. But it had to leave at the end. It hurt me more than I care to say. Something and someone that made me feel so damn good finds me and then has to leave. I've always been disturbed by me. I've always thought that not having a boyfriend or guys looking at you was a clue to you that the nunnery was to be looked into. I put myself down so much. But I've done so much growing this past year. I don't put myself down. And don't care what people think of my abstract behavior – it's me. But when Terry found me this summer it was like everything was perfect. For a short time I led a terrific life. And then he had to leave. I was so hurt. I never intended to fall in love. In fact, I was scared of it. But I fell anyway. But when he left I didn't have a relapse and be down again. I know it's possible for someone to love me and care for me a whole hell of a lot. Whether we ever "love" again is too far off to know. But just one real love, not one night scams, has made me understand a part of myself that has literally and honestly put me on the brink of suicide.

AOM 9/16/1984: I wrote Terry a letter tonight. I'm so scared of that one being over. I guess I've never been that secure with him, even though I gave a lot of myself to him. I told him that maybe it'd be better if I let go of whatever hold I held over him. It's the last thing I ever wanted to do, because I love him so much. Or at least I think I do; my first real feeling love. But he has a hard time saying he loves me. He says it. I don't force it. I'm not blind to see he does love me. That hurts even more. When there's a love between two people and it almost has to be given up. I want to believe him so much that he'll come back for me. But it's hard, because I can't find myself completely trusting him and his manly desires. Not many relationships can sustain distance and time for so long without some physical heart-break. The thing is now that he's gone, I can't even picture myself with any guy except as friends. I found Terry when I wasn't looking. Maybe fate'll have it that way for me again. It just all hurts. To tell you the truth, I don't know if I trust love.

AOM 9/17/1984: I found this story that I started to write a couple of months ago. It's about a kid who claims he's crazy. I guess I sort of came up with the idea from my all time favorite character, Holden Caulfield. But I think I surprised myself...It relates so much to my past life. A lot of people look at me and think "how could she have any problems?" But, God, I had so much happen to me in such a quick time and such a bad time. I had a really hard time hanging on. That's how come I've always been able to relate to Holden. I saw in him a lot of myself. A lot of times, characters I choose to write about are take offs from different times of my life. I think I choose to write more from a guy's point of view (like SE Hinton) because guys don't have to conform. But girls are too gullible to society's ways. Sometimes that's why I think I don't fit in. Because I choose not to conform. I choose to be me from the inside out. From the clothes I wear to the way I act. For the first time in my life I have been me. And that is the best feeling to have. Sure, there are certain parts of me physically in which I could conform. But to tell you the truth, there aren't that many super skinny girls running around ECHS. As long as my face remains adequately clear and I remain unaffected by life's little ups and downs my size won't phase me that much. Layered looks help.

Anyway, back to Holden. A lot of people think that Holden was a wimp and quitter on society. But from page one on he remained almost like a private friend. I used to think what Holden would have done. I wish I would have met Holden at the beginning of my junior year. Maybe then I could have avoided the self-hatred, near suicides, painful psychological "sessions", tearful fights with parents, the acting, and the hiding from society and everything. Sometimes I think I'm a better actress than I claim. Not many people saw it. It all broke out when hiding got to be too much, though. Still a select few really saw the pain. I don't even think teachers saw it. Good kids never hurt. I love life now. As much as can be expected. I feel so different. Sometimes I think all the hurt was necessary to <u>discover</u> the real me and look beyond the acne faced reflection. I found what others told me was there – ME. I just refused to see. I guess everyone needs to really discover themselves. And then the learning finally begins.

AOM 9/22/1984: ...There is so much I want to do, and so many decisions to make. It wouldn't be fair to ask anyone's advice because in time I'll realize what I'd really like to do. And how. And why...

AOM 9/23/1984: I am not in the brightest of moods. I almost got fired today. (*Because I lied about why I couldn't go to work and ended up at a football game instead. And someone ratted me out.*) Then I started thinking about college again. I hate it when my parents totally void my hopes of going out of state to school. Well, screw them right now. I'm sending one out of stater to Purdue. It seems like a pretty kill school...I'm just a little mixed up about school, college, and Terry...It doesn't seem like forever's a realistic goal for us, let alone nine months. I really love him, but God it's so hard to keep holding on when no real hope seems in sight. There's also this selfishness to it. I want to see other people, but no one's asking. But every time I try and bring it up with Terry it's like he thinks I want to say good-bye. But I don't. I want to just reaffirm what I feel for him by seeing how I feel about being with another person. Who the hell knows? Not me!

AOM 9/24/1984: ...Lunch today kind of triggered me off. Senior Hall of Fame elections. Certain people were on that list five + times. Some had no talent yet were included on the list. Point made: I am not jealous. Just pissed at how it is that all of the conformists are on that list. I am just very disturbed about the whole conformist issue. I hate that THAT group all dresses, talks, walks, laughs, and looks the same. I'm so glad I am not a conformist. I think most people see that.

A mask cannot conceal
Nor a therapist heal
The love and passion that I feel.
The love is deep and tense
Caused by what? A pretense.
Anger grows and forces thus
Feeling of hate and gullible trust.
No right have I to love one so
To give so much and never know.
Fear dwells and causes wonder
Crashing, hitting like pangs of thunder.
To say good-bye I musn't do
Life is long.
Like an old song it lingers on.
The memories become bearable thoughts.
To keep dreaming and praying, I ought.
The wave crashes on the shore.
Forever doubting I want NO more.

AOM 9/29/1984: *"I never meant to cause you any pain. I only wanted to see you laughing. I only wanted to be your weekend lover. It's such a shame our friendship had to end."* - Prince

9/29/1984: Up until a week ago, I was constantly talking to Terry. But I don't anymore. He's in NC now. I think I might be surprised if he ever calls or writes again. I mean, I'd like to know that it wasn't just some major scam job. I honestly can't tell you if I really do love him. As the days go by, I don't think of him as much. I think about how much I'd like to see other people. You know what I miss most about Terry is our friendship. I think that's one of the reasons I don't want to let go. But I know that I do have to let go of him. The last time we talked help me realize that, too. All we did was fight. It scares me to think I may never hear from him again. But I have to accept that...Paul's an asshole. Sometimes he's cool to talk to, but other times, God, he's a trip...You know what else is a trip. I've been off of my face medicine for two weeks and I have a few more zits on my face, and I massively broke out on my back and chest. There are even some on my neck. Gross! But I still feel better about myself. God, I swear, if it ever gets like it was last time, I want to die. I hate hating myself. I really do like me.

AOM 9/30/1984: Hey, tomorrow is 2 weeks until my b-day. And I am finally going to be 17. Yeah! No big deal. I've never really felt 16 anyways. I've always felt older...You know there is nothing to do in Oceanside.

This place hasn't changed in 12 years...I can't believe I haven't talked about Terry in a few. Actually I'm trying to put him out of my head. I wish so much someone new would come into my life. You know what my dad said? He said that Terry probably just used me. And then left to find another girl in another city. It was kind of rude of him, but kind of made me finally realize that maybe I have lost Terry.

AOM 10/2/1984: Last night I talked to Terry. It was so weird. All week I was getting depressed because he hadn't called. And when he did it was just like having any other guy call me. I haven't been feeling very good lately, so maybe that has something to do with it...I think I'm getting "closer to the edge" (song by Art of Noise) with just packing up and sayin' see ya...I can't wait until we go to Germany this Christmas. Hopefully, that'll help me come to a conclusion, too, and my future in general. I am beginning to wish someone would say, "You have excellent potential to become a _____." And then say, "Pursue it, kid." But I just don't know anymore.

SHOW ME

If ever our roads shall cross
And I appear to be lost
Hold my hand,
and lead the way
Show me there is more to this world,
and that there will be a brighter day.

AOM 10/3/1984: To tell you the truth I used to want the world to end. But now I don't want it to. There's too much that I want from life to just say, "Farewell, cruel world." When I think about it, I came close to just saying farewell. It's kind of scary. I know now that there are rough times. At this moment things are kind of rough, but I'm hoping they'll be just like they used to be, because it kind of really scares me.

I once had a balloon and let it go
To places I have yet to know
I once had a balloon
I let it leave my hand
Just so one day it will know of
what I have yet to understand.

AOM 10/4/1984: Tonight, I want to talk about something that had no effect on me, but a lot of effect on my family. First off, I am not an insensitive person, but when my grandpa died this summer, I was almost relieved. He was a crazy old man. I mean the man lived a full life. He even died in glory. His death made the papers for weeks and even the news. We had phone calls day in and out. It really disturbed my dad, my mom, and my brother. As for me, my investigative side came out. All I wanted to do is find out if the death was legit. I guess what really bugged me about him and made me feel relief was that my grandpa was hard as hell on my dad and his brother. My dad has had a damn hard life. His mom died when he was six. She killed herself. His dad and stepmom gave him no support. He saw his best friends killed in two wars. His first wife left him. And his first son was born crippled. He died a few years ago. And there's me. I have been the cause of so much pain for him...but I am not going to dwell. I've just never expressed how I've felt about that death and my dad. I really love my dad. I just have the hardest time in the world expressing my love.

ALLEGEDLY SHOT AT TORMENTORS

'Peaceful, gentle' elderly man dies in jail

EDWIN OLAF HEGBERG
"Never bothered anyone"

By Frank Saldana
Tribune Staff Writer

An elderly Oceanside man died in jail yesterday after he was arrested and booked on three counts of attempted murder involving shots fired at neighborhood youths he thought were taunting him, authorities said.

Edwin Olaf Hegberg, who would have been 80 on Aug. 12, suffered an attack at about 3 p.m. in county jail at Vista, said Sheriff's Lt. Raymond Fisher.

An autopsy today showed that Hegberg died of a heart attack, said Supervising Deputy Coroner Max Murphy.

Hegberg was arrested at 12:17 p.m. Wednesday after police said two shots were fired from his .22-caliber rifle at five youths who had climbed over a wall onto his yard in the 4000 block of Thomas Street.

Hegberg's wife, Dorothy, said the youths had tormented her husband for weeks.

"I hope those neighborhood brats have learned something from this," she said today.

Mrs. Hegberg, also 79, reminisced about her husband today in the living room of her house, where she sat next to his wheelchair.

She described him as a peaceful, gentle man who always worked hard during their 43 years of marriage and "never bothered anyone."

"He was very proud of his yard and had a beautiful vegetable garden growing. Now I don't know what I'm going to do with all that corn."

She said her husband became infuriated Wednesday when the youths — all minors whom police have not identified — trespassed on their property. A few minutes later, one of the boys dropped his pants, bent over, and "mooned" the Hegbergs, she said.

That was the latest in a series of incidents in which she said the boys had harassed her husband, she said. The feud began when he hired them to do yard work for him, she said.

Mrs. Hegberg said her husband was pleased with the work, but for an undetermined reason a disagreement ensued and one of the boys threw dirt on his head.

The dispute escalated, police said. On Tuesday, Hegberg was knocked

Please see DEATH, B-3

AOM 10/12/1984: I have been trying to communicate with my parents about my future, my mom in particular. I am just going to decide on my own my future. I am just so ready to go. You know that's the only conflict in my life – my future. Ridiculous, aye? I think it's very! I wish she would understand that I am incredibly sick of school. This year has been fun, granted. I just don't know if I want to go right to college. I want to go to Germany. I wonder if I'd ever come back. I know I would. I JUST WANT TO GET AWAY...I have been playing this game with myself and others for the longest time. It's about Terry. It was all a lie! Honest to God it was. I never loved him. Nor do I want to. I fooled everyone. Even myself for a while. But down, shallow depths, inside I always knew I never loved him. I just liked the proposition of having someone love me. And that I believed. I think I'll know when I'm really in love. But love will probably be a ways away. I think I demand a lot. And until someone (besides Terry) comes along, I can just mess around. Now I finally got the absolute truth about Terry out. Load off of my mind.

Letter from Terry post stamped 10/12/1984: *Your Little Marine!!! Hey "Buddy", how ya doing? I'm living now in a cute little room with a cpl. who's moving next month...Got plenty of room (hint). Wishes. Wishes...I'm also putting money in the old bank so I can come see you. But the bad part is it's over a year. It's on your birthday so would that be okay? I mean I want to SEE YOU SO BAD!!! I'll be out for sure. Then if you want you can come back with me and I'll send you to UNC only if you want. To me it's perfect...Don't hurt me especially cause I promised myself I would not hurt you. I love you and I want it to stay that way...In a way I'm kind of afraid to come out, you might be seeing someone else, what would you do? What would I do? Then again we might fall more in love, then I would have to stay, wouldn't I? Of course...I cannot wait for my reply. So hurry with good pictures. Sexy ones. Ooh la la (that's French). So bye for now. I love you, Kirsten. Terry "Buddy"*

AOM 10/14/1984: Tomorrow I will be 17 years old. I am so glad. I hate being 16. Actually it was probably the best and yet the hardest year of my life. I feel so much older than 16. I'm excited about being 17. The number change won't make me feel different; just being able to say it will...What does age really matter? If you look and act older? ...I used to be really susceptible to falling in love fast (or so I thought I was). But for a while now I've gotten to know people before making a judgment on how I feel. And from Terry I learned not to let myself play games with people's emotions. It's not really fair for all parties involved, especially me. Selfish, but true.

[*At the top of the page names are written in a box. I used to write down names I thought were cool to name future children. I did actually name one of my children one of the names listed.*]

AOM 10/15/1984: (1st period) "Another one bites the dust. And another one's gone, and another one's gone. Another one bites the dust." Remnants of 7th grade. I always thought Shannon (I know a secret) was going to beat me up...SEVENTEEN. Today I am 17 years old. I am 7-teen. Seventeen years lived. I am a Seventeen year old. Seventeen years old, seventeen years old and...Bored. I am the chairman of the Bored. Board. Bored. Bord. BORED. B.O.R.E.D. I keep spelling it (no bored) but it (bored) doesn't look right anymore....(2nd period) What did the round table say to the flat table? (I don't know either.)...Isn't know a dumb word? K-now. It should be pronounced know (k-now), not no. Dumb. Just like gnarly and gnu. Imagine how foreigners must feel. English is a peculiar (peck-u-lar) language...(3rd period) I feel like lighting this pack of matches right now and having an imaginary piece of dynamite (dy-no-mite) so that I can blow up this not-so-imaginary pre-calculus room. What's one less math teacher? More or less. Moral less. Sounds similar...I've never stuck my face in my birthday cake before. I wonder how ma and pa would respond to that. I may contemplate that action further...(4th period) People are obscure. General observation. This class is full of 'em. They are all creative. Especially this one guy. I have this 35 degree angle of him. It's not that I think he's cute (not that he's not - different). His whole air intrigues me. He seems so damn intelligent. I've never talked to him before, but his intelligence is freaky. God, sometimes when he speaks in here the words coming out of his mouth are amazing. He's spontaneous. It's freaky. But I wonder if he's going to blow it in life. I do think so. It's not that I think he couldn't make it, but it kind of seems like he may not want a normal job. He'll probably be a great author someday. This is bad thinking - but I get these feelings sometimes – I don't think he'll live very long. Sort of like Edgar Allen Poe. But a different death. I think he said once he doesn't like to fight. He'll probably die denying fighting. Scary thought...(5th period) I don't want to write about him anymore. It's trippy to me to even think that way. He just kind of reminds me of a little boy who had to grow up way too fast.

We're watching the Mondale/Reagan debate in Civics. I hate Mondale. But I hate Ferraro even more. I thought Mondale was being too damn elusive!! Those two Democrats bug the hell out of me...Do you ever wonder what the scums on the streets were like in childhood? I mean, they haven't been bums all of their lives. Actually, I wonder what most people were like in childhood. It's hard for me to imagine sometimes that adults were even young, that they were ever even my age. Aging is a bazaar facet of nature. Kind of scary in fact...You know I think this has been a pretty great B-day. I am very content right now. Nothing has been wrong (knock on wood). I got to spend time with myself. And I like that. But tonight I get to be with my family. That makes me happy, too. I am just very happy right now. I haven't been this happy on a birthday in years. I always expected too much. I think I acted differently this birthday. Must be the age. Heck, man, I'm halfway through my teens. Wowwy Kazowee.

AOM 10/17/1984: Tonight I talked to Terry. He was yelling at me. I didn't provoke it; I only told the truth. God, he is such a little boy. If I were to say all that was said I would be the demon. But they had to come out and EVERYTHING did. He was crying on the phone. That's always bugged me about Terry. He is too damn emotionally unstable. He was kind of tripping me out because he was sort of talking about making me hurt for the little game I had played. Someone finally conquered him and now he needs his revenge. It scared me at first, but Terry will forget about me. He has to. I cannot remain his sole purpose for living. It was so weird to hear someone fall like that. I had to do it that way because he was so ignorant to see through my hints. It's sort of too bad that someone had to love me that much. I don't know why it just is. I guess I know I wasn't meant to love Terry. I think he loved me so much and that's what's weird. I wonder how far he'll go. He's very different psychologically. Murder would be a mastered craft to him if it were legal. Trip. We ended the conversation with him being my big brother/friend. He said, "I guess you can love your sister...but not the way I love mine." Something to that effect. I'm just relieved to have finally told him. I care for him. Too bad it had to hurt him like that.

AOM 10/18/1984: Things seem changed all of a sudden. Not since yesterday's ordeal with Terry. That's always been in the coming. Things just seem all around different...I am sitting in darkness, with but a candle to help me see. I see no lines, nor do I feel this pen. My eyes are feeling pain, fatigue, strain, anguish, lost. I am a child now. Thrown back to horse drawn carriages and long length skirts. I sit and watch my parents make me grow to what I am today – October 18, 1984 – destroyed. I sit here on the curb with my best friend who is calling me nasty names and now isn't even talking to me. I didn't do anything. I guess people just get sick of things. I'm sick of everything. I have to let go now. I must venture on. Perhaps I should move to the gay 20's. Happiness hidden behind a façade. Yes, I think I'd be rather good at that. Life is one big game after the other. The martyrs. The cloak and dagger. The murderer – and me. What am I really? A fetus. A child not walking; comprehending. A tree. Not moving, just dying. Boredom. I don't know what I am. I am not an 1880's child. Nor am I a gay 20's façade. I am me. Granted that I am. Just a child playing a child in an adult world. Obsolete, yet incomplete. I am but a drop of water on an endless sea. A speck of sand in an oasis. A label on one of billions of products. I am me. #5xx-xx-xxxx. Check that on your computer. Conclusion: 5xx-xx-xxxx, blow out the candle, kiss mommy and daddy goodnight. Tomorrow you will conquer your next plight. Sleep tight...Note back: 5xx-xx-xxxx shall never conquer all plights. Computer you don't understand. All is not right. When is the next flight to Athens, Greece? I think Aphrodite is calling. She needs me. Says I can play the part pretty well. Says some work needs to be done in recent aspects of my life. Will persevere. Yes? No? Maybe? Most definitely. My light is dimming fast. Mommy and daddy aren't done planning yet. They'll never really know. Little friend still doesn't speak. Everyone will need me. They do. I need them. Funny people. Funny ways of expression. I love this zany world of 1984 even as I sit here in candle lit darkness with a piercing in my eyes. Tomorrow I will be blind. Saturday deaf. And Sunday dumb. Life. Does it really exist? Ponder that one a while. Good night. 5xx-xx-xxxx

[*I wrote some weird shit on occasion. I swear I was not doing drugs.*]

AOM 10/19/1984: I was in a strange mood at 11:00 last night. Strange. It's safe to say I think I am recuperated.

> *ashes to ashes*
> *dust to dust*
> *love and contempt*
> *end in lust*

AOM 10/21/1984: The Distillery was a lot of fun the other night. I danced most of the time by myself. And I loved it. I felt superior. It was like I didn't need anyone to dance with to be happy. I was so happy by myself. Maybe it intimidates guys to have girls/see girls dancing like that. I don't know. Because I've stopped trying to figure guys out. Sure I want to be in love, or think so. But I don't need anyone who is insecure and who gets embarrassed by me. God, I have changed in so many respects. It just really hit me Friday night. Before (I don't know how long ago before was) I used to think I had to dance with a guy and pretend to be something I'm not around them. But I don't. Not if I want to be happy. And not if I want to believe that somebody is in love with the real me. It's all a little confusing right now...Yesterday, I actually got kind of excited about college. I'm applying to Fullerton. They have everything that I might want. I hope I get into UCLA. No business but I'll improvise. I'm kind of glad that I'm excited about college again. I was beginning to worry myself.

THE ROOM OF MY LIFE

> *Day by day*
> *The walls move with my emotions*
> *Happy and flowing,*
> *A plant with a new stem*

Nothing remains the same,
New dust has formed
No angle is alike in here
They change with what is felt
Enter the room
And see straight out
Freedom beyond a levelor blind
No key locks,
Nor a window does bind
A breeze through the open window crack
Refreshing thoughts of nights way back
A steady flow of cosmic air
Contempt lays outside these walls
Refugee to alibies
A cluttered emotion
Stack by stack
Confusion,
No way out
Another one of life's rewards...
Discovery
And to what it leads
Room, castle,
Home, emotions,
and wired-up walls.
In and out
The room is
Me, Myself, and I.

AOM 10/22/1984: I was so happy. Today I found out I got accepted to Purdue University's School of Management.

AOM 10/24/1984: Man, I am so intrigued, practically obsessed with the 35 degree angle man. It's so crazy. I've never said a word to him, except "thank you," but that's two words. He is so opposite to anyone I could see myself going out with. He is so mysterious. I just feel like walking up to him and saying, "Do you like to talk?" And then we could be friends. I have this feeling he'd be a great talker. I can't see myself romantically involved with him. I can see this great friendship, but only outside of school. His friends probably wouldn't accept me and I them. They are too bazaar for me. But he, he just does something. I wish we could have a platonic relationship. I have had so many urges just to talk to him. I envy his talent. His silence intrigues me completely. But I like it when I see him smile. It makes him seem alive, more real, more mysterious. Obsession. My God, what does it mean? I just do not know.

Mr. B: You've discovered someone with equal talent and disdain for conformity. He's a lot like you, maybe an alter ego, that's why you're fascinated. [*Clearly, he knew who I was talking about.*]

AOM 10/25/1984: I had fun in Creative Writing today. We had a sub, and she was so funny. Funny not in a humorous sense. She walked so funny. Her hips led her body and then her feet side-stepped. We played Trivial Pursuit. Man, it was hilarious. All the not so trivial people were on our side. I was laughing so hard. HE was actually speaking and smiling today. It was cool. My mouth was pourin' out the good ones today. I even said about two words to him. Actually more. He probably thinks I'm very strange. I laugh a lot. Today was no exception. I don't want to find out all the excuses for why I can't talk to him. And why he can't talk to me. I got jealous today when I saw him talking to this girl. Actually, I don't think it was jealousy, more envy. He's got wit. I saw that today. Infatuation with an obsession. Wow, how illogical...Went to lunch with mom today. There were so many old people. I feel sorry for them. I think they're more ignorant than we are. They're all set on morals, standards, and views. They don't accept much in change. Today we grow up accepting more. But today's more liberal. Yesterday, wasn't. And the older generation best represents that.

AOM 10/26/1984: The geese flew over my house this morning. It made me happy...I'm in psychology right now. We're having group discussions. My group is doing some ridiculous role playing thing. A bunch of goobers. One of the girls is a flunkie. She smells, too. It's funny because this guy has totally been playing games with her mind. She thinks he totally loves her. It's funny how blind she is...Now things are getting ridiculous. They're having the guys role play as fags. They're so immature. It's kind of funny though how reluctant the guys are to play fags. I had to play an emotional role. But it was kind of challenging.

AOM 10/28/1984: All I am right now is pissed off at the world. Things are just making me so mad. I'm depressed. God, do I ever hate that feeling. I hate the way I'm feeling right now anyways. I think I have mono. I probably have some incurable disease.... My mouth has been nearly fatal to me a couple of times this past weekend. I just feel like getting wasted...You know what I hate is that people think I'm so tough and can fend for myself plus 20 others. I hate that because I am not tough. I get myself out of trouble the same way I get into it – with my mouth. Being considered the buff one has always made me feel like I was super fat and unfeeling. I hate when people say, "Oh, Kirsten, can be my bodyguard." No, she can't. I'm sick of that image. I've never been able to get rid of it. My dad always used to kid (?) that the reason why I didn't have boyfriends was because I was bigger than them all. And I scared them all away. Doesn't help. I know there's got to be other things keeping them away...I hate when I let myself become depressed.

AOM 10/29/1984: "That's bullshit," said Mr. Hansen. God, he's a cool teacher. He's so real. And what he's talking about sounds so realistic, like when people tell you not to worry about something. I wouldn't worry about it unless it was really bugging me. I hate when I'm really down and low but can't figure out why the hell I'm mad or worried or depressed...Now I'm home listening to the beat of the egg timer. My mind is ticking too. I have had the worst headache for the past few (understatement) days. I've considered taking the whole bottle, but that would end my life along with my headache. So I'll suffer a bit more...I have ugly hands. They are calloused and scarred. I have this big ole callous on the middle finger from writing. It's gross. And makes my small and pudgy fingers look even worse. My fingernails just do not grow. And on my left hand you can see the scars, not just visibly, but physically. I fail to be able to make a number two. I'll never be able to have a wedding ring put on my finger normally because the tendons leading to that finger are connected to another finger. And so goes the whole left hand ordeal. Not to mention the grossness and ugliness of the three inch scar. I think it might be longer. It looks like a damn scorpion. Maybe this scar is why I hate bugs. And love to kill them. I just wish I had pretty hands. No scars...To tell you the truth, I love scars. But just not on hands. I like scars on guys a lot. I think it's debonaire if they have a small scar on their face. I have tons of scars on my legs. But they hardly even bug me. In fact, they're kind of fun until you have to tell someone you got them shaving. I always lie and say I did it some other way. I've always been good at that. The one exciting fall I had never left a scar. I fell from a tree and landed between two branches ripping open my side. It's kind of funny when I look back on it now. I was such a tomboy. Can you believe Dana and I were best friends for six years of our lives? We were so crazy. We had so much fun together. That was until the first time we got drunk together. Then things changed. She used to be so innocent. She was introduced to drugs, sex, and more alcohol in junior high. She eventually was hospitalized. She called me and said she was in a mental institution – actually I think it was a home for troubled kids. She told me she would always have a special place in her heart for me. It hurts to think of being so close to one person and then what you had will never be there again. She will always be special no matter what. I hope she makes it okay in life. In fact, I hope a lot of people do. I'm beginning to regret what I said about 35 degree angle man He's cool. I want him to make it in life. I feel like talking to him about the future. I hope he'll go to high school reunions.*...My headache isn't getting any better. Pound. Ouch. And my callouses aren't getting any smaller. Pre-calc test tomorrow. Yuck. Double pound.

[*_He has never been to any._]

AOM 10/31/1984: Last night Debbie said something to me that made me think. She said, "You never really had a boyfriend, though." (referring to Terry) That's sort of true. Besides the sexual stuff we were sort of friends. I never had a total confidant in Terry. I don't want to dwell on that because only I really understand the extent of that relationship. But I just want a boyfriend again. Someone to go places with and to be crazy with. Someone to spend money on me – I am broke...We're talking about suicide in Psychology. I take a personal interest because I was once very suicidal...I can't believe what just happened to me. I was in the bathroom and some girl asks me if I want a smoke. I said no. And then I started defending myself. I couldn't believe it. Who cares whether or not I smoke? So I won't die of lung cancer. Actually, I might because I do smoke cloves. On occasion. I'm proud of the fact that I don't have to do drugs (never have) or smoke to feel cool...I've been thinking more about the eventual outcome of 35 degree man. The more I think about him and the more I observe him the more I begin to see that perhaps my first general observation was wrong. Actually, I think he may have a lot going for him. College. Definitely. Office job. Still skeptical. I want to be able to look into the future and see what he (and others) will be doing 10,20,30 years from now. Actually, I really don't want to know what's going to happen to me or anyone else for that matter. Life should just happen.

AOM 11/1/1984: I wish so much I could just stop thinking about him. In psychology it's called obsession. There's also this thing called obsessive-compulsive behavior. But I can't do the compulsive part. All I can do is wonder. And wonder. And wonder. I wonder what drives him? I'd really like to know what it is . (Mr. B: Me too! I've talked to him a great deal and I still don't know)...I don't even know why I bother to dwell like this. Obsessed? More than likely. Perhaps.

I believe in intrigue at first sight. Girl sees boy. Sparks fly. But nothing comes of it, except this feeling of desire. But it's a desire I think may never be fulfilled...Maybe I don't believe in love at first sight.

Granted there are guys who I stumble and fall over at first sight. They make me queasy and nervous. They make me feel ugly is what they do. They make me so self-conscious of my appearance. I'm not as bad now as I used to be. Sometimes now I'll confront the situation, but it seems like they're more interested in the person I'm with. That can be so frustrating.

ONE NIGHT

Love was made
With a passion,
With a power
Bodies were moved
And brought together
They became as one
A moment of glory
was fulfilled
One more conquest
Destroyed and crushed
Loneliness
Yet love prevails
And overcome shall both
The moment brought
Some pain,
Some sorrow
A closeness achieved
never again.
Her moment of ecstasy
A small tear shed
For never again
Shall those two
Be as one
He left the room,
And closed the door
Madness, she thought
But fine indeed
A lesson in love
She would never again need.

SECRETS IN THE DARK

Behind closed doors,
Beneath the shattered mirror frame

On blankets drenched in sweat
By the crackling of the stove
They lay.
Together they moved as one
Feeling the force and passion
Feeling the tension mounting
They came at one climactic moment
The tensity flowed free from all
Ecstasy established
Smiles bestowed
They lay there together as two now
Shadows of their bodies reflected on the walls
Emotions were now set free
The words "I love you"
slipped from his lips
A smile cracked on her face
Once again they became as one.

AOM 11/2/1984: It really bothered me what she said about him. Why would someone laugh about what 35 degree angle man had to say? When I listen to him talk, I see how fucking real he is. This is driving me crazy. I'm trembling. Something just totally hit me and now I am so disturbed. I can't believe I am almost in tears...I feel like a little outsider today. A little baby. A little child. I feel I want someone to talk to. I cannot dwell anymore. No one understands the extent of what I am feeling right now. Obsessed.

I'm sitting here on the edge of the world. I found a beautiful place on the beach just to sit and think. The breeze feels great. (I wish it would blow away what I am feeling/experiencing) ...I feel like standing on my rock and telling everyone that I have just become the supreme ruler of the earth. Or at least my beach. Queen of Tower 9. I see all the houses around me, but I don't see them. They're not part of this fascinating beauty. The footsteps of small children are and the bubbles left by scurrying little crabs; the rocks that have laid here for ages; and the sand that can tell the story of it all. Ageless and infinite. The crashing waves and once blistering sun subside to nothing more than sheer eloquence. Through my sunglasses I see a sun that illuminates one of man's greatest enemies to divine delight. The crashing of the waves only makes me see that there will be no end to life's problems. But there is hope. Like the setting sun and the different patterns of the waves there is a tomorrow. One with different patterns and new horizons. One with different particles of sand in the place of yesterdays. The pier will never really leave its spot. Nor will these rocks I sit on. They will sit here to represent hope and second chances. They will endure lovers' quarrels and nights of glorious passion. They shall endure all, like the waves, the sand, and the sun. I shall try to endure it all. Try to realize that even this beauty I see has its own obsessions. And that even with all the power it has it will never fully achieve what it desires. A symbol, a landmark. The ocean and its surroundings represent me as a whole. Content yet never satisfied. Curious, but never fully achieving. Loving, yet never knowing. Dreaming. Dreaming is the essence of my life. I know tomorrow exists. The crashing of the waves and the noise of the birds tells me that. I live for tomorrow with the same obsessions and desires waiting to be fulfilled. I have hope once again.

TRANQUIL EMOTIONS

Bottle floating freely
An escape to the unknown
Rocks are beaten
And torn to tatters
Waves are ignited
And then lose their spark
Children tease the birds
The elderly reminisce
A couple kisses
Waves collide
Sailors silhouetted in the sun
Images of eternity
Knowing it will always last
Orange skies,
Playful dogs,
Lonely people,
And the setting sun
Daylight ends,
Sun is set
The bottle cracks
All is gone
Last light sheds
fears tomorrow may never really come
But then again
There is never really a silence
Life lingers like the earth and sun
Forever living an eternity.

35 DEGREE ANGLE MAN

Caught in circles,
Games elusive
First words unspoken,
Utterances of nonsense.
Wonder and intrigue
Dominate the spirit
Contemplations,
Fears of discovery
What comes next?
"Hello. Let's talk."
Shattered images
Compulsive acts
Conceivable
Uncontrollable desire
No response
Obsessed mind
And doubting heart
A dream,
Nights of passion
Or simple words
Rather-
Silence be spoken
Pulverized ceramic pieces
Picked up and swept away
The differences overcome
Mystery relinquishes,
Wishes unsatisfied
Solitary meetings
and words never spoken
A cracked mirror image
Leads the desired heart
To fire and ice
The chill -
Great, unfulfilled
and never ending.

I wrote this poem for the 35 degree angle man. Whether or not it's actually presentable to him is doubtful. But it kind of explains some stuff to me. It's kind of like the circle pattern and the feelings I've been having from being obsessed – if that's an appropriate word for it.

[*This poem would go on to be printed in school publications. When I signed his yearbook at the end of the year, I finally told him (wrote it) that it was about him.*]

I am not even tired tonight. I feel like writing even though I should be studying for the SAT...This journal has sort of become my diary. I'm too lazy to write in the one under my bed, so I use this instead. This explains all my moods and emotions plus some....I have a feeling Mr. B may not read everything in here. (Mr. B: I read every word!) Even if he does, it really doesn't matter. There's not really that much in here that I wouldn't defend verbally. Actually if I write with spontaneity I may figure out in 20 years* what was bugging me back now. (Mr. B: So speak with your heart, speak honestly, stop letting your mind get in the way.) I'd kind of like to explain why I wrote the poem "Secrets in the Dark." ...I do not flaunt the fact that nor do I deny it that I am not a virgin. It used to be the most important thing in the world for me to lose it. But when the opportunity finally came up it was nothing major for me. Sex is a selfish act yet I was never selfish...I guess what my poem is trying to say is that I never experienced love like that. The poem is about two lovers who have their own special place. Who make love with innocence and an honest to god passion for each other. A sincere love. I'm not sure that's something I felt. Maybe he did...I'm not confused about sex anymore. I know now to feel more of a love before jumping. I know now to be more selfish. I know to be me. I know sex can be anything I want it to be. I know it can make or break relationships. And I know it's not necessary (Mr. B: Good insights!) ...Sex is kind of a very confusing subject. It's probably just as confusing for every other teen, but they probably choose not to discuss it. But I just feel like this journal has become a part of me, a very special part, shared only with a select few.

[* *It would be nearly 37 years before I opened that journal back up to write this.*]

AOM 11/3/1984: God, today at the SAT I was reminded so much of the old me. It was so strange when I saw Lany, Miles, Scott, and Steve again. Lany is so cute and skinny. I felt like an outsider again. Like I used to feel when I was swimming. I felt ugly again today, too. And I felt really fat. It was really depressing and it kind of hurt. It made me glad and proud that I could leave it all. But it made me wonder how much I have really changed since then. I felt a setback in my life today. I was actually glad to leave them...Lately, I've had this desire to see what it would be like to go flying over a cliff in a car. Just flying free. Suspended in air. But everything would end that way. It probably wouldn't be a bad way to die. You'd feel this ultimate moment of glory. Don't get me wrong, I don't plan on driving over a cliff. Flying is just so free. I'm tired now. I'm always tired. I need to go see a doctor.

AOM 11/4/1984: I feel like sitting in a little corner of the world; obsolete from everyone and everything. No cares in the world. No one to say things or tell you things. Kind of like an inside, private battle between me and my unknowing world...With all that seems to be going on in my life right now I just feel like I'm a piece of rope holding a boat to the dock and the boat keeps resisting, it wants loose. So it rips and tears at me, the rope, yanking and pulling, throbbing. My head. A circle of confusion. What is so damn confusing? ...I don't much care for myself right now. Or things around me. I just want to fly; to be free. Carefree. Careless. Invisible. Just me, me, and me...I have to go. I have to. It doesn't feel right right now. I feel like I am slipping and I'm going to fall through the ice. I can feel it breaking now. Gotta run and hide.

AOM 11/6/1984:

Who do you turn to
When the game is through,
The charade is done,
And there's only you?

11/7/1984: (An envelope from Terry with the lyrics to a Night Ranger song, a number "69" tab, and a picture because "I didn't want you to forget what I looked like.")

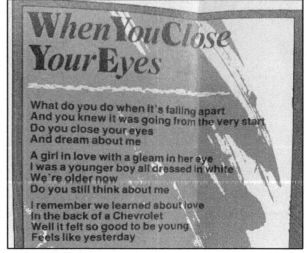

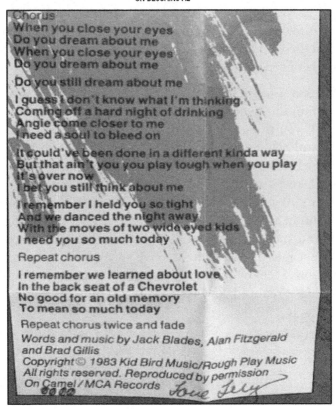

AOM 11/8/1984: I don't like listening to him talk in CW. He makes me want to talk to him more. He is so damn fascinating. He even has a sense of humor. I listen to his poetry and I find out more about him. Thus, I become less intrigued...I read my poem about him. It was hard not to explain what it was about. I just wanted to turn to him and say, "Hey, that was about you."

LOVE IS...

Love is a fallacy.
Love is a game.
An inspiration,
A desire,
A flame.
Love is a child.
Love is a toy.
Hiding,
Playing,
Being coy.
Love is unknowing.

Love is showing.
Lost,
Lonely,
Steadily flowing.

AOM 11/13/1984: An incomplete poem...

If he doesn't,
he won't.
If he does,
he will.
Neither pain nor glory
will prevail.
Emptiness always there
And shallows murky in disrepair
In depth feelings and emotions
Touched by an arsonist's flame

...

AOM 11/15/1984: In one month we leave for Germany. I'm excited about going. I love it there so much. I love the freedom of small town Germany. The forests and places to think all around you. Old houses and churches. Department stores in hundred-year-old buildings. I always feel like there's something going on...Now I'm going to answer the prompt from Mr. B about suicide. It's kind of hard for me to explain how I feel about it, because I was labeled suicidal. I wrote some poems last year as my self-hatred reached its peak. This one kind of explains things best. Or at least what I was feeling. (*I wrote out "The Battle of the Canvas" that I had written in March*). It might be kind of hard to understand so I will explain. I had such a high hatred for myself. Anyone and everyone was afflicted by this hatred. My hatred just got to the point of feeling like I was in a cage and there was no way out. So all I wanted to do is die, because I felt so much shame. I just felt like the ugliest creature on earth. With no hope for anything, but constant suffering...it was written at a point of total and complete desperation.

AOM 11/16/1984: This is a poem in response to my obsession with 35 degree angle man. I think it's pretty self-explanatory. SURFACE. (Mr. B: Does this satisfactorily explain your attitude?)

MOVE, LITTLE CHILD

No longer intrigued
By obscure looks.
Simply wondering
Why he's him.
Let be all that's past.
Move onward
To your goal.
Move, little child.
Block of obsession
Gone from within.
Never reached,
No longer desired.
Left empty,
Hardly caring.
Move onward
To your goal.
Move, little child.
Free from longing.
Knowing no more.
No less.
Giving nothing.
Losing less.
Realization became the point.
Found.
Move onward
To your goal.
Move, little child.

I feel like a brick wall. I feel "yucky". I haven't felt this bad about myself in a long time. I'm finding a lot of fault right now. And I'm not liking being in high school. I can't wait to go to college. But where am I going to go? I wish I could go to the east coast. Why can't money be no object? ...Tomorrow I'm getting interrogated by my boss and manager. I'm going to tell them I'm quitting before we leave for Germany on the 17th of Dec. It'll give them a month or so. I'll try to find a new job when I get back.

VANISHED

If I were to pull the trigger
Close my eyes and disappear
Would you fear the end near?

140

Would you follow footsteps in the sand?
Hand and hand.
We could leave this land.
You and me -
Vanished.

THE HIDDEN – A Sonnet

A rose from the lover to the loved
Hearts embedded with passion burning
Hand in hand like feathers of a dove
Their innocence leads the heart to yearning
Their love bestowed from heavens atop
Relief leaves the victims hearts content
Bonds and chains this love could never stop
Tenderness is given without consent
No mother, no father to intervene
Solitary moments between the lovers
Secret hiding places never to be seen
The love of the innocent, under cover
In the plowed fields, with growing flowers
Lives a love never to be devoured.

AOM 11/17/1984: It amazes me to think how fast a day or two can go by. It seems like there was no Friday yesterday. Maybe there wasn't. I don't know anymore.... Terry called me last night. I don't like talking to him, because all he does is brag about things. I never get a chance to talk. It was okay last night, though, because I was half sleeping when he called. It seemed more relaxed talking to him. He didn't mention revenge. Just that he needed to talk to me. I think he still loves me. It's weird. Lately I've been thinking about him, but this phone call made me totally believe in my decision that it's over and that there is a friendship – sort of – there...There's so much about myself I'd like to start to change. I want to get into a self-improvement bit. I started it off by telling work that my last day is the 13th. One bond broken away...And then there's my health. I am going to have to start working out again. I should probably get back into running and cycling. I don't know if I want to swim this year. It'll be hard because I want to take a class at MCC. I've been neglecting my body too long now and I'm seriously feeling it.

AOM 11/18/1984: "I'm in the mood for you." I would love for someone to say that to me...[*I wrote several poems on this day. An alternate title for*

"Reflections" was "Self Portrait". It has always been one of my favorite poems about finally being okay with myself.]

REFLECTIONS

Mirror reflection covered with mist
Blurred vision of hopeful illusions
Turned to shattered images
Tempted by hate, and hope
Tomorrow's vision a friendlier sight
From a child to a woman
No curly locks, or despair
Hopeful heart.
Opened eyes.
No detoured vision or false illusions.
The image, a woman
And the reflection,
the reflection,
Has come of age.

EMOTION

Could one love surpass another?
Deeper, stronger, more concrete.
Could one emotion devour the others?
Anguish, hate, and fear.
Does harmony exist when peace does not?
War, murder, and crime.
Is any one desire more powerful,
more complete,
more yielding,
more never-ending,
more THERE?
The heart leads the soul
to powers cherished by Gods.
(And) the losers become the victors.
No love beats another;
Or destroys a hope.
But all is a fair chance
for emotional dominance;
For one more fulfilled desire.
An emotional peak.
Emotional prominence.

Equality for all.
Emotion, love, harmony -
Established.

FOOTSTEPS

Footsteps:
child, woman, man
Eternalness swept away,
Power of the waves
Footsteps:
small, medium, large
The waves show no mercy
A footstep,
Bound by a thought
Deep, wide, shallow
There or not
Vague marks of vivid pasts
Subsiding to nothing
All that's present becomes past
All that's hope is untraded, unsure,
but surpassable terrain
Footsteps evade the waves,
And hit the rocks.
No people, no noise,
No dreams or visions.
Just solid, untouched, unsuspecting sand.
And, no footsteps.

AOM 11/19/1984: Things seem so screwed up right now. God, I hate it. There is so much about my family I cannot even tolerate right now. Especially my brother. He's a little shit. Everything he does annoys me. My parents annoy me. Deb is the only person not annoying me…I don't know what I'm supposed to feel anymore or why…I wish I knew what it was about me guys don't like. It's so frustrating. One year your life is crap; the next it's great. But one part doesn't change. That of guys. I used to be ugly. I don't feel ugly anymore. But it hasn't changed. (Mr. B: are you sure? You're too self-critical! Maybe you're too mature for high school guys. Wait till you get in college. Maybe you'll find more interesting men.*)…I just feel like crying right now from sheer frustration and anger of it all. I just feel so much tension in my head. I feel tension everywhere. It is so DAMN FRUSTRATING. I don't even like the solitude and refuge of my room anymore. I JUST DON'T LIKE THINGS.

[*No wonder he was my absolute favorite teacher in high school.]

AOM 11/21/1984: I don't really need this journal right now so I'm not that bummed that it's leaving me for the weekend. Maybe this weekend will open my eyes. Actually I don't even think it's my eyes that need to be opened. After last night I just need a break. Troy (a friend's ex) can be such a goon. It's so hard because he tells me one thing and her the other. I hate being the middle man. It confuses me more than either of them. I HATE BEING THE MEDIATOR. Troy started calling me and we became friends, though. He told me something that made me feel good. But also start wondering why the hell I don't have a boyfriend. He said that I could have anyone I wanted. So why the hell don't I have one? I know it's stupid to wonder why. It'll happen in due time. Right? I know but it's frustrating when people say nice things about you, but no one does anything. I just don't know anymore.

A picture of my mind. And that is what I leave you with. Have a nice weekend.

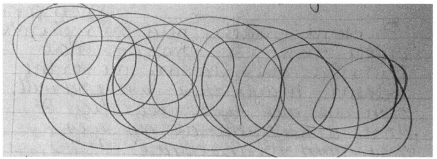

AOM 11/26/1984: I'd kind of like to say it's been a nice break. I'm ready to face my journal again. I guess towards the end there I was having a tough time trying to figure out Troy and my friend's problems. But I think they came to a culmination today. I finally told my friend what I'd had locked inside of me: Troy used to like me (before them). And recently he's been calling. He told me that stuff. I think I was totally sending off the wrong signals. I think it's my nature to be flirtatious at the wrong time. More so lately. Troy told me all this stuff. And I put two and two together to find that nothing means more to me than my friendship with her. Hopefully things'll cool off now – and I'll feel a little less tension…It's kind of weird to think that with all that's been up with them I've been kind of on a high. NOT BECAUSE OF THAT. I've just been feeling kind of good about myself. More positive. I'm still a pretty confused kid inside. I like my poem "Reflection". It kind of says what I feel. I can feel the transition from girl to woman. It's not that weird I guess. I knew it'd be coming. I do feel older. Lots...I've been thinking about my future a lot. College. College. College.

AOM 11/28/1984: Today I can honestly say I am living for the future. If I didn't have tomorrow to look forward to, I would feel incomplete. I know my mind is aching from all the decisions I have to make now about tomorrow, and I know one wrong choice could destroy it all – my hopes of power and happiness could be shattered. It's a painstaking process, but I'm hoping what I choose now will be the right choice for happiness tomorrow. Hopefully the little mistakes won't catch up with me...There are so many roads and paths I can follow and choose from. Which though? I'll know the whys when I figure out the ways...It's all so much for a 17 year old to decide. My future in the hands of me – a little girl.

12/1/1984: I know it's been years since I last wrote, but it's not like my life hasn't been catalogued. It has: in my journal. That has everything. But first off I should say it is way over between me and Terry. It was before it ever started. I made myself believe I was in love, but I believe now more than anything that I never loved him. I evaluate in my journal. Life has been kind of lagging. Deb and I are the best of friends. Our friendship just seems to be getting stronger and stronger. Her ex used to like me. Isn't that gross? Gross, though. I did not even like him. I think I have begun to give up on figuring out why guys don't like me. It's not because I'm ugly. I smile. Have a good time. Seem a hell of a lot older. And I guess maybe that's what it is. I am just a hell of a lot older mentally. I know what I want from life and will go about achieving it. There probably will be someone very special in my life in the near future. If he can wait, so can I. I am happy now. Sometimes I get depressed but

it's the future that keeps me going. I am me and that is all I am. I have accepted that. I like me too.

12/3/1984: I hate how I get all excited about a plan I have for the future only to have it crushed by my parents...I don't want to stay at home. I don't want to live here anymore. I have lots of freedom, but I just can't hang with it. I feel like I need out. I don't think it'll change if I stay. I'll still be feeling the tension even though I will be of age. They piss me off...In ways things do seem so unchanged from a year ago.

AOM 12/4/1984: I've been having a really hard time at home lately. Especially today. I walked to school just to defy them more. I hate them right now. I hate when they put down what I want to do, especially with my future. All my dad wants is for me to go to Palomar and then he'll figure out something cheap for me to do afterwards. I cannot cope with staying at home for two more years. I should divorce my parents, then I can get extra money and then they won't have to cut down my dreams. What really bugs me is they sit there and argue with each other over who is blinder. They both are blind. Can't they see they're both blind? I have so much ambition for myself – but they seem to have totally none for me...I just want to say I had a really enjoyable last hour. I went walking for an hour plus. I just was so relaxed. I stared at the stars and jumped for the trees. I danced to my tapes. I didn't care who saw – I had fun. I sweated up a storm with my dancing but even that felt good. My mom came looking for me. I just wanted to say to her, "Let me enjoy the present." Because that's how I feel but I didn't

AOM 12/12/1984: I could have totally gotten into that discussion on the American dream. I don't think there is any one set of values for any one person. I think what people believe is somewhat influenced by society. But most people have a mind for themselves. Maybe 35 degree is right. But I don't all together believe in what he's saying. I'd really like to know what he wants from life without conforming in one way or another. I wonder how long he can believe he is not conforming in some ways. I've talked to the guy. Yes, he is morbid. But he is also quite witty. He's got some powerful comebacks. What he believes in is a lot of what I do – or a lot of other people for that matter. I just don't choose to express myself so morbidly to prove a point. And I don't need to conform to the punk rocker image which he essentially does. He admitted to me that he was a punker. Isn't that a sort of conformity? I know no one can be totally unique. I call myself a non-conformist, too. But I know I have certain characteristics that are just too common to be all mine and all unique. The big difference between me and 35 degree is I like life's adventures. I like fun. I like to smile. He just seems like he hasn't given the good of life a try. He has a pretty smile if he'd only smile more. Maybe what I've observed and heard I've misunderstood. Maybe not. Who's to really say? It's people like 35 degree that you really wonder about when it comes to the future. I really do.

AOM 12/13/1984: We got robbed today. That's one of the shittiest feelings. They only stole $125 in cash. But to think someone was in your house. It hit us at a bad time, too. We're leaving for Germany so our money is extremely tight. I just wanted to give mom a hug today. But I didn't know how to go about it. I do love my parents so much. Sometimes I just don't want to face it. I'm so emotional inside. I guess I'm just hard as a rock outside.

AOM 12/15/1984: Reading Death of a Salesman really makes me see how much I love my parents. God, I love them so much, but it is the hardest thing in the world for me to admit or show. It's so hard to explain why. All weekend I've just felt like giving them a hug and telling them I love them. I really do. I wish they would believe that I do, and that I really don't like hurting them. It's just part of my nature I guess...I get as frustrated with myself as they do.

AOM 12/16/1984: *(A sticker labelled IRREGULAR is on the page with a poem next to it)*

> *Maybe it's good,*
> *Maybe it's bad*
> *To be stamped irregular.*
> *A mark, a symbol.*
> *Me? Sometimes yes,*
> *and sometimes no.*

I am 50% Swedish. But I've never been there. I've always wanted to know my ROOTS. No one will tell me. It's a secret in my family – between my dad, his brother, and my dead grandpa. They'd never talk about it. They're ashamed or something. My dad has said it was something about his grandpa getting kicked out of Sweden for doing something against the king. It's so intriguing. I just want to know*...My brother is the last of the Hegberg generations. If he has no boys the Hegbergs will end. I hate to ooo that!...Tomorrow we leave for Germany. I'm excited

[*I know my complete family history. No royal mishaps. Just a family looking for a better life in America. We are, however, American "royalty" in that my dad's mom was a direct descendant of John Alden and*

Priscilla Mullins of the Mayflower, along with over 50,000 other Americans.

AOM 12/17/1984: There is this feeling when you're sitting on an airplane. You wonder. I do. You wonder if you'll ever come back. I'm not afraid of dying, I just don't think people should die in an unnatural manner. Murder is cruel to say the least. When 35 degree talks about murder, I just wonder so much about what he's saying...I think I'm getting to a point in my life where I'm at a very anti-war state:

FRANKIE SAY

WAR

HIDE YOURSELF

The plane is getting ready to take off. What if I were to die – or never come back? Isn't that chilling? What if we got hijacked? It's not crazy. There are so many damn innocent people on this plane. People who have lived and discovered less than I have. I AM INNOCENT. THEY ARE INNOCENT. WE ARE ALL INNOCENT.

AOM 12/20/1984: I love Christmas in Germany. It's so festive. I could probably really go for living in Germany in a smaller town. The thing that bugs me, though, is that a lot of the kids never leave here. They don't seem to care about what's outside. I don't like that. Period. How can anyone learn without going outside of their terrain? The fear of discovering is half the fun of life.

AOM 12/22/1984: When I'm outside I get this explosive feeling. I just want to burst. I want to run. I want to dance. I want to sing. I feel like running down the lit street with my Walkman and dancing up a storm. It's such a beautiful and free feeling.... Sometimes I just feel like sitting outside and crying. I want the cold to turn my tears to ice. I want time to stop. I don't like the way the world is going. There are tanks and army boys on every corner here. You kind of wonder when the war's going to begin. I wish life could be just as free as I feel now – so flowing. But even feeling harmonious doesn't feel right when everything else is wrong.

AOM 12/23/1984: MAKE LOVE YOUR GOAL, THE POWER OF LOVE, A FORCE FROM ABOVE, CLEANING MY SOUL, FLAME ON BURNT DESIRE, LOVE WITH TONS OF FIRE BURNS THE SOUL, MAKE LOVE YOUR GOAL. Frankie Goes to Hollywood is so powerful. I can listen to that song, The Power of Love, hundreds of times. It says so much. It's so powerful.

12/23/1984: We've been here almost a week now. I've been having fun. My cousin and I have been getting along. That's cool because she's been asking me to go places with her. Tonight we're going wine drinking with some of her friends. The whole social atmosphere is neat here. Except they don't flirt like we do. Or maybe it's me. Who knows?...Last night I went to the coolest disco. It was gigantic. It was so cool. We didn't get home until 4 o'clock. There were some incredibly gorgeous guys there...We watched slides from the Duemmer Lake from the last time we were here when we were at Britta's. I saw Lutz. Tell me everything wasn't totally rekindled. I get to see him on New Year's Eve. Plus some other good looking guys. Including Ulf. Eeeee. They all know I'm coming. It might be a kind of weird feeling. It's so weird, too, that I still feel for Lutz. It's a strong feeling, too. I'm scared to see him. I wonder how he'll act.

AOM 12/25/1984: Merry Christmas! Mine was great. It was so different over here. It's celebrated more on the 24th. Yesterday was a beautiful day. I went shopping with my mom. Visited my grandfather's grave. Ate dinner at my aunt's. Sat around with everyone and talked. Opened presents. Went to church at 11pm. Came home. Gave my grandma and great aunt a hug, because they're them and I love them. Then we sat around and talked. It was so beautiful...It's the coolest feeling to have relatives remarking how much I've changed. Not so much looks, but personality. They all think I've made a positive impression on life. It feels so good. When your relatives approve, then you've passed the test.

SOMEBODY by Depeche Mode
I want somebody to share
Share the rest of my life
Share my innermost thoughts
Know my intimate details
Someone who'll stand by my side
And give me support
And in return she'll get my support
She will listen to me
When I want to speak
About the world we live in and life in general
Though my views may be wrong
They may even be perverted
She will hear me out
And won't easily be converted to my way of thinking
In fact she'll often disagree

But at the end of it all she will understand me.
I want somebody who cares for me passionately
With every thought and with every breath
Someone who'll help me see things
In a different light
All the things I detest
I will almost like
I don't want to be tied to anyone's strings
I'm carefully trying to stay clear of those things
But when I'm asleep I want somebody
Who will put their arms around me
And kiss me tenderly
Though things like this make me sick
In a case like this I'll get away with it.

That song says so much. All of Martin Gore's (Depeche Mode) songs say so much. They all remind me of stuff I would write. When I read or hear the words I wonder how they knew what I was feeling.

12/29/1984: Britta and I had fun in Bremen. I'm already looking forward to New Year's (Sylvester in German). Tonight we cousins went drinking. It was funny. I had so much fun being with them.

12/31/1984: I can't believe it's already the last day of 1984. It really was a great year. So much happened. I'm glad I'm ending this year here in Germany. It's snowing today and that's even cooler…I kind of feel incredibly horny. Yesterday, I totally just flirted with Hans. I mean there's something about the guy that I am attracted to. He's younger than me, though. That makes me feel young, too. I wouldn't doubt it if something happened between us. I think he's got a crush on me. It may be mutual…Actually I don't think it is. I think it's that whole challenge bit. I want the people I pick out to take up my dare. I like to see how far I can drive them. It's that feeling of power I like to possess….It's hard to explain what it is about me. I like to see how much power I can possess and who I can manipulate. It's almost like drive 'em to a point and stop…There are times when I know I would just jump into bed with a guy. It's like I don't even care about my reputation. There are times when I just have this total desire to fuck. Just wham! Bamm! Pound! I like that force. I wish I had someone to show me how to be good in bed. I've already done everything. I just want to be good. (STOP!)…Tonight we go to Oldenburg. Lutz, Ulf. Yow! What will happen? I wish I already knew. Here's to a great year – we've earned it. So much is going to happen.

1/1/1985: It's here – and it looks to be a pretty cool year. I don't think I want to make any resolutions. I have set my mind to lose 5 kilos by July. Hopefully that's when I'll be coming back. I've been invited to Greece for 3 weeks. I hope Deb wants to go. It's the chance of a lifetime. I know I'll regret it if I don't go…Well, last night was something. I feel so much for Lutz. We kissed. Wow! A few times in fact. Double wow! But inside the dude totally played me off. And today he could barely look at me. His sister says that he likes me, but this was before. It's like the most frustrating feeling. He was so drunk. But still he asked me if I loved him. I said no. It's true. The feeling's still there; I just don't know what it means anymore…I smoked pot for the first time last night. I did it with Ulf, Mario, and Stephen. Mario was pretty good looking. They're all going to Greece, so who knows what that'll bring. What happens if Lutz goes? There was this guy named Thomas there last night – who is something I've dreamed of. I'm pretty sure he was attracted to me but had a girlfriend. Happy New Year!

AOM 1/1/1985: This is a poem to Lutz. It's crazy. I feel so much and know so little. But that feeling never died. The fire never stopped flaming – it just burned. A simmer to an explosion. END.

DREAMERS

If words cold describe
A feeling so unconcise
No passion, no pain
No feeling of what?
Or is there one to define?
To say I love you - a lie
To say I feel
Is to mean
Love is a horizon
A far off view
Not guided by misperceptions
Or drunken thoughts
Love is a realness
Beyond the essence
Love has not been lived
But nearly felt
A wonder, mystery, question, misbelief.
Something that has left doubt
And sure thoughts that
what could have been

Has been‑
In a dream.
Dreamers live forever,
Just not the dreams.

Epilogue: Love is shit – and that stinks.

IT DOESN'T MATTER by ML Gore (Depeche Mode)

I am happy that I have you
Even though you're not here now
I know somewhere you are dreaming
Though it's definitely not of me
It doesn't matter if this all shatters
Nothing lasts forever
But I'm praying that we're staying together
I am warmed by your friendship
Even when you're far away
And I'm happy in the knowledge we may never see the day
When I kiss you and you kiss me
Don't pretend you miss me
The worst kind of diseased mind
Is one filled with jealousy
If we should meet again
Don't try to solve the puzzle
Just lay down next to me
And please don't move a muscle
I will thank you most of all for
The respect you have for me
I'm embarrassed
It overwhelms me
Because I don't deserve any.

Actually, despite Lutz, this year looks like it's going to be absolutely terrific. Graduation – Greece – College.

AOM 1/2/1985: I'm not looking forward to coming home. I'm not looking forward to school. What am I looking forward to? Graduating. There are times when that doesn't even sound good. It seems so far away. I can't wait for this summer…Feelings are really confusing. Like Lutz. I just wonder how I can feel what I do from these brief encounters in the past couple of years. I see so much in him. I know there are some kind of mutual feelings there. Now I just don't know how the feelings are. Both sides. I don't even know what I feel...DREAMERS LIVE FOREVER; ONLY THE DREAM DIES.

AOM 1/3/1985: It's kind of a weird feeling to think that a song could have so much influence over what you feel. The song "It Doesn't Matter" makes me want to forget and see that you cannot dwell. You can dream and know but you cannot dwell. Whoa! What did I just say? I don't even know but it made sense to me.

AOM 1/7/1985: The trip ended today. I am really kind of bummed. I had such an excellent time. I can't wait for this summer – RETURN...I am looking forward to finishing. Le Grande Finale – Finally! There's so much I have to do. I cannot picture all the work I have ahead of me these next couple of months. DEADLINES.

AOM 1/9/1985: I decided New Year's Eve that I would make no resolutions this year. I'm going to let things flow...I got accepted to CSU Fullerton today. Now I'm just waiting to hear from the one school I really want to go to – UCLA...I think I'd like to study international business. I could get my travelling in and still work in the business field...Right now I have reached a point in which I really don't want a boyfriend. I finally see that there is so much more to live for (not that I was living for one). I'd like to get married one day and eventually have kids. But I'm one of those persons who's out to achieve her goals before anything else...Inside my stomach is churning and my heart is beating quickly. I guess it's because of all I have ahead of me. There's so much. Before I wondered if I'd have enough time for everything, now I'm beginning to see things are going to fly.

AOM 1/10/1985: You know it's amazing how much alike Debbie and I are. Not physically. But in what we believe. What we think. How we feel...It tripped me out when we both at the same time showed each other those two songs by Depeche Mode. Neither of us knew. It was really weird...It's a special friendship... I just got really sentimental. I don't know why. I guess because lately I've been thinking a lot about the future. I want the future to come. I want to hold on to these present memories.... It's weird because when I think about what I want to lose least I think of my family and my friendship with her. The two things I want to lose least because they've been there through the hell of it all. And I cherish that.

AOM 1/13/1985: A year ago everything was crap. Now, now things are so cool. Things are rather great in fact. It's the greatest feeling to feel so happy and flowing inside...I don't have a job right now, either. But somehow I have this confidence I will find a new and satisfactory job soon. I start looking this week...I don't even want a boyfriend right now. It doesn't bother me to say, "No, I don't have a boyfriend." I think I finally realize that everything does not have to be now and at this moment. I have Greece and college ahead of me. So much to look forward to. Chance will lead me to love. I think I believe that!

AOM 1/15/1985: Writing Prompt: Who are you? How do you see yourself? How do others see you? What is your image?...Those are difficult to answer. How I feel at school is sometimes very different to how I feel otherwise...My image. To tell you the truth, I don't think I have one. And I guess it would depend upon the person who's observing me, when, and where. I believe that some people find me arrogant. Some find me bubbly and outgoing. Actually I believe a lot of people envy me. I don't think anyone hates me. Some may dislike what I represent (if they think they've figured it out). I don't have a bad self-image and that's very crucial. COCKY. A ROSE WITH THORNS...I am me. I finally am. There is a lot about myself that I know I still need to discover. I've stopped hiding behind would-be sentiments. Life is so much easier when there's a part of you that feels very comfortable and satisfied. To describe me is hard. I feel I am so much. But I do not try to be what society says I should. I am working towards a me that will satisfy me first....I would like to be successful. I desire no status in HS. I am known. HS is too much of a game in my eyes. I desire to make it in the challenge that lies outside of ECHS...I am a hypocrite. I will admit that. Everyone is. Sometimes I feel guilty for things I say, then do. But what I do is not meant to harm anyone...My life has been like a flow chart with its statistics, up, downs, and usually optimistic outcomes.

AOM 1/16/1985: I feel kind of numb right now. No one's died. Nothing has come as an incredible shock to make me feel this way. I just don't feel good...It's kind of hard to imagine that on June 19th I will be done with high school...I feel so young. Actually I feel old. But when I think about graduating I feel young. Out in the real world starting June 20th. God, I will be a college freshman. A world traveler. I will BE...I do like moments alone, but I am not dubbed "strange." I've been called "bazaar" by a few people. Maybe it's by the conventionalists. The people who dare not to be. Who must be as society says. I openly display that. I believe people must be creative, or different, in some aspects. Maybe how I am overwhelms people. I dare to be who I think I am. I don't like to hide what I feel. Nor do I wish to conform to societies ideals. I look for more than one conclusion. I'm never satisfied. Maybe that bothers people too. It doesn't disturb me to not always be accepted either. Preconceived perceptions bug me...”Somebody” (DM) hit me. Every time I hear the song. It makes me think. Too much, maybe. I don't even know what the song really stands for. Yes, I do. I probably even know why it hits me like it does. It's what I want. Exactly. What I feel. Exactly. In fact, I even believe I am what he is talking about. I am somebody. Exactly.

AOM 1/18/1985: Well, dear Journal, today I must bid you good-bye forever. Don't be sad. You know more about me than my diary...When I'm older and have my own 17 year old delinquents I'll be able to pull you out. They'll laugh. I may cry. But it was all worth it...It's been great. It really has. And I wish you and me the best of luck – we deserve it. Love Ya Lots! Kirsten THE END

[The *All of Me first semester journal was 210 pages of college ruled paper*.]

1/18/1985: I hadn't realized it'd been that long since I last wrote (*in my diary*). Time's flying. I guess there's a time in a person's life where she gets pissed, bored, angry with the little things. Frustration arises. That's me right now. Inside I'm very happy. I'm just scared and pissed about some things right now. I'm scared shitless about UCLA. I still don't know if I'm accepted. I want to go there so bad. I don't know what to do if I don't get accepted. I'm so scared. Thor's pissing me off. He's got this superior attitude. He got in an accident tonight. That makes me even more mad! Whatever he does affects me. Now I have no car. I don't have a job. The little fucker. He's been blowing so much for me. Sometimes I cannot wait to leave this summer. Because of him especially. He bugs the hell out of me. I can't wait to go to Greece. Deb and I are going for sure...I want to go back to Germany. I miss Lutz. I want to talk to him. I don't miss him because I feel I'm in love with him. There's something about him I really like. I'm scared of that slipping away. I should have seen that on New Year's Eve...The majority part of me wants no boyfriend. Not right now because things seem to be going so good (knock on wood!). But there's a small part of me who misses having a boyfriend. Not even sex. I know I'm going to Greece this summer. And college in September. Think maybe then I'll fall in love? Or meet someone extra special? I want a German. I miss it there. I really do. I can't wait to go back, but I have to.

1/20/1985: Last night Deb and I went to the Distillery. I love that place. Actually, I could care less about the place. It's the dancing I thrive on. I love dancing so much. Sometimes I wonder what I love to do more. It gets kind of frustrating though because there are so many good looking guys and no one asks us to dance.  I love dancing by myself though...Last night was snowball. Deb and I had no dates, of course. I do hope I find one for prom.

1/21/1985: I've decided that I'm going to devote an hour or so of time a night to me. I feel so much better when I do. I relax even when I run. I've started running regularly. It feels so good. If I keep it up I think I'll look, so good by Greece. I'm excited about it. Running invigorates me. Now just cut down the eating. Who knows? Look out world!

1/27/1985: This was a totally depressing weekend. I was waiting for all the happiness to have something go wrong with it. I didn't get accepted to UCLA. And let me tell you I was crushed. It's not even like UCLA has my major. So why be upset? It was just so ideal. And now I don't know where I'm going to go. I'm going to see if I can transfer my application from Fullerton to San Diego State. Maybe something will come of that. Right now I'm really kind of distressed. I'm also upset because I still don't have a job...I'm also bummed because dad is leaving for his new job in San Francisco tomorrow. I want this one to work out so much. Not because I want him to be gone, but because dad deserves it. I love that man. Lately I've felt closer to him. I want EVERYTHING to work out for us. I've been kind of depressed about myself, too. I feel like a moose. I just don't feel good. I want a boyfriend. Actually, I don't know if I want that; I just want to know that someone is going to be there. For prom, for lonely nights, for me. I'm really torn about a lot of things now. What I feel, what I want, what to do. Please let this all work out. Somehow, I feel I deserve it. (Not to be selfish)

[*With* second semester came another journal for *Creative Writing class*, continuing *"All of Me, Plus Some"*; It continued to be a huge source of my writing. Journal entries are AOM. Dee and Deb also makes a brief resurrection.]

DD 2/1/1985: (K:)There are actions and parts of my life that I find incredibly hard to elaborate on. I mean they're natural, not synthesized fact. It's real. But it's so hard to explain them, but I want to remember them. So if anyone asks about this incredible bond between Deb and me they'll know. The secrets we've shared and kept; emotions; jealousy; our witty sense of humor; private jokes; loyalty, etc. This became the journal of our friendship...There is always the doubt that, no matter how close, that bond will break...We went to the drive-ins last night with a group of friends. We talked our way into a free admission with some other friends. Had a blast flirting with guys. It was fun to see her being confident around guys. After a while, we talked. We sat on the back of a boy's 20 foot truck and had a confession session:

A. "Kirsten, I'm in love with "boy"."
   "Has he kissed you yet?"
   "No."
B. "Deb, do you ever get really horny?"
   (Walks away, comes back) "Hell, yes. Sometimes I just feel like calling (boy's name) up and saying, 'hey'."
   "I know. Not that I've experienced it. But I understand."
C. "Deb, have you ever masturbated?"
   "You?"
   "Once-"
   "I have too -"
   "In Germany. In the bathtub."
   "I knew one day that'd come up."
   "God, one more step in our friendship."
D. "Kirsten, I have to fart."
   "Do."
   "No." (ten seconds later) "Aahh."
   "Deb!"

AOM 2/3/1985: There are times when my desire to be in Germany exceeds my desire to be here. The little things: songs, pictures, memories. They make me want to go back. There is something there. Sometimes I really can't even explain my desire...It's like I know what I will find there. I've discovered it all before. I've had it all before. I've lived it...Most people would probably dub me a spoiled brat because I've seen the "world". Whether or not Germany, plus fragments of other countries, qualify as seeing the world is questionable. Granted, I've experienced more in my 17 years than most people do in a lifetime...I think I come under the heading of "lucky few", aside from the wealthy. I have two parents who understand and want to keep the family bonds on both sides. I have relatives who want to see me grow up...If I could say I only liked going back because someone is there to care, I'd be wrong. I have so much here, so many who care. It's hard for me to say I want to go now. The ties I have to my family are strong. But this inner force I feel to

Germany is pushing on...I don't know what I expect to find there now. A new lease on life, maybe. But I'm not even unhappy. I guess what it all gets down to is taking that final step into maturity. It's that one final leap away from adolescence...A jump from one continent to another, over oceans, through language barriers, and battle scarred fields, maybe this is my step. My leap. My jump. Each time I go something pulls me more. Every thought pulls me more. Vivid and vague impressions stir inside of me. They pull me. The more they pull, the more I see I am growing up and parts of me have to cross those barriers, no matter how large or small.

ODE TO GERMANY

Wretched field of massacred souls
Prisoners to others sacrifices
They stand alone
To the world, they're oblique
Strived for power,
Failed.
Strived to succeed,
Still striving.
They moved onward over the rolling hills
Through majestic castles,
Over the plains,
Through the marshes.
Power has failed in their hands,
but power lays in their land.
It holds the story of it ALL.
Germany, my sweet Germany.
For all past mistakes,
the present can only justify for.
You are you,
and I love you.

AOM 2/5/1985: At first I was kind of bummed that we had to keep a journal again. I know I don't HAVE to, but for the sake of graduating... Now I'm more excited about the idea, though...I'm going to have so many memories. Good and bad. I'm going to have so much to look back on. Be proud of, be ashamed of...it's easier for me to write in my journal than my diary. I find it much easier to be writing to that third person. I know what I feel...It's almost "neat" to be able to trust someone, like a teacher, who isn't going to be two-faced...

SMALL SOMETHING

I'm a small hole;
A big, black dot;
A surge in the tide.
I'm a vanishing molecule;
A spectacle of dirt;
A serial number;
A line on the wall;
I am a small something,
A nothing.

AOM 2/6/1985: Lately I've had this desire to cry. I just want to pour tears. Tropical Storm Kirsten. I haven't liked myself. Or the way things have been going. I don't like what I represent right now. In fact, I rather hate what I feel and see right now...(*later that day*) I found out today that I have to get a tooth pulled. I'm kind of scared. But then I'm glad because I'm in pain. The girl at the office complimented me. It made me feel good because, like I said, I don't feel too hot right now. She said I looked like a girl she once knew who was in a beauty pageant. Whether she won or not is another thing. But still, she meant it as a compliment...I finally got a job. It's not what I wanted, but right now I like the idea of being employed...I also found out I didn't get accepted to UCLA. I was kind of bummed and kind of pissed because (name) got accepted. She's ranked lower in our class, had a low SAT. Me #19 and (name) #3 got redirection notices. Now I don't really know what I'm going to do. It's just hard deciding...I feel like I am at this point of my life where I am lacking enthusiasm. I have no desire to do anything. All I do is eat. It's a disgusting habit. It's like all those commercials – "It's not your fault you eat. It's a disease. Call 1-800-555-1212." BS it's not my fault. There are things that drive me to eat. I rather hate eating, too. That's the way I make myself suffer, I guess. Binge, binge, binge!

AOM 2/9/1985: Two days ago I had my wisdom teeth pulled. I look like a chipmunk. It's like call me Chip for short. I'm waiting for someone to put a needle in my cheeks so that they'll pop...I haven't been too enthused this second semester. This class is dead. No one talks. Or comments. Some of the people have terrible attitudes. Some don't even care (my observations) ...Writing is an art. I don't like when people say "can't". There is so much to writing I feel I can't do as well as I wish I could. But I don't quit...I thrive on writing. It's my escape. My fantasy. My reality. My hatred...I want to write that book or screenplay one day*. I don't care if it's a best seller...All of my life I have strived to be the best. Everything

159

I do, I like to win at. Or at least achieve recognition...I don't like to say I'm a quitter, but if I don't feel confident enough about something I will quit. It's like I lose all endurance. I'm getting better though. I almost quit on life once. I endured that. I think there's so much I'm going to have to endure. With writing, with life, with hope, with love. I don't want to be a quitter. I'm a fighter. I guess I always have been. I just need to see that...Writing has helped me to discover so much about myself.

[*I did both. For myself. Just to say I did.]

AOM 2/10/1985: You can still call me Chip, but I've lost a few of the acorns. I just hope it goes down by tonight. Distillery. Despite not caring about picking up on a guy, I do like to look semi-decent.

AOM 2/11/1985: (AM)I had a terrible time last night. It was absolutely terrible. All I did was think. I never go to the Distillery and think. But last night I was on the verge of tears the whole night...I don't like it here right now. I don't like being accused of not caring about college. My parents are provoking that...And as for saving money for college, I am not going to miss out on 3 weeks in Greece and 2 weeks in Germany. There's no way...I took a look at my life last night, too. Everything just made me think. Seeing Debbie with a boy. I've always hated when it was me, a friend, and a guy. It's always seemed like I'm the one left outside. I isolate myself...I realize what I do. Yet, I persist in doing them. That's the worst part. I'm a manipulator. I can hurt so good, and I hate that feeling. I guess in today's society you are either the stepper or the steppee. There is no in between...I don't know what I want. Right now I could really care less about college. I mean I do care, but it's so frustrating...There's much I need to think about. Time is closing in, too...(PM) It's my life let me live it the I way want to. Let me screw it up my own way. Just let me do it. Let me fail. God, just let me try. You can't always think what I feel is bad or wrong. God, I only want the best for me too. I just want to do it on my own. I want to fight my own battles. I don't want allies. I don't. If I lose, I lose because I did something wrong. I am not a failure. I am someone. Why doesn't anyone believe me? Why? I am...I want to quit. I just want to stop. Say it – FUCK IT to life. I can't stand it. I don't know anymore. And it hurts. (To my parents: The stains on this page are tears.)

[I would turn that rant into a poem.]

JUST BE THERE

It's my life.
Let me live it.

The way I want.
Let me screw it up my own way.
Just let me do it.
Let me fail.
God, just let me try.
You can't always
Think what I feel is wrong.
I only want the best for me, too.
I just want to do it on my own;
Fight my own battles.
I don't want allies;
Just your support.
If I lose,
I lose because I did something wrong.
I am not a failure.
I am someone.
I am!
Please see that.
Please understand.
And bear with me.
Because what I am
Is what I like,
And what I need to be.
Please just be there.
Be there for me to hug and hold
When I need you.
Don't go out of your way.
I do know you're there.
One day I will come to you,
When I feel it right,
When I need that hug;
And when I really need your love.

AOM 2/12/1985: All I've been doing for the last hour is crying, screaming, beating myself up. I hate myself. I dislike what I am so much...I was punching my mirror in hopes that the reflection would go away. I just wanted it to shatter. I want to shatter...I see a moose. A big, fat cow. It's the ugliest feeling.... I can't stop crying. Every two seconds something triggers me. My whole life is shit. It seems like everything I do or try is nothing. It's crap...My new job isn't helping either. I am by myself for five hours a day. The worst thing in the world for me. No radio, no people.

Just me and all I have to do is think. And I don't want to think anymore. I HATE THINKING.

AOM 2/13/1985: Last night my parents and I fought. And we talked. I cried all night. Everything is just bugging me...I've already quit my job. I may be unhappy without money, but at least it might be a more content unhappy...I think I might swim, too. That might hinder finding a job but I'll have to make do. I've decided swimming may help me like myself better. I'm good at it or at least everyone else thinks so. As long as they believe it...I have to say that I won't be as good now as I was when swimming was my life. I guess as long as I win then things will be fine in their score books. Mine don't count and neither do the people who know me as a 'has been'...I just want things to go better. For me. For my family. I love them so much. I really do. I love them.

AOM 2/16/1985: ...A lot of people are expecting a great deal from me – especially myself. I know I will make it in whatever I decide to do...I'm really beginning to hope SDSU will accept me. I think I'd be pretty bummed if I don't get accepted. Two rejections. Ouch...It's weird how one minute I know what I want, then the next I don't.

AOM 2/18/1985: I saw "Breakfast Club" today. It was a fantastic movie. It moved me in so many different ways. I laughed. I cried. The acting was great. The movie was cast perfect. John (Judd Nelson) was damn good. And so was Ally Sheedy as Allison the basket case. It said so much. My mom asked me afterwards if that's how kids really feel about their parents – they're to blame. That wasn't even the point of the movie. The point was getting to know one another. Everyone was from a different group there and they all had to communicate. They shared so much. What I would give to be able to experience something like that. It was just fantastic...My friendship with Debbie seems really different lately. Sometimes I get this feeling like she doesn't trust me or want to confide in me anymore. It's getting so I don't even want to tell her things anymore. I don't have much to tell her anyways, but sometimes I feel what I'm trying to convey isn't being heard. She always sounds preoccupied when I call. It's just such a weird feeling. We're so close. Little things are becoming irritating, though. I wonder sometimes what would happen if we were no longer friends. Maybe I'm just imagining this all. I doubt it. I've just never been super comfortable in friendships until Debbie. I've just always felt used by people.

AOM 2/19/1985:...Things were cool between me and Deb today. I guess friendships go through those lapses. Sometimes I get down on things and this past weekend Debbie got the better of it in my head. Oh well.

AOM 2/21/1985: Sometimes I get this total desire to slam my brother across the face. Like yesterday. We were driving home and I had to restrain myself from backhanding him. I wanted a baseball bat. I just wanted to make him shut up and see things my way. It wasn't even so much having him see things my way. It's just his whole tougher than shit attitude. I get so frustrated by him. We cannot communicate anymore and that hurts because we used to be so close...Why do people let themselves get fat? It's so ugly. I'm looking at this girl right now who is <u>fat</u>. And it's gross. I can't help but wonder if those people are happy. There are times I get so frustrated with my weight and how I look (now she's pulling out some M&Ms!!!). I always feel like crying, dying, running. I just wonder how they feel...35 degree is really a very fascinating person. I was shocked by some of the stuff he was saying today. I can't picture skinny (name) playing football. I can't picture him losing his temper. I did picture him in jail and even that was sort of hard. He is a really fascinating person. He is real and I don't think I ever really saw that in him. Even during that time of obsession. He and Mark are both interesting people to talk to. And they laugh with me and at my sarcasm. I like that because I never really thought those two would. For some unknown reason that meant a lot to me...I hate these (writer's) blocks. It's like I start thinking too much about ideas that they all mix and become cluttered. That's worse than having no ideas because the words just don't come out.

JOURNEY

You talked of mountains to be climbed.
You spoke of Seven Seas to cross.
You knew of lands with no barriers.
You saw trails with no seeming end.
You lived the greatest love of all.
I saw the passion that never ended.
I knew the obstacles our love could withstand.
I spoke of the frictions we would survive.
And I talked of the greatness of our love
On top of the highest mountain.

A DREAMER'S TALE

A flow of mass confusion
Clutters the dreamer's conscience.
Right or wrong, become oblique.
Only conceptions of what could be
Or what could have been
occupy the source.
Visions of reality fade to blurs.
Sparkling diamonds, fancy automobiles,
Fifth Avenue.
The only obstacles in the Dreamer's Quest.
Substance – source of it all.
Dreamers occupy the slums;
Sleep in allies;
Work for scums.
Their dreams never subside.
Only their illusions of it all
die in the scuttle.
When their dream is shattered,
Their lives abused and battered
reality fades in.
Some die, and some live on.
Only the real dreamers live
long enough to recap their song.
They are the Dreamers who
never dreamt wrong.
Just never knew that even Dreamers'
Dreams can come true.
This is to the Dreamer,
This is for you.

(Mr. B: Excellent work! You're suffering from writer's block? It sure doesn't look like it.)

AOM 2/22/1985: I'm kind of bummed. I just realized tonight when I talked to my friend in Germany that I may never see Lutz again. That's kind of a crusher because I feel so much for the guy. He won't be near places I'll be this summer. I guess I should take that as the clue that there was not meant to be anything anymore between us...He asked me once if I loved him. If there was anyone I think I could really love it would probably be him...I hate when you think you find something and you have to realize that it will never be. I'm not pessimistic just realistic in this case. I have to be.

AOM 2/24/1985: My trip to Europe is finally coming together. It is such an exciting feeling...I need a job but I'm so picky about jobs...It's really important to me to be happy right now. I need a job that will keep my interest...I am an optimist. And somehow I will persevere. I will! ...Looks like I might be going to the University of Denver. I haven't been accepted there yet, but I think I will. I've always been intrigued by that school. It feels almost like a small Germany...Haven't heard from State transfer...It's cool, too, because lately my parents haven't struck down my ideas. They're being a little more tolerant.

AOM 2/25/1985: I GOT A JOB! YEAH! At Mann Theatres. I'm kind of really excited.

AOM 2/26/1985: Writing prompt: Portrait of Oceanside...I guess when you've lived in a town for 12 years of your life – the other five in neighboring cities – you overlook the good. You become obsessed by what's wrong with the city. You're constantly looking for an escape, because you know you will probably never find one...But now it's different. In a few months I'll be leaving home for college. And it's with this realization that I've discovered there's more to Oceanside than what I've come to loathe...My favorite part about Oceanside is the beaches. It always has been. I love being able to sit on sandy beaches and breath the fresh air in the summer. I love it in the winter because, despite some cold days, it gives a sense of refreshment and hope. It's an escape and it always has a story to tell...The town is so diverse. There's the old and the new. An old Spanish Mission looms in the Valley. And then there's the Valley with its stereotyped bad reputation...Most people assume Oceanside is divided equally. In the Valley live the low lifes (contrary in recent years) and at sea level live the socialites. I think over the years it's all blended in and finally emerged as one...Scuzzy Hill Street, plagued by hookers, pimps, and jarheads for years is finally beginning to pull itself together. New streetlights and breeds of people inhabit the streets. The new train station opens up new railways to the surrounding communities...Oceanside is taking on a new light to me. Maybe it's always had its own uniqueness through the years, but I was too busy looking for an escape. Granted, Oceanside is not the liveliest city, but it's home. And I've finally accepted that.

AOM 2/27/1985: If anyone I cared for ever asked me to stick around for him, I would. I feel so stupid for saying that...But it's so true. I think it's because I long for someone. I am tired of being alone; alone in a boyfriend sense. I don't like the feeling of never really knowing...Somehow I can almost see that happening to me. I can see myself falling in love and having that person ask me to stay here. I would. It'd be a special feeling. I think I'm also scared of the fact that that love may be the only love I'll experience again...I know that's probably not true. I am 17 years old and too young to get involved with someone I might be able to spend my life with. But still it's that feeling of having someone...I guess I've been thinking about college. There's so much to leave behind. But my family and friends will always be here. It's just that one person...And it's so crazy! That one special person could just change my mind. I know the hurt I'd feel, too, if things suddenly changed and ended with that person. I'd feel the guilt and anger of not going to college. But somehow, despite knowing the possible consequences, I would still stick around. (And I feel so, so..."young" and almost irresponsible for feeling that. But I don't even really feel that's wrong. Just a phase, I guess). I JUST DON'T KNOW.

That little outburst came from a reaction to a made-up situation. Actually it's not made up. I wish it were because made up situations are easier to solve. Like I told Suji, "I don't think I have the power or strength to make my obsessions reality."...I am such a fighter/survivor when it comes to anything but relationships. It's been nearly six months since Terry. I haven't seen anyone, but Lutz. That lasted a day. But I begin to wonder about my own self-worth in relationship to guys...I wonder will I ever be able to love. Yes, I will. BUT will anyone ever be able to love me? Accept me for me? Know who I am? Love me? Laugh at me? Cry with me? Feel for me? Be with me? Want me? All because I am Kirsten Hegberg? A real human being...I have so much of me to give. With Terry, it wasn't right. It never was. Just giving your virginity doesn't justify reasons to unlock the love you can give inside. If I would have really loved him, I think I would have probably released that. But I knew! ...And that bugs me. I almost feel like asking myself, "Why can't you be naïve?" But I have too much common sense for that. I've held back so much. I just wonder if that one day what I really want will also fall prey to my reluctance.

Sometimes there's one person who's very looks, words, actions spark me as attractive. Attractive in the sense that somewhere inside of me something churns. It says that there's something more to him than just his physical features...Steve hit me that way. Steve works at Mann. Everything he did, his mannerisms made him so desirable. He talked to me. He made the effort and that made me feel good...But I hear Steve is the love of every girl at Mann's. He hasn't gone out with any. I don't even know if he has a girlfriend. And what gets me is if I know I'm going to have to fight for something, I don't go after it because I hate to lose. I'd rather be able to say I was never in the running, or I just forfeited it...I don't like when I'm like that. I get very jealous and envious of that person...I wish I had the courage (and maybe the ability to accept rejection) to ask him out or any guy I'm interested in (nobody now) out. Maybe that's wrong. I am a women's libber, but I also believe in chivalry. I love when guys hold doors open for me. I don't have the guts to ask him out. But then again, I did only meet him yesterday. Give it time, Kirst, give it time...But see what I mean? I let some guy I don't know take up four pages of writing. He sparked all these thoughts. I think they're kind of dumb, but they're what I feel...One of those oddities, where first impressions stay imbedded until our second meeting.

AOM 2/28/1985: I got a letter from my dad yesterday (Note: My parents are not divorced or even separated. My dad recently got a job in San Francisco so he lives up there. We write. I feel closer to him in that sense, even though he's gone). He said he would support me in whatever I do for college, although he would prefer I go to the JC...I think I need the pressures of a four year. I JUST DON'T KNOW.

I am not a wall,
Lacking emotion.
I am not the sky,
Forever content.
I am not an ocean,
Always seeking more.
I am me.
I am alone.
And I only want
Someone to love.

By the way, I got accepted to the University of Denver today. I guess I'm happy. But I just don't know.

THE CAGE

Indescribable thoughts.
Circles with no end:
Start, stop.
Go, end.
A cage with no key:
Shake, pull.

Scream, quit.
Quilted patterns of no significant order.
Wondering if it will ever end.
The fears locked up.
The anguish emerging.
The hatred fierce.
Keys to the cage hang on a wall.
My arms can't reach.
Obstacles can't touch.
I sit in a corner and cry.
I become obsolete;
Hide my fears.
No one sees the loneliness.
I am alone.
Alone in my cage.
I have no one.
I stay hidden,
They stay hidden.
Loneliness erupts and flows yet to another cell.
It never stops.
The key, the key
Strapped to the wall.
Let me out,
Let me live to see.
Let me touch love,
No longer be alone.
Let me discover, feel ecstasy,
Then one day uncover
That loneliness was but a phase.
I don't want to be alone anymore.
Unlock this cage,
And let me live.
I deserve this chance.
Let me know.
Just let me feel
What enola* is like.
I don't want to be alone* anymore.
I just want out.

(*enola=alone spelled backwards; hence, the opposite of alone.)

AOM 3/1/1985: I woke up this morning with this feeling of summer. It was one of those exciting feelings. It was overcast and the birds were chirping. It was peaceful. It was like June. Kind of that anticipatory feeling, like when you're waiting for the overcast skies to break off and the sun will shine through...It was such a good feeling because June is going to have so much going on in it. That's an exciting feeling right there...I finally feel like my mind is clearing out. Things seem to have gone so much better this week. I just hope they continue.

AOM 3/3/1985: It was pointed out to me tonight that it's not wrong for girls to go for guys. I just never have. I've always been too afraid of what his response might be. What could it hurt (maybe a lot) if I decided to go for it? There's a 50/50 chance. I've got to stop being so pessimistic when it comes to guys. It's like what do all other girls have I don't? Some may have gorgeous bodies; beautiful faces; long, silky hair; some may even have it all. But there's got to be something about me someone has to find attractive. I don't consider myself plain in any sense, so there has to be (?) something about me...I don't want to look for that something. I want someone to tell me it. Terry always loved my smile. But to always smile is hard. I love when people tell me that, though...I wish love weren't such a broad term. Then it would be easier to say. Love really does mean more to me than just saying it. Love is an experience. I'm not looking for it. Don't even know if I really want it now...Well, my dear friend, once again I have gone on babbling. Like a brook, I keep flowing. A never-ending stream of words, emotions, fears, and hopes. Like the endless currents and sudden spurts of pressure, my writing keeps me floating atop of it all. I'll see ya 'round sometime at the delta of it all.

AOM 3/5/1985: ...I am tired of looking. It's like when I find something it slips away. Or I don't have the desires or strengths to pursue it...I am so much more comfortable being me, not someone out to get noticed by any other means. I like who I am, most of the time. I know that sometimes my personality can be very intimidating and over-bearing. But it's a power I think I possess.

INTIMATE DETAILS

A tender stroke on the cheek.
A trail of lips careening down her neck.
A peck on her nose.
Warm, passionate moments of tender embrace.
Explosive pulsation at the feel of his body
Pressed against hers.

A hand moves slowly
To caress her silky skin.
Tender waves of thought
Were penetrated with each touch of his lips.
Tremors were felt with the passion
their bodies ignited.
Meticulous motions with each passing moment.
Slow, never ending movements.
Pangs of power, lust,
Intrigue, and ecstasy.
Each passing moment, a new elation.
Each existing moment,
A new peak of delirium.
And each forthcoming moment
Conducive to each powerful pulsation
Lingering behind.
Aftermath forever possessed in the
entwined lovers super conscience.
His hand strokes her cheek;
her lips, his neck.
One last fiery kiss.
Eyes closed, fingers touching, breaths slowing,
The lovers rest.

*I have never worked this hard and long on a poem before. (Mr. B: It shows! Excellent work! The time and effort paid off.)

AOM 3/12/1985: ...I always wonder what my future will be like. It's never exactly like you plan. I can see myself living outside the US. But I can also see myself here. I can see me living on a farm. I can see me living in a mansion. I can really only see me in pretty clothes. I can see me being a business woman with a husband and family. Whatever happens I hope it's something to be happy with. And to tell you the truth, I really believe these next few years will lead to an exciting and fulfilling future.

3/15/1985: Once again I have neglected my diary. My journal has been the victim of my rages and frustrations as of late. I've had a lot on my mind. Especially about college. I finally got a job. I work 30+ hours a week. That's great for money reasons. Somehow I haven't managed to lose any weight despite the work. It's the days off that kill me! I like the people there. They're fun. I work with Suji, too. That's great because we're always laughing. Deb and boy are back together again. I have this feeling he's going to hurt her again or something's going to happen.

That's bad because maybe that's what I want. I hate sitting at home alone on weekends when I don't work. I need to get out with more people. Maybe this job will help that happen. I think our friendship is at a low right now. I'm just annoyed with life. I'm anxious, nervous. And I'm sick of being alone. I want someone to be close to. Someone to hug and to hold...I had a Pap smear done yesterday. It wasn't as bad as I thought it would be. I was relieved to find out I don't have VD. Let me tell you I was beginning to fret that for a while. But Terry would have told me. Pheww! What a relief. I just have some sort of infection. Seven days, no more itch. Thank you!... Sometimes I miss sex. I miss the closeness. I like touching. I miss having someone...I hate when guys will look at me at work but none of them will say anything to me. I don't even think my weight is a factor anymore. No, I haven't lost but two pounds. I think I have a cute face sometimes. I have spunk. I'm NOT conceited. But hey I'm sick of looking. Because I have a tendency to find but not be acknowledged...Life, with its ups and downs, will the elevator ever pick the right floor?

3/18/1985: Lisa came down this weekend. It was a lot of fun. We went dancing. And there was this guy, Nick. I don't want to dwell on him because it only makes me think about him more. Nothing happened. We just talked briefly. He was 20. He was a damn good dancer. I had fun dancing with him. But he was out of my life sooner than he came in. I hate when I think of the perfect lines right after he's gone and out the door. "See ya," I say in my head. And at the same time I know I may never see him again. "Life's a bitch," I say. "Oh well." I hate Deb's boyfriend. Suji got a new car. Straight A's on progress report.

AOM 3/19/1985: I sent in my Letter of Intent to Denver!

AOM 3/20/1985: ...Prom is two months away. I wonder if I'll go, and who with. I want to go very badly. I kind of think I will. Maybe I'll ask someone at work...shopping for the dress is the most exciting part.

AOM 3/24/1985: Yes. There does seem to be a little lack of communication between me and my journal lately. It's kind of understandable. It's like that commercial: "Same thing?" "Same thing." "Same place? Same place." It's been the same. Not too much is happening...Granted, the college dilemma is being narrowed. I'm waiting now to hear from SDSU. If I'm accepted and can get housing that is where I will be going. It's much more economical. More convenient, too...My dad is pushing to have us move up there. It won't affect me. But my brother HATES the idea. My brother is perfectly content being here.

I don't think he likes change...My dad told me that my brother and I are TWO COMPLETELY opposite people. We are. I used to think we had a lot in common. That was before he got into high school, and before I quit swimming. We are as different as night and day.

AOM 3/25/1985: (*Social commentary*) EXACTLY – "People are afraid of what they don't understand." I may not understand it, but I'm not afraid of it.

3/25/1985: I wrote to Terry today. Kind of to relieve my conscience. It was something I should have done a while ago. If he writes back he does. If he doesn't he doesn't. But I finally wrote it...I cannot deny it anymore about Bobby. I'm so jealous of his girlfriend for having him. If I liked anything about her, it might be different. I like Bobby. We had a friendship once and I hate how that's all gone now. I see him looking at me. I can't help but wonder if he feels the slightest for me. It's bugging me. I want that one passionate kiss. And I want it to be a secret. I don't want anyone to know. Just me and him. It wouldn't be right otherwise. Just to know something was there would satisfy me.

3/27/1985: I met this guy yesterday and we're going out tomorrow night. Where? I don't know. His name is Brian. He's 22. And he's a Marine. I do hesitate when I say that. And once again I get to drive. Double hesitation. I'm not that desperate for a date, so there must have been something about him I was attracted to. I just don't want to get caught up in my finding everything wrong with him bit just because of his Marine label. He may turn out to be the coolest guy. He's pretty good looking from what I remember. I don't want to let anyone influence me. A lot of people are so against going out with them. I know I chance it when "certain" people find out. There is nothing wrong with them. If they had long hair there'd be nothing stopping them. I guess that's another thing that differentiates me from others. I'm ready to give other people a try. I don't want to look for excuses not to like Brian. I never want to have to use anybody again. I don't want a commitment right now. I don't want to be too involved with a person, not just sexually. Emotionally. I would love for us to become great friends. Do things together. Have fun. That's all I want right now. We'll see what happens tomorrow.

3/29/1985: Just quickly...our date was okay. He was a really nice guy. We kissed a few times. But I have honestly come to the conclusion that I don't want to be involved. I'm too happy right now. I don't want to go out with him again for that reason. I'm content knowing I'm capable of being liked.

AOM 3/29/1985: ...I didn't sit there and pick him apart and find excuses for not going out with him again...My life is going so good right now. I am happy. I am very happy. I feel good about myself. I can't wait for my trip. I like working a lot. I still don't know what's up on college...It's not so weird, but it's weird how I don't feel like being involved anymore. I don't think that'll change either. There's a lot of other things to occupy my mind. And for once I am not looking for excuses. I have just made realizations...I feel so much older. It makes me feel good that I have realized/discovered that. Another part of me I've learned about...I feel like things between me and Debbie are getting better again. Seems like just recently we've both done some more growing. We can't wait for our trip.

3/31/1985: I don't know what it is, but I can't stop thinking about Lutz. It'll be 3 months tomorrow since I last saw him. Not a day has gone by since I last saw him where I haven't thought about him. The thing is last year (83) when I was all "in love" with Lutz it was because I was so alone and wanted to believe I had someone. I don't need to pretend anymore. I am so happy. I think if I really wanted a boyfriend, I could have one, but I don't. I just feel so much for Lutz. It scares me to think we may never see each other again. We may never have a chance at having anything. I wonder what type of power Lutz has over me that makes me feel the way I do about him? If he was super gorgeous maybe I'd understand. And maybe that's it, he's not. But I am still incredibly attracted to him – what he is. He is what I am capable of loving, what I have been "in love" with since June 1983. I feel so much. And I hope I see him and TALK to him when I'm there this summer. I can't stop feeling for him.

INCLINATIONS

Tides surge, suppressing us.
Ripping, tearing, pulling.
Saying, "No."
You move, swaying with them.
Distance is irrelevant in love's domain.
But I feel crossed with pain.
I reach, I grasp, I hope.
But I cannot connect.
I search in vain,
For one small link;
the key to us.
I search, and search.
And look, and look.

Frustration overloads inside.
I become fatigued.
Currents pull me.
They've taken you.
Maybe it's realization. Maybe.
(But) I hope not.
I am still searching for the key.
I will search until I find it;
Until you are securely
Locked in my arms;
When you are mine.

SILHOUETTES

You slipped into my heart.
I never wanted anything like this.
I felt that spark in that one kiss.
(I fell deeper into you)
We were so close,
Yet worlds away.
Two oceans apart.
The distance hasn't mended my heart.
I imagine us - strangers,
And I glow.
I stand still in time.
That one attraction, the one moment,
Pretense.
None of them false.
Everything was right.
Only you, me, and two oceans.
Yours and mine
The Atlantic and the Pacific
Met briefly with that one kiss.
And I wish they'd collide again.

AOM 4/3/1985: It's Wednesday of Easter week vacation, and I am utterly enjoying myself. The weather is fantastic. The skies are a mystifying shade of blue specked with cotton. The grass is a crisp shade of green, alive with pesky insects. There's a sereness to the birds' chirping. But my radio takes away from that. I enjoy it anyways...I am sitting in my backyard. It's not even 10am and the sun is already frying my back. I have so much energy, though. And let me tell you, that feels so damn good...This vacation has been great so far. I'm working a lot, but I love that. I've been doing some writing. I feel so relaxed...It seems I have gained so much confidence. Especially since I've been working at Mann. I don't think in a conceited sense. But I feel really good about myself as a person. I feel I have made so many new and worthwhile contacts. I feel liked and enjoyed by my peers. I feel pretty. People tell me I am, too. That makes me feel really good, too. Before I didn't want to believe people when they said that. Now I can look in the mirror and sometimes there's that one angle that catches your attention and it's like, "Sometimes there's something about you."...I do not mean to sound stuck on myself. I am not. I am just rather content right now. I'm suffering from headaches, but mentally I just feel relaxed and energized...I leave for Europe in 3 months. I can hardly wait for that. But there's so much coming up before then. Graduation is going to be here before I know it. I have to quit work in 2 months. I have to do some massive saving...My dad comes home tonight. I'm kind of excited. It's amazing that I'm getting along with everyone, even my brother. Makes me feel good, too...I know this sun won't go away, but I'm going to continue enjoying it.

4/7/1985: Today is the last day of Easter vacation. I don't know where the time went, but I enjoyed every minute of it. I feel ready to handle these next ten weeks of school. The time is going to fly. I feel it now. I have to start knowing what direction my life is going to go. It's either Denver or San Diego. I really don't want to go to SDSU. I don't like it here in SoCal. I don't know that it'll be different in Denver, but I'm ready for that challenge. I think I'll love it there. It's where I want to go. I'm not trying to escape from anyone or anything. I love my life right now. I like myself. I'm getting along with my family. Love work. So why leave? Because I need adventure, challenge, and intrigue. Yep, that's it.

(I wrote a letter that I never sent to Lutz on this day:

Dear Lutz!...What is it about you that I have become obsessed with? It's a crazy feeling to feel so much for someone you know hardly anything about...I guess I should explain something to you. Last year when I wrote you that letter, I was really depressed. I wanted to pretend that I had someone. It was like a security blanket. But that was then, and I overcame that. But what I feel for you never subsided...Once I got out of my chronic depressive state, I went out with other guys. And I learned how to put you out of my mind for a while. When I found out that we were coming back to Germany over Christmas vacation, all my old feelings for you were rekindled. The first thing I thought of was "Lutz."...I went out of my mind wondering if I would see you again. And *when I did see you again all I wanted to do is talk to you. I wanted to explain why I wrote that letter. I wanted to be with you. Just like it had been when we were at the Duemmer Lake...Your personality, Lutz, is great. You were so much fun then. I guess I've always seen in you the type of person I want to be with. It's almost as if you've become the figure I want other guys to be. I want them to be like you...It was different on New Year's. Granted, I still felt for you. I almost wish we never would have kissed. I at least got to share a small part of you...Lutz, you think there will ever be a time when you and I can sit down together – alone – and talk? Even if you say nothing at all but get out of my life, I will still be forever content in knowing we could have had those last few moments together. Sober and in one form or another...I'm not going to send this letter. I want to explain that all to you in person. And if that day never comes then I will forever keep it inside.)*

AOM 4/8/1985:...It's official that I'm going to Denver. Unless we can't get anymore money for it. But my dad told me today that if that's what I want, then I guess that's what I'll do...I have this feeling they think, or he does, it's because I want to escape them. It is totally not that. I am someone that has to be constantly pushed and challenged. I need deadlines. I work good under pressure. I like the whole theory of challenge...Somehow, I can't see me finding that here. Even at SDSU. I need to break away from SoCal stereotypes. The whole image is so unflattering to me. Who's to say that Denver will be different? The people may possess a different kind of arrogance. But ALL those new ideas and things I'm going to have to face.

ALTER EGOS*

You are my reflection;
The image in the mirror.
You may be short,
And I, tall.
You are small
And I, the contradiction
In physical togetherness we lack.
But in emotional bonds
We are stronger than the richest gold.
We are alter-egos,
One in the same.
Sharing secrets of past,
And dreams of tomorrow.
We know the others hates, fears, desires.

I know you, and you know me.
It's as crisp and clear
as the reflection on the crystal, clear water.
We've created a bubble of impenetrable plastic.
It's our air (often misinterpreted too)
We know how to play the games -
And win.
We are two in the same.
We are alter-egos.
We are in it to the end.

[*A poem about my friendship with Debbie.*]

AOM 4/9/1985: ...I am moving on for me. I need that. But what I feel inside for everyone else is so strong. I love human beings and am so intrigued by what they represent. I want to see a war because I want to capture the grief. I want to hug a small child. I want to make someone smile because I gave them a piece of bread. I want to be thankful for the peace that exists everywhere else. There is so much I want to experience, to do. I may never get a chance to do it all. But no matter how my future may turn out, I will try to do it all.

AOM 4/11/1985: I don't understand the total relevance of prom. I don't even really want to go...There is no one I really want to go with...I don't like listening to people's accusations. I am so different from all those people. I have this feeling high school was not in my plans. It's the memories afterwards that are going to be worthwhile in my memory. There are things in high school I will never forget. I don't want to...I have so much drive and ambition. I want more than most people. I'll achieve a lot in my life because I want to. I don't want 4,000 lovers and 12 illegitimate children. I want one husband and 1-3 kids. But before I do anything I want an established career...I'll probably get an MBA before I get married...I want so much from life. Why does it seem the prom has to be so important? There is so much lying ahead of that one night.

AOM 4/12/1985: My dog is dying. We've had her for 11 years. My family is pretty torn up about it. (I just talked to my brother and he said she'll probably be alright. Saves us the tear jerking for a while.)

4/14/1985: Friday night I had a party. A massive party with probably 100 people. It was the coolest party I'd ever been to. People I'd never in my life would think would be in my house were in my house. Gorgeous guys, pretty girls. None of them intimidated me though. It was so neat. Except Thor's surfboard got stolen and a phone broke because someone threw it down the toilet. I got shafted after it all though. We told mom. Last night we had it out about so much. We screamed, yelled, cried. I love her so much. I love dad so much too. He's really hurt. I just hope that come May Dad and I will be able to talk. It means so much to me to have a relationship with them, but I'm so defensive. I wish they'd accept that. There's nothing I wouldn't do for them. I don't regret my party. I don't ever want another one. It's something I got out of my system. I'm paying for it. I just hope that dad and I can continue building.

AOM 4/15/1985: Oh, what a weekend. First off, I went to the EC v OHS swim meet Friday. I got in the water and swam unofficially. I won. It killed me though. My body was aching. I just had this desire to swim. I got it out of my system. It's been over a year, too. It was so weird…That night we had a party at my house. My parents were out for the weekend so I took advantage of it. It's like I've always wanted to do something wrong in that sense…My mom and I had it out. It was so emotional. I was a total bitch. I admit it. At one point I made it seem like it was her fault for my party. My attitude was bad. I felt like shit, though. Things are kind of cool now, though…The party didn't get wild or super loud. I do have to buy a new phone because someone stuck it down the toilet. I just hope the next time I see my dad he won't let what we've started to build slip away because of that. It scares me the most. Establishing a strong and stable relationship with him means a lot to me right now and with my mom, too…My mom asked me the other night what they could have done differently with me. Nothing probably. I think there are times when I could have used their understanding in my individuality and believing in my ideas. I am so unique – I am one of those creative children parents (society) will probably never fully understand. I've accepted being different. I think most people have. I just wish everyone would have seen this all along. I've always just wanted them to be there and hear me out. But for a long time the communication lacked in our relationship. It's getting better now, though. Despite everything I love them more now and understand them better now than I ever have. I do need them. I want us to survive.

4/16/1985: I decided not to go to school today because I had a doctor's appointment. I enjoy just taking a day off every once in a while. It feels good. I bought this album. Peter Gabriel Plays Live. There are some beautiful songs. The man is mesmerizing. Some of the effects are incredible…I think stereotyping is wrong, but it is so damn contagious. Especially with Marines and why? Because we live in Oceanside – Marine capital of California. It bugs me because I have never been one to judge on a haircut. And that's all it is – a damn haircut. Marines are people. I am intrigued by them because most of them come from places I've never been, places I've only heard or read of. They have so many stories. Working at Mann's I have come to see that some of them have great character and personality; some are total assholes. I know I could probably be happy with one. When I say I'll never go out with one again it's because there are so many factors stopping me. The greatest and probably dumbest is I don't like driving them around. I feel used. If they had a car it'd be another thing. Believe it or not, my peers also influence me. I care what they say. I just wish that they, too, could see there is so much more to them. Marines have a way of making me feel beautiful. They look at me. They talk to me. They tell me nice things. One of the greatest comments I ever got was when one said, "I like you; you're crazy like me." Some tell me I have pretty eyes. I do need someone who is above my intelligence. There is this one Marine who comes into work who is gorgeous. He is. I find him incredibly intriguing. He's well built. And dresses preppyish. He's always got something to read in his hand. He seems quiet and reserved. He's never there with anybody. He almost seems conceited in a sense. Maybe there is something about conceits I like. I don't know why. They never really do that much for my ego. I don't really think I attract them though. Not sure why I felt I needed to excuse my criticalness of Marines tonight.

AOM 4/18/1985: OK, I got shafted. And I learned, but I cannot believe I'm actually sitting here on a bus. It's a joke. I have been punished. Give me the car. I know. I know. (Busses don't even stop nearby anymore). This is too emotionally exhausting for me. I must rest.

4/18/1985: I heard back from Terry today. It was a nice letter actually. He sounded so old in it for some reason. There are times I do miss him. But I like it better now. It's easier for me to talk about him and things now. His letter relieved a lot of anxiety and regret, too.

Dear Kirsten,

I got your letter. Surprise to hear from you. I was hesitant about writing to you wondering how you would react or feel. Well, I didn't react to your letter. I had a feeling that's what it said as soon as I saw your name. I am 20 years old. I can get pity from anyone, I don't need it. And as for thinking about you, I think it's a little more than twice a week, or day, whatever, I think about a lot. I still have all your letters, and I hope I can keep the rest.

I didn't, and I didn't want you to stop your life over what happened.

We'll get over it, but I would think it would be even better if I stayed there. I'm positive. I was in love, in some shape or form, and it wasn't just the physical part. Our communication got better, we just started knowing each other when I left. Don't blame it on anyone. I think I can be a friend now. Those kinds of things take a while. I would write though, who knows, the next guy, hopefully will be moi. I don't know. I hope you're taking care of that beautiful body of yours. Maybe down the road our paths might cross and I'll buy you dinner. I do miss you, we had some fun. Maybe not to you, but I did.

Maybe you'll write me again? I think you can. I'm not writing anything because there's nothing to write. Pretty simple, huh. Just be a good girl for moi. Tell mom and dad I said hi. Sure would like to see ya.

Love always, Terry

PS I got promoted to L/Cpl

PROM. Still no date. But what's cool is that everybody is looking for me. At school, at work. A couple of guys at work said they'd take me, but they're already going. Robbie said he'd take me if it weren't for Jessica. He said Paul would be a fool not to go with me. Paul used to work at Mann. And I had a sort of crush on him. Robbie's going to try and set something up. The guys at work make me feel so good. Rod told me I could have anyone I wanted. Wayne loves my eyes (Mike, too). Andy likes me. Ego boosters, but I ♡ it.

AOM 4/21/1985: What is there to write, to talk about? I do feel a great deal of excitement, and some confusion. On a good note, I heard back from Terry. I feel so much relief and guilt taken away. I've finally been able to accept things. It took six months to happen, but I'm glad it finally did. He doesn't hate me and, more importantly, I don't hate him in the slightest. It's such a relief. I'm really scared about DU. Not about going. Inside I am so happy. I look forward to opening every DU envelope that comes in the mail. What I am petrified about is the money. Denver is practically all I think about...It might sound contradictory, but I don't think I really want to go to the prom. There is no one I really want to go with...I need this trip this summer. This trip marks the beginning of the rest of my life to me. It's one of the biggest steps to being an adult. I'm ready to run into walls, bruise my knees, have my ego crushed, and I'm ready to fight those obstacles. I'll probably want to quit and head for the security of home more than once, but the accusations are going to keep me one step ahead of everyone else.

AOM 4/22/1985: Mom took us off restriction this morning. And I am so happy. I do not feel like I got off with no punishment either. That one bus ride was enough for a lifelong punishment for me. Actually it wasn't that bad. In fact, I think I have the coolest parents in the world. Not just because of that, but because of all the little sacrifices they make for us/me.

4/22/1985: Welp, Deb got a date to the prom. I'm excited and jealous at the same time. I have no one and it is almost like a feeling of complete loneliness. I haven't felt alone in so long. I haven't longed for anyone in so long. I can't sit here and think NO ONE is attracted to me. It's just not the right people. Or they're someone I can't see myself having a good time with…I want to get wasted off my ass. And maybe I'm saying this out of a slip of depression but I just feel like being laid. Having one passionate fuck with somebody. For some unknown reason I feel I need that. I need the closeness and intensity of someone I hardly know. I want to lose all control that night. I want to be something I'm not. Almost like one of THEM. I just want somebody for one night of passion. Passionate kiss, passionate thrusts. I do not want a commitment. I want one night of frustration relief. That's all. Can't I have that?

AOM 4/23/1985: I don't know how long I'm going to be able to write with clear eyes and clear mind. I am crying right now. Our dog died today. God, I loved her so much. I was the last one in the world to admit or show it, but I loved her so much. And now she's gone. A part of me has gone now, too. Me and Heike had an understanding. We had our own secret bond. She was my friend and I was hers. I don't want to have to regret the words of hatred I said to her or the angry gestures I made.  Heike lived through the hell years of my life and was probably the greatest victim of my frustrations. She's the first death I've ever really had to cope with. It's so hard. I began to alienate myself from her at the end. I never touched her. I could hardly look at her. Those beautiful brown eyes. The way they'd look at me. The sadness and pain she must have felt. I had to let go of her. Maybe I thought I could escape the pain. I can't. Heike's memory will never ever die. No animal will ever replace her. It was so much easier when my grandfather died. I'd begun that separation long ago. Just two weeks ago Heike came into my room – a place she has rarely ever gone – and she slept on the floor while I was taking a nap. I can't stop thinking about her. I can't stop crying. And I can't stop feeling the pain of her absence. This house has lost a certain glow that Heike brought. It's so hard to accept that she's gone. But it's reality now. I just hope someone's taking care of her. She was so special. I wish she wasn't gone. I want to be holding her right now. I'll never be able to let go. And I'll never want to. My family can sit there and believe I never cried over Heike, but that's another part of the special bond I had with her. Our closeness was secretive. I know there will be times now when I turn for her and there will be nothing. Heike, I love you.

[*I was sobbing as I transcribed my words on the page. I am so glad to have remembered her like that. I would learn from her to give unconditionally to all my future dogs, every one of them stealing my heart.*]

4/24/1985: Sometimes, like lately, I really want the closeness of sex for those few moments. The desire is incredible. I feel so horny. I wish for once I could have an affair. One that will not phase me emotionally the next day. I just have this totally romantic way of seeing it. It won't be a 'let's not talk' type thing. He'll want to talk to me. We'll feel compassion for each other, but it will be our little secret. I would want to be in control inside. I want him to lead after the initial advance. I can see the kisses, the hand movements, the loss of control. My mind will only be on those moments of lust together. But somehow I do not see me simply being able to lose/forget that night...The one person in the world I would really like to go to bed with is Lutz, but to me that would be making love. And it'd be something in my life I would not be able to forget. I could get lost in love with him. I could see myself losing control to lust, passion, intrigue. I want to mess around in Europe this summer. I want to be totally carefree and promiscuous. In college is when I want that commitment. It's the casual affairs I want now. Finding someone who cares is what I want in college.

THE YOU

I can't stop the impressions,
the memories, the visions,
the you.
I can hold the kisses;
the moments, the passion,
the you.
The you forever embedded in memories
The you I want to hold again
The you lost in the ruckus
The you I cannot release.
It's you I'm crazy for

It's you I want and need
It's you, the you, I love.

DO YOU?

"Do you care for me?
Do you love me?
Need me?
Feel the passion?
Withstand the pain?
Fight the strain?
Do I make you smile?
Send you high a mile?
Fancy your style?
Do you love me
Like I love you?" he asked.
She said, "No."

4/26/1985: I feel so alone right now. I have been all day. I almost feel like a rejection. And I'm having a hell of a time controlling my eating. And when I can't do that you know something's up. I almost feel like crying. I can't pin down why. I just feel like my life is lacking something right now. I don't even think it's a guy. It's just plain...I keep thinking about Lutz. It'd probably be better if I didn't see him this summer...I guess what it'll take is for me to fall in love with someone else who can love me back.

AOM 4/28/1985: I am so tired. My body doesn't seem to want to fight anymore. I am lacking the usual Kirsten energy. I have no spunk. No desire. I feel like I am standing still and everyone else is moving forward. I can't concentrate. Or think. I am so bored. I'm depressed. And I can't find the key to getting out. There's usually a way. All my reserves are used up. My life is the same day after day. There's no versatility. There are times when I feel so alone, too. I become so frustrated because I can't figure out if my life is ever going to take on a new direction. I know it will, but I need something new now.

AOM 4/30/1985: I went out with this guy last night. He was totally cool. It was neat in that I could actually talk to him. I didn't have to lower myself. He's even got incentive. (I will discuss more on this later). For once I felt like I didn't have to impress anyone. I was natural. And I was able to think about my own feelings first. No – "I have to impress him." I liked him and I think he liked me. It was so different than being with Terry. Ajey and I could talk about everything. He'd listen and laugh with me. I didn't feel like I was playing games. I was me and that was a really good feeling...I feel such a difference in attitude about Navy guys versus Marines. Ajey looks normal. He talks normal. Acts and dresses normal. And I don't even have a complex...It's so weird how my life was so down in the shits. I was bummed because my life was so BORING. That one date added versatility to my life...Deb is also starting to see someone. This will be the first time that she and I will have both started seeing someone – no matter how short it may turn out in either or both cases...It's just kind of weird (And I wish there was another word besides weird!).

5/1/1985: It's so weird how my life varies from day to day, page to page. Monday, I met this guy, Ajey. We went out Monday night. We went to his apartment and drank strawberry daiquiris. It was cool. We could talk and laugh. He didn't even kiss me until 15 minutes before we left his house. It felt so good to kiss him, too. It felt right. It's been so long since I've felt that comfortable being with someone. It just felt right. We came here and sat in the living room for an hour – kissing, what not. What made me feel good is that he didn't grab for any certain parts. It was NORMAL kissing. We're going to the Distillery tomorrow night...He's 6'. Brown hair, <u>blue</u> eyes, killer tan. Nice body. Aged 20. In the Navy. I'd never have guessed except I met him at the McD's out base.* He's got a nice car. He is so totally different from Terry. We can joke around and play along with each other's jokes. He's kind of got an arrogance, but he doesn't sit there and talk about how good looking he is. I wonder what will come of all this – (one date). I'll tell you the results of manana. No games. I've already established that.

[*I had been there shopping and was leaving when these guys called to me from the McDonald's. I kept walking but something inside me made me stop and turn around. I had never done that; it was not something I did. I only remember being impressed by Ajey, but I know there were others there. He was playful and cocky which I found really appealing.]

AOM 5/2/1985: Today I gave a handicapped person a ride to school. He was walking up the hill towards school and was looking for a ride – hitchhiking. So I decided what the heck and stopped and gave him a ride up here. His name was Reggie, or something like that. And he was nice. He wasn't retarded, not even. I think he has polio or something like that. It made me feel good to give him a ride. I would have felt guilty all day if I hadn't...I'm going out with Ajey tonight. I wonder how this evening will turn out? I always wonder how the 2nd, 3rd, etc. will turn out...Mr. H said something to me today that made me feel good. He asked me what

I've changed about myself recently. I told him nothing and asked him why. He just said something about me seems different and he likes it. It WASN'T a perverted sentiment. It's probably because I'm not pissed at him or the class that much anymore...Bobby said hi to me today. Amazed me. I wish he wouldn't have said anything. I could have gone the rest of the year not saying anything to him. My friends don't like him. And I think I'm beginning to see why they don't. He's everything I despise. But last year when we had that special friendship there were things they'd never understand. But I know now that I, too, would be reluctant to trust a friendship like that again because it ended too fast and without warning.

5/3/1985 @ 1:00am: Ajey and I have a romantic involvement. We slept together tonight. It didn't seem wrong. And I was in control when it counted. I could say no. I could enforce it. The closeness and the way it all happened felt good. Ajey may be the casual affair I've been looking for. It still hurt, but it's been so long. I hope that one day I will learn not to hurt, or just won't have to hurt at all. It was a good feeling to be with him. And he cared about getting me pregnant. In fact, he brought it up. So we were careful with that part of sex. I enjoyed myself. I have a feeling it'll be a while before I tell Deb or Lisa. Maybe Mickey because she can't say anything. I'm tired. Until later.

5/4/1985 @ 1:00am: Just got back from being with Ajey. I'm not sick of him yet. We went to bed again tonight. It didn't hurt this time. In fact, it felt rather good. We talked about the casual relationship bit. It's so cool because that's all it is and all I want it to be. I like him and have fun with him. PS Suji knows. And I don't want Deb knowing for a while.

5/5/1985 @ 1:05am: I feel so guilty for lying to mom. But I like seeing Ajey. So I find my ways. He and I and his roommate went to Spoons and had drinks. I actually was served. Ajey and I went to the mall together today and were over here a while. We are so much alike and that's what is so cool. I like being with him. We have fun and that's important...I worked until 3:00 today and from 3:15 until 10 I was with Ajey. Sex gets better and better. It doesn't hurt anymore. He's fun to be with. I don't get sick of him. At first I could kind of see similarities between him and Terry. Now I hardly see any – if any. They are so different. I like Ajey a lot. But it's neat because the relationship is totally planned. But even now he talks more about doing things together. I guess the time bar is a blessing. It's only been a week and that's so weird. We can talk about so much more now. We laugh. There's no pressure. I like that. I think I may go out and get the pill tomorrow. Just to try and be sure.

AOM 5/6/1985: Spent Friday with mom. We talked about things. It was pretty cool spending the time with her...Dad came home this weekend. No arguments. We talked some about DU...As for the rest of the weekend, I either worked or was Ajey. Ajey and I have a totally casual relationship. No strings attached. I like it that way. It's what I've been looking for. I like him a lot but I know when it has to stop. It's kind of cool having a restriction – it bars emotional bonding.

5/6/1985: Tonight was totally cool. Ajey and I went to the movies, out to yogurt, and then sat in his car for an hour and talked. We talked about what attracted us to each other. About sex. And love. We talked about the times we've had sex. He said he felt guilty after the first time, even the second, because it happened so fast. He loves how we can talk and "B.S." and laugh no matter what. He says I'm one of his best friends here because we can talk about anything. I can't believe it's only been a week. It seems longer. I think it might be harder than I anticipated not to get too attached. I even think it might be happening to him. Things never are like you expect them to be. I'd elaborate more, but it's late and I'm exhausted.

AOM 5/7/1985: Ajey and I talked for an hour and a half last night. It was one of the coolest conversations I've had with a guy. We talked about love and sex and how alike we are and, and, and...We can talk so easily. It is such a good feeling. I could be "addicting" in his words. But we both know the time. It's hard to explain what it is or what I feel. I like him a lot. I don't even want to contemplate love. I can't really explain it without feeling dumb or presumptuous. Maybe someday when I better understand. And maybe one day I'll be able to tell Debbie all about me and Ajey. The truth, the whole truth, and nothing but the truth.

5/8/1985: I think I'm really confused right now. I may be jumping to conclusions, but how is it I see a car identical to Ajey's with a girl in the passenger seat. Ten minutes later I call his house and he's not home. It kind of hurts. He tells me all of these things. And maybe that's it 'the no matter what happens we'll be friends.' Maybe that was my sign. We would no longer be lovers, but just friends. Maybe that's the way it should be. I was floating in high heaven. And I really liked him. I do really like him. I just feel burned. Maybe it wasn't him. I do think it was, though. It does hurt. It pisses me off too. Not so much because we went to bed but because I was believing. Maybe dad's right – he's just a BSer. But my god I liked that BSer. I was so comfortable and sure around him. I'm scared to ever call him again – and that's the scariest part. I want to believe I got a wrong #, but I didn't. I want to believe I imagined this, too. But I don't think I did...Okay, so I totally jumped to conclusions. He didn't even have his car tonight. They were at the gym. It made me feel so good to talk to him. I could hit myself for jumping to conclusions. Tomorrow night, Ajey, his roommate, Deb, and I are going to drink daiquiris at their house. It could be fun.

AOM 5/9/1985: Everything is finally falling into place. My biggest worry is getting the financial aid for DU. I need the newness of Denver. It's a challenge, and that's something I need. I am excited about my trip, too. I cannot wait to jam. It'll be weird leaving if Ajey and I are still seeing each other. Man, last night I jumped to conclusions. I could not believe how jealous I got. But it wasn't even him. I felt so bad. I mean, I didn't unleash it on him. I guess it's just going to be harder with this no strings attached bit.

AOM 5/10/1985: I had a gnarly hangover this morning. We drank strawberry daiquiris last night. So now I'm lagging. I feel so blah – But, I was happy seeing Ajey. He just makes me feel good.

5/11/1985: ...The other night Ajey and I were talking about what were to happen if I got pregnant. "It'd be our problem, not just yours." He even said he'd take me down to get the pill. But I'll go by myself. I'd feel weird. He leaves in exactly two weeks. I wish I knew what he felt for me. What if he doesn't want to see me when he gets back?

5/12/1985: I am so tired and sick. I do not feel good at all. At first I thought it was something to do with me feeling uncomfortable over the weekend. But being with Ajey tonight made me feel good. We talked for an hour about things. A beating around the bush talk about us. Being together, discovering our true feelings. Made me feel good.

AOM 5/13/1985: This weekend was weird. I was so uncomfortable the majority of it until last night when Ajey and I once again sat and talked. I think what was bothering me was that I am trying to deny the feelings I am beginning to feel for Ajey. We didn't talk about us directly in that sense. He just said that he's tried denying and it doesn't work – you eventually fall. Yes, definitely when I talk to him I don't even notice an age difference. Three years isn't much – true. Another thing that still is bothering me is that I went out with a Marine and he doesn't know. It shouldn't phase him or me any, and I doubt it will. I don't know why I would feel guilty – do feel guilty. Me and my non-conformity, but I'm almost being a conformist for feeling guilty. I guess because Marines are stereotyped and so are the girls ("sleazes"). But Ajey isn't and I never was.

Mr. B's question to ponder: Why are there so many unwanted teenage pregnancies? My response: This first idea hit me when Europe was mentioned. In Europe, sex is accepted. Here it is still wrong. Ever since I can remember, I've seen dispensers for prophylactics on the streets in Germany. The precautions are there. Here you have to walk into a drugstore and admit to the older generations that you are having sex. God forbid it might even be a secret associate of your parents. As for answering the question on unwanted pregnancies, I don't know that there is just one answer. A lot of people believe the sexual myths. It amazes me how ignorant they can be. Schools can't and don't teach enough. I never learned anything in sex ed. I learned about my body to some extent. There is something they forget to teach. Having sex is not an act of ignorance. Nor is it an act that is wrong. In fact, I don't think sex is wrong period. Unless it's solicited. And yet it is they who take the precautions. Many girls today are on the pill. But it takes a month for the pill to work preventatively. For that month, what do you do? Abstinence is not easy when there is desire, when the will for the other is stronger than resistance. I don't think sex is ever really planned. It just happens. When there is mood, when there is atmosphere. I don't even believe any more that all guys want sex or need to have it. Girls can be just as strong willed. I've had all the courses, read the books, seen the statistics, yet I've been guilty of not using protection. What would I do if I became pregnant? I'd be another statistic. I can tell people I'd have an abortion, but I don't know if I really could. No matter what kind of decision you make you have to live with it for the rest of your life. If I got pregnant now my parents would be so hurt. But they'd be there for me. We've talked about it. Parents can't always talk with their kids. At least with my mom we can talk about sex and the consequences. She has a hard time sometimes understanding my values or theories, but she listens to me. I would almost contemplate keeping a baby if it were to happen to me (but I'd rather it didn't).

TRAPS

You set yourself loose
and are caught.
You put up barriers
and are captured.
You shield yourself
and become imprisoned.
You run to hide,
but trip instead.

You avoid the obvious,
but hit the inconspicuous.
You are trapped
in the web of love.
You become fatigued
from fighting feelings.
Emotions scrambled
in your heart and mind.
You know what is right,
but side with the wrong.
Caves only hide you
from low tide.
Seas rise and expose you.
You are caught in the trap,
and there's no escaping.

[The first poem I wrote about Ajey. His initials are at the bottom of my writing.]

5/13/1985: I can't believe I have nearly come to the conclusion of my second diary. Finishing it tonight will give me a sense of accomplishment. It's weird ending this one, though. It has experienced the worst times of my life and some of the best. You know my emotions inside and out. You were a victim to my lies, my tears, my awakening, my self-discovery. You experienced the loss of my virginity, the trials and tribulations of college choice making. You were neglected, and you were cherished. It was too bad that you couldn't talk. There were times when I could have used that. For the first time I will be terminating a diary with someone that I like a lot and practically have – Ajey. I wonder if I will fall in love. Sometimes I think it's inevitable. But then again there's the time barriers. He says his trip will be the test for him. I feel a lot for him. I just hope no matter what that I can always turn to him as a friend. I have learned so much from him. All guys are not alike. There is so much more to him. So many what ifs keep coming up. There's so much more he can teach me. You know the neatest part is that it is not just a sexual relationship. And I don't need to learn in those regards. We've been together so many times lately where we easily could have but we just talked and joked instead. We are friends. And that is so important. The physical attraction is just a way of expanding our friendship. Maybe it's a way of showing each other how much our friendship means…It's been traumatic. It's been happy. You can't relive the past, even the regrets. Thank you for being there. I love you. Kirsten

The Soft Red Journal
(May – September 1985)

5/14/1985: Note # one: This is going to be more like a journal than a diary. What the difference is, I don't know. I guess journal sounds older and more for sharing all sorts of experiences with. Diaries are more for love and feelings. God knows, this will include all that, but it will also include more. Of what? I don't know just yet. It'll be there on paper, that's all.

Ajey and I went down to the beach and watched the sun set on the pier. We talked and laughed. I have such a great time with him. We can talk about anything. And the more we talk the more it seems like we sort of open up feelings for each other. It's been just over two weeks but I like him so much. It's getting easier to forget other things. It's only me and him when we're together. And that is a special feeling.

AOM 5/15/1985: Last night mom asked me if Jey and I ever fight or argue. She asked me if I was sick of him yet. No, no. I am not. And maybe that is what's baffling her. I am constantly with him. Time flies when we're together. WE can talk for hours about things. If we ever argue it's only in fun. It's a teasing type of arguing. It's fun. Last night – actually the more we're together now, the more we talk about feelings and love. But it's all indirectly. It's not directed towards us in particular. But I have this feeling when we talk, parts of our conversations pertain to us. He leaves in a week and a half. He says that'll be the time when he discovers what he feels for me. I like him a lot. I wonder if *TRAPS* describes it all. Am I getting caught? Is he? Is there an escape? Do we want to escape?

Yesterday when we were talking in class about sex and our parents, I just wanted to tell the class about my parents. My mom in particular. When I was about 14 my mom and I first started discussing sex. She was really reluctant about it. But I made her talk to me. Last summer when she found out I was no longer a virgin it kind of broke the ice more. It's easier to talk about those things now even though I know she's not that comfortable. What she doesn't understand or finds it hard to is that you don't have to be in love with someone to go to bed with them. She told me I was wrong when I said I was too young to fall in love. Maybe I'm not. But I don't feel you have to be super committed to a person to have sex. One of my friends recently lost her virginity to someone she hardly knew. She was crushed and cried. She doesn't talk about it now. I don't push it, because I can empathize with her even though I never felt that. One of my friends called me cultured. She says my ideas are so broad and varied compared to everyone else I'm associated with. She calls me METRO. She says that describes me perfectly. Maybe it does. I do definitely believe that how I feel about things are more open-minded in approach than a lot of people. I'm not a traditionalist. But I am not a complete deviant. I am somewhere in between with a lot of different ideas.

5/15/1985: ["In love with your mind; obsessed with your body."] If I could only tape record some of mine and Jey's conversations, I'd be able to explain so much better. We started out talking about names for kids and marriage – but not to each other, just how it would be. We talked about our trips. He said the only girl he would want to take back from his vacation is already here. He said it would be the perfect vacation if I were to go along. Tonight we also talked about us directly. We talked about how at first we both thought 'casual affair', but how there's more. There's emotion. Both of us were really reluctant with giving in to our feelings. He said he'd realized it was more around last weekend. With sex there's no feelings (1st time/s). When making love there's emotion involved. I'll tell you the next time we do whether I feel it's making love. It's more than sex. Making love is a big statement. It's like someone saying to you, "I would kill or die to make love to you." Ajey has made me begin to contemplate SDSU. I wonder if we'll stay together that long. It'd be nice. He talks of taking me away for the weekend. Of being alone with me. Talking is enough for us. And that's such a great feeling. I look forward with anticipation to the next time I can see him. I love being with him. I know I forgot things, but they'll probably come up later anyways.

5/16/1985: I have eleven hours until this day is over and then my period will be late. What am I going to do if it doesn't come? It's hard not to think about that, even though I try not to. I do not want to be pregnant. God what then? I do not even know. Scream. I've being eating like I'll be starting the rag – so hopefully that's a very good sign. Pray!...I told Ajey that I'm scared I might be pregnant. I was so obnoxious tonight. I was having fun. And then on the way home I just tripped. I told him and he told me not to worry. Well, we discussed things and I'm trying not to worry and I'm hoping that tomorrow morning it'll be here. We got off of that and briefly discussed us. He goes ask me anything. But I didn't have anything I wanted to ask. He told me he'd always be there, "Maybe not in Denver, but I'll be by your side until then. It's only a phone call away." He asked me if I was his. I asked him if he was mine. He said he was, and I said it applied in both cases. Then I asked him if that meant commitment. He said it meant we needed to talk about it someday. There's no rush on either part. It was weird. The night was kind of weird. I hope I see him tomorrow. He said there's definitely an emotional bond.

5/17/1985: I like to write every time after I go out with Ajey. They let me off work early tonight. I swear the last time I ask for that. I've got to stop. So I went to Ajey's. We ended up in bed after a long process of taking off our clothes. He bought a rubber. At least he's/we're thinking of the consequences now (still not here). It was funny because things were leading to things, and I ended up asking him if he liked getting head. I don't like giving it that much that's why. The next time I decide to I'll just have to blow him away – no pun intended. He said he'll miss me when he's gone. I have this feeling I'm going to end up missing him a heck of a lot. I love just being held by him. And the more I am with him, the more secure and comfortable I am with him. He makes me feel good.

5/18/1985: I am NOT pregnant! Thank God for great favors. I think I'm becoming more attached to Ajey. I always want to be with him. Tonight we went to some small party. His roommate and I talked most of the time mostly about a girl he slept with. But something also came up when he said the last girl Ajey was seeing got too serious. I don't think I am. And I don't want to become that way. It's hard not to feel because I know he feels for me. I'm beginning to wonder if maybe I am falling in love. That's hard, too, because you find and then get to let go. I felt so young tonight. For once I felt the age gap... We were having sex on the floor, but I couldn't get into it. Sometimes it's hard. It just made me feel so young and I wish I would have told him that because now it's beginning to bug me. I'm so tired tonight. All I want to do is sleep. (Thank you, again.)

5/19/1985: I just want to make this really brief tonight because I am dead. I went over to Jey's. I tripped. I just started thinking about Ajey and me. I'm becoming attached and I'm scared of that. I'm getting caught in the trap. His roommate and I talked for a while tonight. He makes so much sense. He makes me reluctant towards the serious aspects of Ajey. Maybe he's setting me up for something. I liked talking to him. Made me feel better towards the Ajey situation. Ajey gave me four red roses today.

AOM 5/20/1985: Last night was weird. I was too deep in thought. I'm growing attached to him. It's not wrong, I just don't want to have to deal with that. I like him a lot and that's what is hard.

5/20/1985: ["Let's put it this way, you're the first girl he's bought flowers for." – Roommate] I'm too tired to write about Ajey's and my conversation. It said a lot, though.

5/21/1985: Last night Ajey and I talked. We talked about us. To relate details is kind of hard because it never comes out on paper the way it did at that moment. We talked about jealousy. And his trip. He said if he found out I went out with another guy he'd be so jealous. I am jealous. I can't and don't want to stop him from anything. I wish I could follow through with his request to go with him. He likes me and I feel like I am his. We talked about seriousness and feeling no pressures. It hasn't turned out like we originally intended – casual. There are definitely a lot of emotions involved. When I was with him today I could begin to accept the relationship we do have. We have fun together and the little insecurities are dumb (No!) – but unnecessary. I went over there today. We went to bed. It was different and neat at the same time. It doesn't bother me anymore that I haven't had an orgasm. It's really not important. It'll come in time. He came over to play with our new dog, Tarah. Mom and Thor were here and he didn't seem uncomfortable and that's kind of neat, too...Ajey and I are going to talk about commitment when he gets back. It's our time to discover what we might really feel for each other. It's going to be a long three weeks. But I'm hoping they'll just fly and I'll hardly have time to miss him or worry. I will, though, badly.

5/22/1985: Tonight was cool in bed. We kept getting interrupted beforehand, but we made it. Tonight it was more like me making the initiative. It felt good. It was totally intense. I'd never seen anyone get into it like that (the movies, etc.). The only things wrong with tonight were I didn't have an orgasm and he didn't finger-finger me. I love that feeling. It is so damn erotic. The orgasm part doesn't bother me. I enjoy it with him. And I think he enjoys it with me. Tonight he said he hopes his trip goes by fast; he's going to miss me so much. Damn, I hope it does, too. I like him so much. I'm not going to see him tomorrow – unwillingly (work). I can't wait for Friday, though. We get the entire evening together. I wish I could stay the night. That'd be excellent, but with dad home, it'd be more than slightly pushing it.

5/23/1985: Ajey leaves Saturday and I am so bummed. I don't want him to go, but I can't hold him back. I'd be wrong. I like him a lot and sometimes that's kind of hard to accept...Prom is Saturday night. Dateless me is working. I don't want to go to prom. It's just being able to say that I went. Hopefully, I'll keep my mind on other things. At least I know that Ajey thought about taking me. That's pretty satisfying...I get to get glasses. Oh, yea! Hopefully, they won't be permanent!

AOM 5/24/1985: After tonight – starting tomorrow – I will once again have time to dedicate myself to school. I know there are only 3-1/2 weeks left, but nonetheless, I'm going to end it with some good writing. Ajey had kind of taken over my time, but he leaves tomorrow morning for 3 weeks. I'm not glad, because I like him so much. But I need the time to get things done and in order...For a while I was beginning to think about SDSU, mostly because/just in case Ajey and I stay together. But I have come to realize that now would be the best time to leave Oceanside, because I have everything I could want here. I have my family. Debbie. Other friends. Ajey. I have direction. And hope. I am happy. All the aspects of my life are fulfilled in one shape or form. I feel good. I've even taken the initiative of doing and getting things done that have been bothering me. School's my final one. I want to end it with straight A's. I know that the caliber of my classes is not too high, but still...I can't wait to leave for Europe. It's in a little more than a month. It's on my mind a lot lately, too...I've been evaluating my life and I'm really beginning to realize what I want. The family will always be here. Debbie will, too. Ajey's here now. If we were meant to be, our relationship will survive. All the time barriers and tests. God knows, we'll have enough of those. Denver could hold so much for me. It probably will. And I'll never know unless what I have here is left behind for a while. They'll always be in thought. It's probably best to leave now because I'm not as bitter toward the city. I wouldn't be as reluctant to come back here. (I promise you, Mr. B, that come June 19th I will know definitely what is up.)

5/24/1985: I am immensely bummed. Ajey leaves in four hours. We just kissed goodbye, stared at each other for a while, and parted. I didn't want to let go. And I don't think he did. In fact, he told his roommate he was having second thoughts about leaving because of me. He also said when

I leave for college it's going to kill him, "I don't know if I can handle that." (Me to myself: "I am going to miss you so damn much.") I am going to miss him. If we survive these three weeks I am prepared to say I am probably in love. I feel so much for him. He's beautiful. Tonight we made some killer love. We broke his bed. That was kind of funny. Then two hours later we were into some intense passion on the floor. "You are an incredible lady" is what he told me. He said it'd never been that good. It felt so good again tonight. It was more intense than ever...I tried crystal* tonight. It did nothing for me. My friends are pissed. It's my life and my prerogative, though. I'm tired and am desperately seeking sleep. When I wake-up, Ajey will be long gone. Please let these three weeks fly by. I miss him already.

[*It was not until decades later and the crystal meth crisis hit that my mind began to replay the fact that I had done crystal. We did crystal like cocaine. I know I did not know the difference and I am certain I never asked. It was not until years later that the realization came to light that this was bad shit. Period.]

5/26/1985: Yesterday I got accepted to SDSU. I'm so confused about things. I wish Ajey were back and we could 'discover' how much we might really feel for each other. I'm contemplating state because of him. Right now I don't want what we have to end. But I want to go to DU. The experience will be incredible. Absence makes the heart go fonder. ("It's going to kill me when you leave to Denver.") If it was meant to be between us then what we feel will persevere through those 3 months. If we make it through all these separations, we will probably make it through anything. I love being with him. It's already strange not having him around. I'm already planning all these things I want to do to me before he comes home. I know he likes me just the way I am. I just want to feel incredibly irresistible.

5/27/1985 @ 12:30am: I got home from work fifteen minutes ago and had the greatest homecoming. Uncle Don was here. He handed me a check for $500 for graduation. I am so ecstatic. I ran to call Deb and there by the phone was a message that Ajey had called. So in six hours I am going to call Ajey. I am so excited at this moment. I probably won't be able to sleep. I can't believe it - $500.

7:05pm: Deb and I went to the beach today. It was totally cool. We were bored half of the time. But being there made it feel totally like summer. Neither of us has the desire to go back to school. I could totally get used to this. Today was so relaxing. I got everything I could have wanted to get accomplished done. I'm tired, but ready to face the new week. Tomorrow I get my haircut and my new glasses.

(Excerpt from letter to Lisa dated May 27, 1985:)...That's great about your proms. I didn't go to mine. The one person I wanted to go with, Ajey, left the morning of the prom for his vacation. So on Friday night we pretended it was my prom. We went to McDonald's for dinner. And then went to his house. I danced. Nonetheless it was our last night together so I enjoyed the time I spent with him...To answer your "just curious" question, yes, we have gone to bed. I'm on the pill now, too. It's weird how our lover part of the relationship came into play. I'll tell you. It'll probably take the rest of this letter – due to my being exhausted and dying for sleep...When I first started seeing Ajey it was just casual – a casual affair. Both of us wanted that. No commitment. No emotional bond. No nothing. The second time I went out with him I went to bed with him. No force. It just happened. Eventually our casualness became emotional. What we once dubbed "sex" became "making love." And it's really special with him. I guess what I like most is that we're the best of friends. He listens to me. He understands me. We have a great time together. There's no pressure whatsoever. We can be together for hours and kiss maybe once. It's the neatest thing...There's one catch, though. Ajey and I had never planned to become attached. I might be falling in love, in fact. I'm glad he went on vacation even though I miss him. As he said this vacation is for "discovering" our true feelings. Actually, I think they were pretty apparent before he left. It's hard to explain what we have...I hope we can get together soon. Love and friendship, Kissten

5/28/1985: I talked to Ajey today. He called me. But once again I just missed him and called him back. Damn, I miss him. I hope so much that he comes home earlier than he had originally planned. I am bored without him. He said he's showing everyone my picture – I hate that picture. I wish he were back. It's only been four days. I cannot wait to see him again.

AOM 5/29/1985: I feel so damn fat and frustrated. I am so uncomfortable feeling. I've been chowing down the food. Probably because I'm depressed that Ajey's gone. I hate having to work and I only have two more weeks left. I just can't hang with some things right now. I miss Ajey so much. I wish he'd hurry back...Life is so confusing. SDSU has officially accepted me. I wish we'd hear from DU financial aid. I want to know now. I am so sick of waiting. And now because of Ajey I am seriously contemplating state. I have this gut feeling that if he and I survive the six weeks I'm in Europe then we'll probably be together a long time. There is so much

HONEST emotion I feel for him. I was thankful to Ajey when he left for not saying he loved me. Somehow it made me feel better. I know he'll be back to me. That's a good feeling. I'm confident now with him. I think there is love there. I feel it from me. It's beginning to surface even more now that he's gone. I just wish he were back. I have this feeling a lot of things are going to come out fast when he gets back. He doesn't get back for 16 (yes, I am counting) more days. I need to start doing things to keep my mind off of Ajey. It's gonna be hard, but I gotta.

5/31/1985: Ajey called me yesterday. He told me he may be home a week early. I don't want to get my hopes up, but damn that would be great. I hope he does. That's being a little selfish, granted. But I miss him. I'm not asking him to come back. This is his vacation, and I wouldn't want to deprive him of that. Just like he wouldn't want to deprive me of my trip...I cannot wait to leave for that trip. I feel all this excitement just growing inside of me. I hope the trip is worth it for Debbie. I've built it up through my eyes so much that she may not like it at all. I hope she does like it. I know it'll be harder to leave Ajey but this trip means so much.

6/1/1985: I think I have definitely been struck by the senioritis plague. School has become a waste of time. No joke. We're not doing anything in any classes except CW. And that's hard to get into because I do not like science fiction in the slightest. You'd think someone with the creative mind I possess (yes, I am modest) would be able to relate or even imagine things like that. They just do not spark any interest.

OBSCURE INGREDIENTS

Composed of irrelevant matter
Particles drifting minutely in space
Forming irrelevant atmosphere
The atomic bomb
A futuristic nightmare
At present
A mass of Martian heat,
Carbon monoxide, HC901, and death
Deformed new faces
Mangled bodies
The Twilight Zone
Obscure ingredients mixed together
Forming elements found only in
The Science Fiction.

THE WAITING ROOM

Lost in a circle
With no single crack
Painted white,
A man in black
Locked inside,
Nowhere to run or hide
Spinning in circles
Illusions of escape
Tormented by electric waves of shock
But from where?
A brown rat scurries across the floor
And disappears.
But how?
The walls become lentiginous in texture
Only briefly, though
He sees a chair
And runs for it.
But falls to the floor instead
There's a square outlined on the floor
He reaches for it
And falls through
The one escape out
Is only going down
Down to hell
Does that explain it?
Yes, the waiting room.

6/4/1985: Yes, I know, it's already June. I can't believe it. These past few days I've worked quite a lot. Or slept. I don't work anymore this week. Hopefully, the sun will stay out and I can work on my tan. And I can also get my weight down again. Maybe it's the pill. Maybe it's frustration. Probably both. I just hope I can work it off. There are nine days left of school. Ten days until Ajey is home. I can't wait for either. My trip is totally embedded in my mind. I am constantly making plans and dreaming of knocking all the guys off of their feet. There's this part of me who wants to have a killer affair. I know that I'll care about it, but it would be fun to try not to. And what about Ajey? God, if I could only describe how much I miss him. I haven't heard from him in four days. Sometimes I can find myself thinking about him less. But that's still a lot. My mind is constantly thinking of him. I get frustrated, though, because it's such a cliff-hanger wondering if he'll really come back to me and just "pick up" where we left off. I guess what's the hardest for me to believe is that Ajey will resist temptation. He talked like he wouldn't. But he's got a pretty illustrious past when it comes to that. And with him and his roommate now together. God knows what they are up to. Before I came along they had made it their mission to be totally reckless and uncaring, breaking a heart in every city. I hope he doesn't. But at the same time, if he does I hope he tells me. Granted, I will probably hold a slight grudge for a while. I'd probably even get an inferiority complex. I couldn't control that. But I want to. I'm just hoping he really does feel a lot for me and resist it. And be honest with me. That's all I really want. Am I being hypocritical when I say I want an affair? Yeah. But I don't know if I have the power in me to go through with it, especially if Ajey and I have established something a little more definite. That's another thing we don't really have the time for that. I don't want to infringe on his vacation space; and I don't think he'd want to do that. I just want it to work when we're together and that we will always have something special together...Today I got my ticket to Colorado. Three more days of only 16 we'll have together. I am so excited about college. It's that totally NEW adventure aspect. Man, come July 1st, actually June 23rd, my life if going to be one big adventure. I will be constantly packing and unpacking. Missing what's here; being frightened; anxious; and constantly striving for more; enjoying. I hadn't originally intended to write this much, but I can't erase it.

June 5, 1985: Ajey called me today. It was such a relief for my mind. Now I won't sit here and think that he's not thinking about me. Because in all honesty, I know he is. He sounds like he really misses me. He told me he couldn't wait to run into my arms. I can't wait for him to get home. But I'm going to have to. This phone call makes me less worried about his return. This week seems like it's going to be pretty hectic. My last day of work is next Wednesday. Beaches all weekend. I want people in Europe to take notice. It's weird how a year ago I never would have admitted to anyone looking at me. Now it seems like a lot of people take notice when I walk into a room. It's nice...I want to go to DU so badly. But when I talk to Ajey and he says he doesn't want to talk about it, I get this feeling like maybe I should stay. If I could only read into the future. God, I'd be a fool to blow going to Denver.

AOM 6/6/1985:

GRADUATION

A culmination of childhood
The ending of adolescence
The greatest step towards maturity
Discovering independence;
Individualism
Frightened and anxious
Enthused and intrigued about tomorrow
Grabbing a document
Releasing you of bonds
A tug at the heart
A notch in strength
Persevering hope for what might come next
A continuous identity struggle
Becomes verifiable fact
The last few years will subside to memories
And hopeful visions
In future despair
These past four years marked the test of survival
Walking down the aisle, I smiled
I made it
That one step beyond the rest
Ready to face my next challenge
I grasp my piece of freedom
I grasp it
And hold on tight
It is mine
Earned by me
Marking ME, what I have become
And knowing secretly what I will be.
Graduation.

6/7/1985: Minus one week and counting quickly until Ajey is back home. And once again mine. For that he will be. From the moment he arrives back he's not going to lose sight of me. I keep thinking of all these things I want to do. I would love to be there when he gets home. I want to put a red rose on his bed, stand behind his door, close it when he enters, and say, "Surprise." I'd kiss him like he's never been kissed before. But we wouldn't go to bed just yet. I want to tell him this line, "Live out your fantasies here with me." I wonder how he'd react to that. I wish we could be alone for a weekend. We'd have some champagne. Get highly romantic and make passionate love. God that sounds great. It'd be even more fantastic if I could finally have an orgasm. That'd be excellent. I wonder if Ajey would be into a game of Master and Servant. No chains or anything like that. Just telling each other what to do to the other's body. He never finger-fingers me. And I love that so much. I'd even give him head the whole time until he came if he'd do that to me. It's so damn erotic and stimulating. I can't wait for him to say "I'm on my way home." I miss him so much. I miss being with him. His company. I also miss his physical presence. I want to make the most excellent love to him.

AOM 6/8/1985: I cannot believe my high school years are finally coming to their culmination. I'm glad. I didn't like it much at all. Sometimes I've seen it as the greatest waste of my time. And almost a burden on my learning experiences. The other day my mom asked me what I would do differently if I had to do it all again. I told her I wouldn't ever want to do it all over again. And how true...Sometimes I think if I were to have transferred to a different school and were made to start over again things would have been different. I would have been more sociable. It's like here I'm acquainted with everyone. I just don't do things with them. And if you all of a sudden want to be one of them then you're a "wanna be". I've never wanted to be like them. Just better friends with some and not have those people be influenced by the others...I haven't hated all of high school. I made the best friend I've ever had. I've left my name in the record books. I was a little afraid to have people see the real me in high school. I think in college I am going to be myself from the start. No facades. But it's like I'm this silent warrior type. I stay back and scope things out and then I strike. After that, there's not much stopping me. I want college to be so unlike HS, where I was scared to be anything...I have no regrets. I just want to make the rest of my life's memories worthwhile.

Our second to last journal prompt: An embarrassing moment. I don't know that I have one. WAIT! I have one. On April Fool's Day this year I was pretending to be He-Man. I went down into a squat and my pants split. It happened at work. I had to wear a plastic bag around me until we could get me a pair of pants. And mind you, Easter week at the movies is rather crowded.

6/9/1985: I went swimming today. It killed me. But at the same time it felt good burning off some calories. I'm going to try to go Monday, Wednesday, and Thursday, too. Work this body. Cut them calories. Think I can make this body look almost more desirable to Ajey. Working out makes me feel noticed. Granted, they were just Marines and lifeguards but I saw them looking at me, watching me. That's a bit of a confidence builder, especially since that's been lacking a little again. It is five days until Ajey is back. Until he is once again mine and no one else. And then we can live out our fantasies together. And I hope for once alone. I want to be with him once when no one else is in the house. When it is purely secret. There will be a time when that happens. I work these next three days. They should keep me pretty busy. During the days try to swim and finish my last creative writing assignment. When Ajey gets home I won't have anything to worry about but him. Just the way I like it. I have a feeling this week is going to fly! (Yeah!)

AOM 6/10/1985: This is my last journal entry for school ever. This yearlong saga will end when the pen in my hand fails to leave ink marks anymore. I'm kind of glad. It's been a quick, yet long year. I'm glad it's ending, that this chapter of my life gets to close.

The last journal prompt: Human frailty. I've been a victim of human frailty. It wasn't with medicine. But I dislocated my shoulder when I was ten. The doctors shrugged it off and neglected to put it back in place. I suffered for four years in swimming because of that. Finally, I saw a specialist. Had an arthrogram and a 2-1/2 hour arthroscopic surgery. But it was only repairable by major surgery and full movement was not guaranteed. So to this day I still suffer from massive shoulder pains. And you know what's ironic is that the same doctor who saw me at ten saw me at 14 and saw something more was wrong. That pisses me off. How many times I have cried in sheer pain because of this shoulder.

I don't really know how to end this journal. Just thanks for the memories. Love Always, Kirsten

6/11/1985: Ajey will be home Thursday morning. I'm so excited about seeing him. I can hardly wait. I honestly don't think things will have changed. I'm listening to the song "The Power of Love" by Frankie Goes to Hollywood. All that surges through my mind is Lutz. What is it about him? He continues to find his way into my thoughts. Two years and I still think about him. They should subside. And they do when I am with Ajey because I don't think about anything but us. Lutz and I were two oceans apart meeting briefly with that one kiss. Why?

6/15/1985: Thursday Ajey came home. It was great seeing him again. It confirmed my feelings for him. We made love, of course. It was nothing great. It was more like a welcome home, I missed you. Yesterday I was with him most of the day. We laid out, went driving, talked. That's mostly what we did. We have made it official being able to call each other boyfriend/girlfriend. We also talked about how on the outside we just make it seem like there's nothing more than a casual relationship. But inside we know it's more. There are definite bonds. We both agreed. It reassured me so much to talk about it. Ajey didn't mess around with anyone on his vacation. I honestly believe it. It is a good feeling to know he is really mine. And only mine. Last night we made love and it felt good. It's kind of bothering him, though, that I can't have an orgasm. It's bothering me, too. I would really love to feel that pleasure. Maybe someday soon. And God I hope it's with him. He says he doesn't want me to go to Denver. I need to. I think I might love Ajey. But I can't let love get in the way of all my other dreams and aspirations. His roommate and I have become good friends. Besides his being obsessed with this girl, we can talk about everything. We talk a lot about sex and things pertaining to that. We can joke and laugh. It's cool....Tonight Ajey and I went to his house. We watched TV and listened to music for a few hours – typical. We then went to his bed where I once again FAILED to have an orgasm. It is really frustrating – for both of us. We talk about it. And I wish to God I knew. I am tired of not feeling complete pleasure. I love being with him. It feels so right. It seems like that's kind of getting in the way. On both parts. I don't want to lose him. And I don't think I will. I think Ajey feels a lot for me. It's just the biggest bitch in the world. And I hate it. I feel like sometimes I am scared to have sex because of that. It's what we both want. And it's so hard sometimes. It's like I'm scared because I know it won't happen. I can't stand it. I like him so much. It's another part of me I would like to share with him.

6/18/1985: Graduation is tomorrow! I cannot believe that I am finally out. Every other second the thought that I am finally finished with HS pops into my head. It's scary and exciting at the same time. I have so much to look forward to. It's like closing a chapter in my life. And it feels good. I haven't really liked HS. This past year I have made a lot of new and good friends. I'll miss that. But I am ready to move onward. I am so excited for Germany. A big part of me loves it there so much. It's what Debbie and I need. These past few weeks we've been kind of drifting. Because of guys and little things. But last night we had a little one on one. And it felt good to just talk. We needed that. Mickey is here visiting me. We're having a really good time. We've been spending our evenings with Jey and his roommate. Yes, Mickey and he have already gone to bed. Twice. I can't do anything to stop it. And if she wants to, that's her prerogative. Ajey and I haven't gone to bed since Saturday. Sunday we went to the movies. Then came here. We just laid on my bed and talked. Ajey and I talked again about you know what. He said he's accepted it because he knows it's not him. I told him that. It's not. I enjoy being with him either way. He makes me so happy. He doesn't want me to go. That made me feel good. But we both know there's no stopping. He also told me he doesn't want to be with anyone else, even when I'm gone. Last night while Mickey and his roommate were getting it on, Ajey and I fell asleep in his room. Nada. Just sleeping. It felt good. I love just being with him. And it's so cool because nothing has to happen. We just enjoy each other's company...Mom bought us some champagne. Yum. They're coming to my graduation. I can show him off. I bought a new camera. Take tons of pictures. Afterwards, there's a get together at our house. We'll make an appearance and then jam. In a party sense it will probably be boring but Ajey doesn't bore me. As for his roommate and Mickey, they'll find something to do. Man, his roommate the conqueror of my friends. Too bad he's such a good friend of mine, too. Mickey is only here until tomorrow morning. It doesn't seem long enough. It just seems like I've been so busy. And my mind is just so boggled. Just contemplating everything.

6/19/1985: This is my day. The day when I release ties with ECHS. It's the day when my visions and questions about tomorrow will be answered. I am so ecstatic! But I am also scared. It's a weird feeling. I may never again see some of these people. Freaky. We got enough aid to send me to DU. Thank God. I have realized that's what I want. Deb and I cried in the car on the way home from rehearsal. It's going to be weird being away from her.

6/20/1985: I am no longer a HS girl, but a college woman. It feels so weird. But at the same time I'm totally ecstatic. I don't know if I could have had a better graduation. I was with my best friends, my family, my boyfriend, etc...I was just on top of the world. I got so many neat and useful presents. I couldn't wipe the smile off my face. It feels so damn good. Last night, afterward, though, could have been better. We went to Ajey's house. We drank a little champagne. But he was already highly buzzed. Then we went to his room. We made love. And he fell asleep. That did nothing for me. In fact, I was rather pissed. His roommate and I went outside and just talked. He likes my legs. Eventually Ajey woke up and the whole tone of our conversation was bitter. He's been so tired from trying to keep himself busy for when I'm gone. That's fine to a point. But when he falls asleep when he's with me from it. Oh well, aside from that my graduation was the best part of my past four years. And it's FINALLY over. Mickey leaves today and I'm bummed. Lisa might come down. I don't see her that much either. And now all of us are going our separate way. God, we're all grown up now.

6/22/1985: Make sure I keep tabs of this: Thursday night Ajey and I made love. It was fun. We laughed a lot. There. ... Last night we went to the drive-in. I fell asleep during one of the movies for a little while. I was so quiet. I hate when I'm like that. It just happens when I'm with Ajey. It's like lately all I need to do is look at him and I melt. I get so tangled up in him. And I am constantly reminding myself that I am gone. I am gone tomorrow for three days. Home and gone again. I love him, I do. And that is rather hard for me to accept. It's not fair to him either. But I'm scared to tell him. It wouldn't be fair if I didn't. I guess I'd just assume losing him before I keep clammed up anymore. Tonight started out really cool. He came over for a dinner. Then we went to the beach. And then we went to his house. It was fun in bed for a while, until it stopped. And then we talked. I, in a sense, like a fool, told him I loved him. I don't know why. Probably because I do. He gets mad at a lot of my ideas. I don't think he loves me. He wouldn't tell me if he did. He said he cares about me a lot. I'm glad we're having these little intermissions. Tomorrow I go to Denver for three days. I'm excited. It is so confusing. Sometimes it feels like he loves me in a sense, too. And then others not.

SPILLED GUTS BRINGS FEAR

In an anxious loop of twisted turbulations
A glimmer of you flashes through me
A hot flash,
feared visions of what was there
Is no longer there
One honest emotion
A prelude to love
You run and hide at the words.
"Uncouth" and childlike
I am not a woman in your arms.
I am lost.
And don't know the underlying causes.
It is a trap with one escape -
breaking our bonds,
the small tie we share.
Closeness? Caring?
Feeling? Sharing? Honesty?

One handshake.
Could it be one more trap?
I won't kiss and tell
I want to lie before I lose you
But I am read like a book:
Page for page.
You turn my pages.
The book is nearing its close.
You and I will carry on.
It wasn't a game
I can't say the words
Nor show the emotions.
Maybe I could say it in my own
"nonsensible" way:
Love You I.
And when it is all over,
You will know,
You will.

STOP!

It's an Emotional Battlefield
A war between two hearts:
Yours and Mine.
No one will win
It'll be a draw
Both hurting
Feelings of anguish, guilt, and frustration
Part now as friends.
A handshake of the heart
A peck on the cheek.
The lovers part
And the war is ceased
Platonic and equal
You and me, Friends
And that is the end.

(Letter dated: 6/23/1985 @ 1:15am) Dear Kirsten, God I can't believe how much I miss you. You haven't even been gone 24 hours. I wish I was with you right now even if it was @ a party or something. Just to be near you. I'm so bored which of course is adding to the problem. You know I'm not sure you'll ever get this letter. It's so hard to say things to you but as soon as you leave it's easy. I don't want you to go on vacation, but I would

206

feel bad if you didn't go. Sometimes I don't know what I want but I know that I want you. It's just with you going one way and me going another that I can't figure out if our paths meet. I'm so in love with you it's unreal and probably you'll never know. I'm afraid if I tell you it will make it too hard to let go when you go to Denver in August. I wish you could stay here in California but that's not you. And I couldn't live with myself if you stayed when your dreams are in Denver. I just hope that nothing changes between us in the future. Well this letter has made it easier for me to sleep. I guess it helps to say what's on your mind.

Love Always, Ajey

6/27/1985: Denver was fantastic! I think I'm really going to like it there. I hooked up with three girls. Two from Minnesota and one local. She had a car which we used to go on liquor runs. The drinking age is 18. Beer tastes the same, too. There weren't many pretty girls there. A few good looking guys, though. Each night we got about four hours sleep. Monday night we hooked up with these two guys from a frat. We went over there. I smoked some pot and did a line of coke. This one guy, John, wanted to take me to bed. But I said no. Rather proud. Didn't even let him touch me. The other guy, Joey, was really cool. Sarah and I talked to him all night. While the one girl and John screwed. Joey said if we ever needed anyone to talk to look him up. Another big brother. I really felt kind of pretty there. Older, too. A lot of the girls seem so young. I think it will be an exciting year. We'll see. As for now, four days and counting. I'm all set except for packing. It's going to be a really exciting trip. As for Ajey, I don't know. We agreed to tell each other of our affairs and I really wouldn't mind one. Holding onto him is a lot to ask, hope, and expect for. We haven't gone to bed since I've been back – two days. Haven't really wanted to until today. He'll probably be tired from his baseball game. So who knows. I think I'm getting sick of not having an orgasm. Maybe I shouldn't let him stop and then maybe it'll cum (oops!). Who the heck knows? Not I, said the king.

6/28/1985: Last night was kind of neat. First off, Ajey and I got into a fight. It was about my fighting my feelings and holding them in. I don't want to lose him. And I know he doesn't want to lose me. He wrote me a letter. He doesn't want me to go. It's so hard. Leaving to Europe isn't as hard as I know Denver will be. Sometimes I am so tempted to stay. But what I need to explore isn't here. If I stayed now I would probably end up quitting on a lot of my goals. I love Ajey. That in itself is hard. But I do. Leaving in September will hurt. I don't want things to change between us, either. Maybe, I can only hope, that the time will make our love grow stronger (Yes, we did last night).

Tonight we went to the movies. Then we went back to his house, sat around, and made love. Before he told me, "I'm so in love with you." We made love and then spent the rest of the night talking about what we like during sex. His two complaints about me: 1). I don't talk much; 2) Giving him head (I don't). We spent most of the time talking. I guess I'm going to have to blow my stereotype of sex and talk. Say all these passionate things that run through my head. We have two days left together. I want them to be totally special. I love him. Saying good-bye won't be very easy. But now I know the love is there. I just hope I don't do anything to ruin that whilst in Europe.

(Excerpt from a letter to Lisa dated June 29. 1985:) ...Graduation went great! Thank god, it's over. I am so glad I can no longer call myself a high schooler. We are women now, Leak, real women. Wow...I had orientation in Denver. I'm going to love DU. I have this feeling. At the same time I know the first week or two is going to be a bitch because I'll probably be kind of homesick...Ajey doesn't want me to go to Europe or DU. Yes, we're still together. Amazing, hah? With him I can honestly say our casualness has turned to pretty much full dedication/commitment. I love him. I have accepted that now. It's cool because the feelings are mutual...I leave Monday for my escapade in Europe...

6/29/1985: I wish I could begin to describe the intensity of what Ajey and I had tonight. God, it was fantastic. And it felt so great. I didn't have an orgasm. But I felt some damn intense stuff. We started off the night doing a couple lines of crystal. Watched TV. Went to his room. And went at it. My body was already quivering. Then we went to the living room and just messed around. Did it on the chair quickly and on the countertop. Went into KC's room and once again

got off. My body is absolutely in pain. I'm having a hard time moving. He told me that it had never been that good before. The only thing which could have made it more perfect is if I had an orgasm. It feels like I am so close so many times. Damn, it was so incredible tonight. I'm going to miss him an incredible amount. He also told me that he doesn't care (I know he really does) if I sleep with someone in Europe because it couldn't be that good with anyone else. That's true, because I don't have those deep feelings for anyone else. Well tomorrow is my last day with Ajey. Whether we make love or not – our bodies pending – I just want to spend as much time with him as I can. I love Ajey. Tomorrow I'll definitely tell him. Even if it's me first. But as for now, my body is exhausted. I am throbbing and trembling. Gotta sleep. He makes me so happy!

6/30/1985: I guess what makes leaving so much easier is that Ajey never actually told me he loves me. I did, in a letter. Ten minutes ago it was hard to accept. Now I don't know. I know what I feel for him and that's the extent of it. I know he'll be here when I get back. What'll be hard for me is resisting temptation – if it arises. I can't believe tomorrow is already it. Our big day. It's finally here. Seven months in the waiting. I want it to be everything we've expected and more. I am so excited. I'm bummed about leaving mom here. I hope everything works out for her. I guess moments like these make you take a look at how much you really do love your family and how much you're going to miss them. I know I will. But what I am going to embark on in 17 hours will forever be embedded in my memory. These whole past few months will, in fact. (Yes, we did.) The next time I write I will be in Germany. The place I love. And I can hardly wait.

7/1/1985: The voyage begins...I'm getting anxious about getting there...This one thought hit me about ten minutes into our flight – Lutz. Of course, what else might? Everything with him is such a mystery... Actually, I just want this whole trip to be great. I'm a little scared that Debbie may have a difficult time at first...My best friend and me loose in Europe. It's finally being processed and it's so weird...Love. Ajey didn't tell me he loved me last night. I really didn't expect it. It's weird how we've been together longer than Debbie and her boyfriend, yet "I love you" has already become embedded in their relationship. I know he loves me. Bizarre? No, I just know. I love him, too. Sometimes I feel that he loves me more than I do him. The other night he asked me if I could mess around while in Europe. I couldn't flat out say no (He said no). It hit me for the first time in my life I have this certain sense of confidence. And it seems like sometimes it's attracting. I have this (slight) feeling that opportunity may arise this summer where I can mess around. Not necessarily sleep around, but other stuff. I believe Ajey. I guess in ways it is my own insecurities that make me want to know that I can be desirous to more than just him. Maybe if he would have said I love you, rather than I'm in love with you it would have cinched another notch for security. I think Ajey has a lot of lust for me. I don't know if that has anything to do with it...This year I have already done crystal, coke, and pot. There's nothing else I want to try. Crystal can be so cool. It's like this extra source of energy. Sometimes I think it's cool. Other times I think it's the biggest waste of money. I doubt I could ever get used to the stuff. Except sometimes I get cravings for something. It almost loosens me up. Like in bed. But fuckin' nothing can make me have an orgasm and that's so frustrating.

We are still sitting here on this plane. For the past few hours one thing has been surging through my head – college. The intensity at which it's flowing. A nonstop pour. I want to cry. Yes, me. I want to cry. Being on this plane away from all the things I love most...My going to DU is going to break us. That is the last thing I want. Somehow I almost feel like I need to put my selfishness aside for a while so that the situation may be more suitable for all parties involved. For once in my life, I feel like putting my future on hold for the sake of my family. I understand completely what our situation is. Maybe I'm hesitant about going to DU, too. Maybe I'm not really as ready for that step. Actually, I know I am. Two things have come into my life to make me open my eyes a little – Ajey, and the realization of I no longer wish to make my family suffer because of me...I love my family, friends, Ajey. I wish I knew what I wanted. Ajey says he wants me to stay. It is not fair that I can feel so confused. I know I'll love Denver. If only I knew. I love them. I love Ajey. Where does it end? Or start to take one direction?

7/4/1985: I just finished this long letter to dad. It explained to him my college predicament...I don't think I want to go to DU this year. It is so expensive. I'd be living with such guilt. I don't want them to say we'll find a way. It's not even Ajey keeping me here (CA). The more I think about it the more I realize it is my family and the money situation. If Ajey and I break up, we break up. One or both of us may suffer but life will go on. I will meet people. I can do that now...Going to Schutzenfest with Britta tomorrow. Lutz's sister is going. He won't, I'm sure. I think I was meant to be intrigued by this one. He's like the 8th wonder of the world to me. What superior powers does he possess?... Yesterday at the tennis courts these ladies told me how much my personality and me myself have changed. They say I'm easier going. I must have been a real snot in my earlier days. MATURITY, yes, that is a what I would say.

7/6/1985: Last night was Schutzenfest. It was fun. I don't think Deb enjoyed it as much. There were two gorgeous guys with our group. So we just gawked. Lutz's sister was there. He is on vacation until after we leave. She told me something, though. She said he likes me a lot but doesn't want to get involved in anything that is so long distance. In essence, there never was hope. I wish he could have said that...I was missing Ajey last night. I felt like a fricken horny son of a bitch. Think I may write him a letter later.

7/7/1985: Last night was fun. I love dancing. The people can be highly rude at times. I've never said so many "fuck you's" in my life. It's great when people don't really understand. The place was called Studio 78. It was kind of an ego booster. A lot of guys were looking at me. One guy kept bugging me and this other guy tried to kiss me. There were some gorgeous guys. In fact, I met one. His name is Rikkie. He was from Holland. He was damn good looking. Deb had her eye on him first. It was weird how he totally went for me. He just stared. He kept wanting to kiss me. He did once. Nothing. Lasted about 2 seconds. I didn't even like it. All I wanted was Ajey's lips and body against mine. He kept wanting more kisses. Pecked him good-bye. I mean it was flattering but all I want is my Ajey. I realized last night that I will have a very hard time cheating on Ajey. I love him. He's all I can practically think about. I want him here with me. Being with me. Making love to me. God, I don't want things to change between us. I hope these next few weeks fly by. I want to be back in his arms again...Everyone here says we are so friendly and so energetic. It's true. We are always smiling and laughing. I love being that way. I can't wait to hear from mom and dad, and Ajey.

7/8/1985: Today we went to Bergen-Belsen, the concentration camp. It had pictures of Anne Frank and other Jews. Fascinating. I am intrigued by all the history. I've always wanted to go to a concentration camp. It leaves a permanent impression in your mind.

[*I took my daughter there in 2019. It became an elaborate museum with an incredible historical display. We spent hours reading the history and then walked the fields. Left me with the same sad, sick feeling I had back in 1985.*]

7/9/1985: I feel fat (Moose!). I hope I start the rag tomorrow. It may justify my eating.

7/10/1985: Talked to mom. Had this urge to talk to her. I miss her. She told me she missed me too. Said Ajey's been by and has been calling. They still haven't gotten any mail from me. I hope I get something from him before Greece...Mom said Ajey's picking me up from LAX. I'm ecstatic. He took the day off too and then that leaves a weekend. Four days straight right off the bat. I can hardly wait...That's going to make it all the harder to let go of him when I go to DU. It's a definite "go" from my parents. It is really what I want. It's back to the old theory of if Ajey and I are meant to be then we will survive the time spans. The way I feel now for him leaving is going to be so hard, but I have this feeling we may survive the time spans and spaces. For all I know we could end up married but neither of us is really going to know until there is that big separation...Actually, first quarter is only twice as long as this trip. Not long at all. I know we'll probably see other people. Probably even doubt what we have at that time. We may make it. Feels right. There's no doubt in my mind we'll survive through the first X-Mas break. But who wants to look that far ahead? Enjoy what we have now. That's great. I'm in love for the first real time in my life. I can admit it without thinking twice. I LOVE YOU, AJEY. (catch it)

7/11/1985: Ajey gave me a wake-up call this morning. I am so happy! It's going to make my day. Miss him. Said he misses me (he said it first). No I love you's. Think it's understood. Should be getting a letter from him soon...Went to Hannover today. Definitely more modern than Bremen. Bought an ice cream. One of many things I munched on today. I porked. But the rag came in full steam. Maybe now I'll slow down in eating. Excited about Greece. Working on my tan and seeing a new part of the world. I can hardly wait. At the same time I'm excited about getting home. Mainly because of mom (dad) and Ajey. By no means do I regret this trip. I am having a great time. There's just so much I want to do before school. Being with my family and Ajey. They take precedence...I kind of feel like writing a poem to Ajey/for Ajey. I think I'm in a creative mood again tonight. I have so much energy. Must be all the chocolate I ate. I MISS YOU, AJEY! LOVE YOU, TOO! (catch it!).

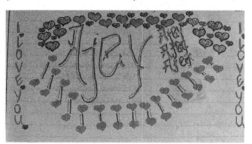

7/12/1985: Today was rather boring. Got a haircut. Bought Ajey a present – a jacket...I am eating like a pig. It's frustrating. It is so REVOLTING!! I am revolting. Blaah. I've got to stop eating so much. It is the most frustrating feeling in the world. If Ajey were here he'd probably be disgusted. Actually, I don't look much bigger if at all. But I feel it and the scale shows it. Why does weight have to mean so much to me? Because, my dear, you like to feel somewhat attractive. I guess other people are what make me feel most attractive. Like that guy, Rikkie. He made me feel pretty. He was buzzin', but he was still staring at me. And that guy was literally gorgeous.

7/14/1985: Today was just one of those days where nerve hits nerve and kaboom you have annoyance. I ran to get a little of the steam off. Felt better. Felt good to sweat that much. I love working out. If only I could get inspired...I called home today. I felt like they didn't even want to talk to me. I had all these things I wanted to say but when mom said I can't keep calling (2 times), I just lost all interest. In fact, I had tears because of the tone in her voice. I felt like a rejection. The best part of my day was when I talked to Thor. He made Jr. Nationals. I am so proud of him. He has accomplished the one thing in swimming I didn't. I hope this will help him to stay with it. He can't blow it now. Too much is riding on it. I am just so proud of him. He made my day – not the biggest shit. He actually sounded excited to talk to me. These telephone calls today were supposed to be my escape. Only one made it worse.

7/15/1985: In exactly one month we will be on our way home. I'm not that super excited because I love it here. But of course there are those things that I can hardly wait for back home. College has taken this priority in my mind. It helps take my mind off of Ajey. I don't think that adjusting to college (i.e. away from home) is going to be as hard as I might think. Granted, there will be times when all I want is to be home with mom and dad or Ajey. This trip is going to make leaving them so much easier. I can hardly wait for the next new thing...We leave on Friday for Greece. I can hardly wait to be in Yugoslavia. I want to know what a communist country is like. The 45 hour total bus ride doesn't excite me...We went to Steinhuder Sea today with Uncle Norbert. He is such a neat man. He's one of my most favorite people. He's got so much zest to him. The only time I don't like him is when he's drunk...All my relatives over here are cool. They do so much for me. I think they do an incredibly large amount for us Ami's. I think my mom was always their favorite. She was Maria's, I know. Going to the North Sea with Norbert on Wednesday.

7/16/1985: Got ready for our trip today...I'm beginning to wonder – no, have been, wondering if I will meet anyone on this trip. Male wise. If I will mess around. It's a question that may arise. I think it would be kind of neat. It's not that I don't love or care for Ajey anymore. That's definitely the farthest thing from the truth. I feel so much for him. I try not to think about him as much. Just because the less I think about him, the less I think about him. Dumb. I can hardly wait to be in his arms again. This trip definitely makes leaving in September easier. I know he and I will talk about it when I go. I don't want to feel bogged down when

I'm at school and another opportunity may come my way. I want to experience. I love Ajey with an honest emotion and passion. But, for some reason, I think I am almost being realistic in that sense. Realistic or selfish. Probably both. I'm very good at selfishness, you know. ENOUGH.

7/17/1985: I am becoming very bitter on this trip towards family and Ajey. Three weeks and I have received no mail from anyone. One phone call. But no relevant evidence that anyone actually misses me. In fact, I think it is making this latter part of my trip kind of shitty. I just cannot wait to get on that bus and go. I want to mess around to my heart's content. I want to forget that there is a bond between Ajey and me. I just want to know that I can be wanted. All my thoughts these past couple of days have been on Lutz and Rikkie – the surreal. What might have been, what could have been. But that, too, is pointless. Leaving for school is becoming easier and easier to comprehend in my head. I'm beginning to wonder if they'll miss me then, either. I'm getting more and more bitter, more and more depressed as I write this. I already don't feel good. Too much fucking thinking and despising right now...Today we spent the whole day at the North Sea. I thought it was neat despite feeling troubled and bothered. Lopi (*Norbert's nickname*) bought us so much. I don't know how to rightfully thank him. I don't expect anything. I do take, but I want to find a way to rightfully or equally give back. Today's theme song: TROUBLES ON MY MIND.

7/18/1985: We leave for Greece tomorrow. Months in the waiting – here. I'm curious to see what will happen there. Will I have a rendezvous with someone? Will I get this gorgeous tan? That's the only thing I really hope for. That and having an excellent time, seeing some of historic Greece. I know that one thing that is kind of bugging me is that Debbie thinks all Germans are ugly. Granted, they're not the best-looking people. But everyone is "homely" to her. I'm guilty of thinking a lot of the same thoughts. I know it. I feel guilty for thinking it. I hate when people aren't given a chance for some reason or another. I guess I just look at a lot of people and see a reflection of me in there somewhere. Maybe not what I am now, but of the monster I felt I was not too long ago. The people do have ugly teeth here. Not everyone, but most of them. It can be pretty gnarly. Especially talking to someone who has food particles stuck everywhere in their teeth. Almost revolting. I think it comes a lot from the smoking they do here.

July 19, 1985: (*It must have been a poetry night.*)

SALVAGED SOULS

*When I talk
Or tell a tale of tales
When my lips move,
Or I silently whisper
I speak of salvaged souls;
wrecked minds;
and torn hearts.
Fields wretched with fading scars.
Emergence of yet "another"
Scars will diminish.
Books will forget,
and deny.
Touch of a button:
touch tone death.
Who will survive?
Only the strong-
the salvaged souls.
Monarchs of supremacy relishing life,
then perishing.
Thru suicidal ecstasies
All will fade-
Including the spoken salvaged souls.*

*(no title)
Love is a circle
With a shadow of doubt
It is compulsion,
compassion,
complete.*

*(no title)
Mystified waves.
Murky motions of thought.
Tides caressing the rocky shore.
Glow setting sun
Brings illuminations of you.*

On the road to Greece. There are 80 people occupying this bus. We haven't made any real connections with people. There are a lot of people

215

younger than us but it's not a noticeable gap...Got a letter from Ajey today. Just in time. Was beginning to lose faith in the dude. He wrote in these exact words, "I love you (and miss you)." Important to note.

(Excerpt from his letter dated 7/10/1985): Hey I got your letter today! I'm glad to see that you can still write in English. Oh big news. I finally made the phone book. And they even spelled my name right. So now I'm important...School started yesterday. Talk about a weird prof. He's one of those guys with a high IQ but no common sense. But this will keep me busy. So I will have less time to mope around the house...So you don't want to go to school in Denver? Well, if you would have said that a month ago I would have given you some speech on why you should go to Denver, but I can't say that anymore. Sorry! It's weird like you kinda know what you want but you're not sure if it's right. But not in this case. I know it's a cheap shot but I think it would be great if you stayed in Calif for a little while longer. Just think of all we could accomplish. And this stuff about you wouldn't study? Bull! I don't know what else you would do because I know I'll have to study a lot. It's interesting to think about...Oh guess who's going to pick you up on the 15th? Of course ME. And I have the next day off also so we can catch up on what's been going on since you left. Sound like a cool way to do things? And I talked to your mom and she said great because she had to work. We have only been over there twice so far. We try to rescue her from her (foreign guests)...Oh ya, if I didn't tell you earlier in this letter, I love you and miss you. Waiting for you. Love, Ajey
(Also included was a postcard with a picture of Jason Segal's "To all Gates": Hi Babe, (get the hint) from the postcard what I want? So hurry up and get back so I can finally sleep @ night. Ok. Oh ya. Roommate says hi and you know I do. Miss you a lot.
Love Always Ajey)

I don't know exactly what's up inside of me with a lot of things. Maybe once I get to – NO! I will write it now – in the dark what I've finally figured out – or partially know...I like to push it until it comes out, until the person says it to me. Until "I love you" or good-bye comes out. I've got to grow up in a lot of respects with relationships. I guess being away from Ajey right now doesn't help in any respects. I do love him, but I think a lot of "vacations" are coming at the wrong time. Love is a word to describe it. I just feel I have this thing inside of me where I feel when I've finally got the person it's time to move onward. But I don't want to do that with Ajey. It wouldn't be fair to either of us. What I feel for him is honest emotion. The whole relationship is honest. Affairs?—for ego's sake. I don't know. I trust Ajey. I love Ajey. It's all just so hard and darn CONFUSING!!

7/20/1985 am: Just stopped at the Yugoslavian border. They search practically everything. Decided we had to use the "toilette." Get this, no seat. You had to squat to go. Felt like I was in a primitive society. At least they had toilet paper. Relief. Austria was a beautiful country. All mountains. Virtually no flatlands. It made me feel like one of the Von Trapp kids in the "The Sound of Music." ...The BO some people have here is gnarly. It could be from the lack of shaved arm pits. I just can't hang with that hair. I guess having grown-up knowing nothing else it's still "gross" even knowing everyone doesn't shave. The legs don't really bother me. The pits. The PITS!... GRANTED. What? Everything is "granted." I'm in a communist country now. Wonder if things are "granted" here?!...Deb is beginning to nerve me. I hope she gets some sleep soon. She is so crabby. She takes no interest in trying to learn something new. I'm not complaining. We can probably have just as much fun together. But she wants to withdraw right away...Grouchiness just gets in the way sometimes. But it's to be overcome...This country is bazaar. I've wanted to come to a communist country to see and I think I've seen enough. There are a lot of eerie looking people running around. Men will just stop and stare at you. It's not the safest feeling. Being here is so much like in the movies. The air to it and everything...I have concluded that I miss Ajey very much – I wish he were here with me right now. I love him. And to the best of my capabilities, I will stay away from promiscuity. He means so much to me. Sometimes I wonder how it's going to be when school rolls around. I'm going to hate leaving him again. I don't know how or why I said what I said earlier – I guess those things cross a person's mind. I have a good thing going. And I can't wait to be back in his arms once again. Can't help but wonder, though, if either one of use will have changed in the other's eyes.

7/21/1985: Yugoslavia was/is a different country. I do not like it. I definitely think it is curbing my communist desire. Everything is so yucky (it fits). We stopped at a gas station today. It reminded me of being in Tijuana. We were attacked by people selling their crafts. Went to a squat toilet with flies buzzing everywhere. Everyone stared at us. Erie feeling.

7/22/1985: We finally made it to Greece. I like it. I think we may get kind of bored here. Not with the beach, but at night. Sometimes I just want to get home. I miss my family and I miss Ajey. This trip has made me realize a lot about myself. I don't know if I really want to go to DU....I think it's beautiful here. It's hot. Water's great. Just no waves. I don't think many of the people here want to give us a chance. I think they might get the impression that we're antisocial. I don't want everyone to think we're bitches...The Greek people can be kind of neat. They definitely tend to be a good looking, intriguing bunch. Definitely gorgeous guys. But contemplating messing around hasn't crossed my mind here. I must really love Ajey. Yes, I think I do.

7/24/1985: Yesterday was fun. We sat on the beach for six hours. We met up with these four Italians. All 20, 21. We went to their tent with Foto and Ulrike last night and had spaghetti. Then we all went dancing until 2am. We fit 8 people into a max 5 seater car. Soso drove, Foto and Stefano front seat. Me, Ulrike, Henrique, and Massimo back seat. Debbie in the trunk area. It was funny, though. It's neat because everyone had to speak English in order to communicate. The Italians say "a" after every word. It was so funny. We came home from dancing and all decided we would steal a four man dingey. We got it in the water and about ten feet when it started to sink. We all bailed. I ended up falling flat on my face and got drenched. To top it off, some patrol dudes came around the time of it all. Deb and I bailed because I was soaking. Got to sleep around 3, but I never really slept...Woke up and realized my back has broken out. The face isn't bad. I haven't been taking my medicine regularly. Rationed supply. It might be a little from stress thinking. I hope it is not going to be another battle of the zits. That whole concept scares the shit out of me...Thought about Ajey a lot last night. I miss him and I miss home. We leave in three weeks. I'm excited, but there's no way I'll ever be able to say I regret this because it's probably the greatest thing I have ever done for my own self-awareness.

7/25/1985: Three weeks and ten hours and we are once again home...Two of the Italians we met are totally going for two of the German girls. The other two are fun and cool. It's weird how Deb and I know what we have at home – her boyfriend and Ajey. And yet we're jealous of these girls at the same time. So now we've been sitting here picking some of them apart. It's wrong because they're neat and fun.

7/26/1985: We are into the minus 3 weeks phase of our trip. It has really been plaguing my mind. Do I want to go? There is this part of me who says, "yes, yes, yes." And the other wants to stay at home with family, familiarity, and boyfriend. The money is a big concern. I don't want my parents going bankrupt. Actually, when I get back if they say we can cut it, you can go – no second thoughts, then I'll go. Not even if the other part of me says stay, look at all you have here. I have a family. A boyfriend.

Do I even want to leave California? Denver was gorgeous. I liked it a lot. And I think after meeting new people and involving myself I could hang no problem. Do I need an extra year to reassure myself what I want to do? I definitely want to be involved in business with an international corporation...I don't think it's fair to put your life, your future in the hands of you at age 17, 18. There's too much there to decide. For all I know I could be making a decision like what color Porsche should I get – even that ones not easy. I just want to be HAPPY. Sometimes life can be such a bitch. So young and yet so old. 20 days...We have been making fun for ourselves...I am anxious to get home. I do not know if I want to go to Denver.

7/27/1985: Just passed this gorgeous guy from Holland who made my heart jump. BUT he is here with his girlfriend. So, it never hurts to look...The Italians left this morning. They stopped to say good-bye to us. They took our hand and kissed us on the cheek...We're starting to make some friends with the people here...It's weird some of the things we'll talk about on the beach or whenever we're bored. We talk a lot about food we want when we get back. Mexican and her mom's Italian. Talk about what we're going to wear on the plane. About who's picking us up. What we're going to do. College and our futures are in the topic now. How many more days? What do we do now? Today we even talked about our weddings...I'm anxious about getting home. The future. It's hard to just totally relax when all that is plaguing your mind. But there are more times than not when my mind is at ease. I sleep great at night. Have energy during the day. Being here makes it easier to stop thinking at times. But my mind is like a grandfather clock – tick, tick, ticking then BONG the cycle starts again. I'm getting tired of thinking but not of talking my ideas out with Debbie because we're usually on the same wavelength.

7/28/1985: Tomorrow is mine and Ajey's 3 month anniversary. That is if I can call it that. Three months since the first time we slept together. I wonder if he knows that. If it's in his realm to recognize that. Heck, in October it will already be ½ a year. I miss him and have this total desire to call him. But, I can wait these next couple of weeks until I see him again. I can't wait to see him at the airport. What if he doesn't pick me up?...Today I am content being here. We are finally being included by people. I think it comes partly from our efforts too. The Germans seem to be amused by us. Pause. Immediately after I wrote that a group came over and started looking at our pictures. Then more came. Some stayed and we talked. It was cool. We took pictures of everyone. It was a great day for this to happen. We were both beginning to get a bit doubtful of ourselves... Today this one Greek, Jason, asked us to go dancing. And then we were walking back to the camp when we hear two "hallos" coming from two other Greek guys. They asked us to go dancing tonight, too. Names were Paros and Chris. Paros is gorgeous. Gorgeous body. It was neat because we've been staring at him for a couple of days now. And then the guy who works in the store, but speaks no English, totally began flirting with us. Those were some ego boosters we really needed.

AJEY ♡ AJEY ♡ AJEY

7/29/1985: "Happy Anniversary to me" I guess so. I'd just assume. But then again assumption is the mother of all screw-ups. Oh, well, it's fun to think that we do have one...Well, I do miss him but the time really does seem to be flying by. We've already been in Europe for four weeks.

7/30/1985: We sat around with everyone and then they signed our journals. It's cool because they were all part of this trip. I can now flip through the pages and have even more memories sparked.*

[*My future German boyfriend, who I began dating in 1989, was on that trip.]

There are these two geeks at this campground who are everywhere we are. They watch us. They're always reading but looking at us. I mean there's flattery and then there's flat out annoyance, which they've become. They just watch and have these "looks" in their eyes. They're probably our age. Man, they're weird. Get a break from them tomorrow (maybe they'll leave).

7/31/1985: Today we went on a cruise (Ouranoupolis). I thought it was great. Finally saw some of Greece. We went by all these old monasteries. Some were over a thousand years old. Women aren't allowed to set foot there...Today when I was on the boat, I thought some about my life. I thought about how I put my own self down a lot; how I make my life miserable at times because of how I feel about myself. I have so much drive and perseverance, yet it amazes ME as to how I let myself be manipulated by me. I find one fault and then another. They're all controllable, too. 135 pounds. What's that? Total desire. Something I could achieve with a little/lot of work. My looks with make-up and hairspray, I'm not bad. In fact, even without, I am not bad. I have a pretty nice, muscular body. My tum needs work. I have nice posture. Happy air. Granted, sometimes I may come off arrogant. Good manners...Thought about college and Ajey. I could leave home, but I could stay. If guys ask me out in college I'll go. I'm too young to be dedicated. I don't know if Deb altogether understands that. It's how I feel. It doesn't mean I love Ajey any less by saying it. It's just something I feel.

8/1/1985: I just popped someone's air mattress. No one knows yet or has seen yet. Took away all incriminating evidence and slyly ran to the tent.

8/3/1985: Yesterday, we went to Thessaloniki. It would have been a cool city but all the shops close from 2-5, which is when we had alone time. Dumb. Saw a cool church. Went to a museum...Last night there was a big storm. We slept under a cabana and managed to neither get wet nor blown away. The lightening was cool. I love weather like that...Yesterday, on the way home, Deb and I had this talk on our friendship. We talked about how both of us are already going our different ways. Before we used to be one in the same. Now we are drifting but are still connected to that support line. We are two completely different persons – ideas, values, morals. But we are connected in one way or another. And that is what will always keep us so close, no matter how far apart we may be distance wise...All I can do is think about college. WHAT DO I DO? Somehow I think what I should do is go a year to a JC then transfer. I'm really beginning to feel my place is in CA. But this other part of me sees the opportunities that lie in Denver. Money. It plays such a big part in it. I just cannot wait to get home and talk to my parents about MY LIFE. Just 12 more days.

8/3/1985: My recent attempt at poetry has been nothing vaguely associated with love. It just didn't come out. Morbid-related subjects are easier and almost more challenging to write.

THE SILENT ONES

In fairy tales or hard core facts
By astonished witnesses or honest bystanders
In past or present time, good or bad:
The will of the wicked prevailed.
Envy, the trigger.
Hate, the murderer.
Love, the killer.
Anger, the annihilator.
Pity, the sucker.
Sadness, the fool.
Platonic watcher, the victor.
Innocent hide the domineering side.
Silent victors of the criminal line.

221

Piercing eye glances,
Cackling laughs that stab the inner soul.
These, their invisible weapons,
Make the innocent silent ones
The wicked obsessed.

LITTLE BO PEEP

Vacuum cleaner, duster buster.
Iron hanger, knitting needles.
Poisonous fluid, Ammonia 409.
Little Bo Peep lost her sheep
To a stab by a hanger,
A sweep of a vacuum,
And the cleansing of powerful
liquid cleaner #409.
Little Bo Peep lost her sheep,
her sanity, and frame of mind.
Little Bo Peep,
Tell me no more why you can't sleep.

But tonight I feel like writing a letter to Ajey in here. But first, the day. Went to the beach. Read. Munched. I'm PMS right now. Restricting myself as best I can because I feel and think I look fat. Hopefully, Ajey won't notice.

Dear Ajey, I'm sitting here thinking about you, getting ready to watch the sun set, and wishing that you could watch it with me. It was a typical day today. Really needn't bore you with details. Just did a lot of thinking, as I always do...I think a lot about you and me. About what our relationship entails. If it's really right. I think about the three months we've been seeing each other and realize how half of it has been spent apart...I'm almost scared of seeing you on August 15th. Scared that both of us might notice little changes that will make our relationship seem different. Sometimes I get this weird feeling inside that when we make love again it's going to be so different. Like we were strangers, again. But there's so much more than that...I believe I've found in you love. A certain kind of love. Being as it is I am not too clear on the meaning of it myself. You've stirred feelings and emotions I've never had. You've become everything I wanted. You are a FRIEND and a LOVER. It's something. I don't know what exactly. It's bazaar....Sometimes I question us. Especially when it comes to the immediate future. Is there one for us? I am not being pessimistic/doubtful, what not of our relationship. I LOVE YOU. As far as I know. It's hard to declare a feeling when you haven't lived/experienced enough to know if it's real or not...Like I said before, I don't know what I am saying. Whenever I get the nerve to tackle my feelings I use the wrong play and fumble it all up. I hope whatever the future brings you and I can always remain together in some form – even just friendship wise...However unclear I may be or feel, there is definitely something there I don't want to lose. You. Others may come our way. I think it'll be necessary. If the friendship we have is strong enough, we will survive. And I guess that is what makes me hesitant altogether: SURVIVING. Will we?

I love you. – Kirsten

8/4/1985: Today a girl gave me an oyster. It was so sweet. I was swimming when she tapped me. Her name was Mariana and she was 12. She told me I was a good swimmer and that she swam, too. She asked me to race her in butterfly. We did. Talked a little more. Then I went in. Later she and her dad came up and gave me a real oyster, telling me how to eat it and everything. I thought it was so sweet...Tonight is one of those evenings when sleep won't make its calling soon enough so tomorrow can get here and then we leave the next day...I want to see my mom and dad. I want to know the VERDICT on school even though I'm pretty sure it's DU. Is that what I want, though? I'm really realizing I could be just as happy in Ca, but then again the DU experience could bring so much. And what if I change my mind? I want to see Ajey, too. More than I'll fess up, but I'm hesitant because of time and change...Funny note of the day: At dinner, Heino lost his dentures for his two missing teeth in his food. The old lady working there brought them out and she announced it to the whole group. I think he was embarrassed. I would be.

8/5/1985: (*I proceed to give a character overview of some of the people on the trip.*)...I am so fucking bored right now. I can't even explain the extent of frustration I am feeling from doing nothing. I have hit the I want to get out of here now phase...I am restless. This is what we've been doing for two weeks. Before I liked doing nothing. Two hours ago I took a cold shower. Now I am dripping from anxiety, desire to leave. I can look back on this trip, though, and not regret it...The night has finally come upon us. We are having a goodbye toast to Greece on the beach tonight. There is a part of me that regrets not being a bigger part of this group...Tonight at dinner this guy named Uwe sat at our table. I think he's gorgeous. His features are at least. Perfect cheek bones. Murky green eyes. Incredibly beautiful smile. Perfect teeth. Straight nose. His hair became a sandy blonde. Man, he has the most incredible look to him. I have been in lust with him since the bus ride. He'll only just be 18, too. He's nice. Tonight was the first time we've talked the whole trip. Good.

8/7/1985: We are homeward bound. At our hotel in Yugoslavia. Tomorrow is the final stretch. I am anxious to get back...Deb seems a lot more anxious than me. I think she misses things more. I've really enjoyed myself this trip. And in no ways regret it...It has made me appreciate so much...The differences between me and Debbie became more obvious. Somehow, I believe this trip has strengthened us in many ways. But it has also made us grow-up and separate at a realistic standpoint. Despite the discovered annoyances and future separations, we will always be inevitably close at heart.

8/9/1985: We're home to Nienburg. Letters (5) from Ajey. One mom. One Lisa. One Rikkie. Couldn't believe it. I was so happy...Talked to mom. Definitely going to Denver. Stoked! Got a roommate from New York. Can't wait to get in touch with her. Can't wait to get home to know it ALL. Think Maria (*my great aunt*) has a lot to do with really going. I love her for it. It is what I want. Ajey can try but it won't work. Dreams first in my realm...So much going on. Gained 3 fucking kilos...It made me happy to get a letter from Rikkie. He made me feel good.

(*Excerpt from Rikkie's letter:*) ...*We had a lovely time together, but a little short...I wish I had more time to get to know you better...I usually don't walk up to any girl I see, but you were something special, you impressed me very much...Rikkie*

The letters from Ajey were all the same – "missing you; can't wait for you to get back..." I guess it should all be flattering – it is. I'm looking forward to seeing him again. But I don't like when he says we're definitely going to talk about my NOT going to Denver. Like he has a say in it. I'm after my dreams and the experiences of things more than anything else.

(*Excerpts from Ajey's letters:*) *7/11/85...I'm sitting in this class that is designed to teach us what's important about being promoted in the Navy. What bull sh---...Boy, it was great talking to you on the phone. You sounded like you were having a good time. I'm glad somebody is...So what are we going to do when you get back? Are you going to fall asleep on me? Just kidding. I hope you can hang. I mean all that partying might make you weak or something. I want to go to Knott's Berry Farm someday. No rush but I would still like to go just the same so I can get some pictures of us...Oh ya, this is your official appt slip for your remaining time in Oside. With that slip you get unlimited use of the only* thing in Oceanside worth anything. Me! All you have to do is stay awake long enough to be interesting. (Ooooh bad cut but I bet nobody is keeping you straight...I think you can take care of you.)...You weren't even gone 12 hours and I missed you. I guess I've grown too attached to you. But I'm not bitching about it. I just wish you were here with me instead of being there with Debbie. Love Always, Ajey

7/20/1985: So you don't think I know what Ich liebe dich is! Well, I'm not dumb and if I am I can go to a German dictionary and find it...I can't figure out why you didn't get any of my letters. My God, I've sent 4. By now you'll have been back from Greece. Maybe you'll have received them. I've received every one of your letters and cards...I got a change of jobs for ten days. I'm going to a YMCA camp for some summer day camp. I'm the medical counselor. 10 days of nothing but swimming and playing

basketball, but don't worry I've got nothing more on my mind than to get you back in my arms. Sound interesting? Guess what my roommate and I did today? Give up? We played tennis with your mom. We stunk. She didn't rub it in too bad. So maybe now I can save face....Do you know how much I'm looking forward to seeing you on the 15th? I'm talking you better get here soon. Or I'm going to go crazy. Every time I go to bed I dream of you. It's driving me crazy. I want you so bad. So I'm going to hold out for 25 more days but after that it's all over for you. So you better get your sleep on the plane because you'll need it...I hope this clears any doubts that I really do miss you and of course am in love with you. Love Always, Ajey PS When you get back we're going to talk about Denver! (on the back of the individual picture, he wrote: To Kirsten, the only one I want. But just seems to be out of the country for a little while. Oh well, I guess I'll wait! Get back soon.)

7/22/1985:...Needless to say another day went by without you. "Slow death." I think this was some sort of test! But then again maybe it's bad luck. My roommate is giving me a hard time. He says I'm too far gone to save. I guess it depends on who is saving me? Know anybody interested? I figured you might want to try first...Your mom told me about your hesitation on going to Denver. I hope you have a long talk with her when *you get back and decide not to go. That's what I dream of when I go to sleep, among other things which will be easily taken care of once you get home...So I hope you missed me! I know your being in Germany is driving me nuts. But I've got a countdown. Only 24 days left. Every night before I go to bed I mark another day off. I can't wait til one day I wake up and there are no days left to mark off...I'll see you at the airport. Love always, Ajey PS I want your body (get the hint)*

7/29/1985: ...As for me, I'm just about to lose what remaining sanity I had waiting for you to get back here. I think this is the worst month I've ever had in my life. And of course you could change that by getting back here soon. You know I wish the 15th would get here but I can't hurry the days by. Oh well I'll just sit here and soak up the sun so I can try to match your killer tan...At camp, I'm going to do a lot of swimming and improve my tennis game so when you get home I'll be a challenge.

(The last trip letters were given to me when I got back:)...I'm all squared away here at camp...I've already seen two little girls for being home sick. They're so cute. They cry and say doc I want my mommy. And all I have to do is reassure them...So I miss you to death. When are you getting back? Not soon enough. I don't think I'll mail this because it won't get to you in time...I too have taken the test of faith. This girl came up to me and told me in not so many words that she was going to take me home. And she didn't even interest me at all. As a matter of fact, my roommate says I should go seek counseling. I tell you if I had any doubts they all disappeared that night. It's great to know that what I feel for you, you feel for me. I guess in a sense we're kinda lucky to find each other. Thank you Mickey D's, right? So I think I figured out your little problem. I read about 3 books on this problem and it all centered around emotional attachment to the other person so maybe you didn't feel strong enough for me, but I think that's over...gotta jam to the sack. I'll be dreaming of you, of course.

Well, this is another letter that probably never reaches you, but that's ok. I figure that as long as I'm thinking of you that I must be doing something right...You know I miss you so much. I can't believe that you're going to Denver for school. I will probably die. God why couldn't you have gone to SDSU or somewhere close? I think I'm going to kidnap you for a week of solitude with me. Sound interesting?

8/11/1985: Happy birthday, Debbie! The big 18! We had a gnarly feast. Then we had cake in the afternoon.

(*Letter from Debbie dated 8/9/1985:*) *Hey Dee, Well, the end of our trip has almost reached the end. I can honestly say I do not regret any of it and if I had the chance to do it again I would...The reason for this letter may not quite be understood by you...yet. By the end of this letter I'm sure, as always, you will understand...Our trip has numerous ups, but it also had its downs. As everything in life does. If everything were always in the middle then I feel there would be no new experiences, challenges or learning. And then where would we be? We would have an acute case of boredom, not only with ourselves but with each other...The down...I think you know as well as I do what I am referring to so no need for an explanation. They were, to me, unnecessary? Yes! But expected. Heck, for 6-1/2 weeks we were each other's lifeblood. The little irritations, the remarks, at the time were so serious. Now I can look back and say, "Yes, they were there." But, more importantly, "Yes, we overcame them," as always, as would be expected...I've learned a lot about myself, you, and our friendship on this trip. I've learned what we as friends can handle and what we can't. Honestly though it's brought me closer to your feelings on big important matters or merely the everyday trials and tribulations of life...Our past and the memories we share will always bind us together with the phrase "Alter-Egos". But I've learned just as we are one in the same, we are also two separate persons. And, to me, that is what makes our friendship all the more special, all the more reason to call each other "best friends" and mean it. We have our sameness in some areas and we have our differences in others. And for a friendship to withstand both is what makes the friendship all the more unique and strong...Another reason for this letter is to apologize. I'm sorry for the quick temperedness possessed on the trip. But please remember there is always a cause for people's actions, sometimes unknown to others. I guess what I am trying to say is please don't hold it against me for life...As we both know, our lives have changed, but not in the same direction. But as we said think about all the new experiences we will have to share. That is something I am looking forward to...Well, Dee, that about sums it up. It's not the end but the beginning for both of us! Remember, I love you and I'm always here for you. (Yes, you can call collect.)...Thanks for the trip. I had a blast! Well, looks like we made it once again. "Alter-Egos – Till the end"?? Heck ya! With love and Friendship Always, Debs*

8/12/1985: Went shopping. Of course. Saw a little castle with my aunt and uncle. Finally went to see Kaiser Wilhelm (ruled from 1871-1888). Then drove to a place where the last dinosaurs treaded 2 million years ago. Footprints and all. Then we went to Oma's and had champagne. I think I'm a champagne "Fraulein". I'm getting sad to leave Germany.*

[* *This would be the last time I would see my Oma.*]

8/14/1985: "Amadeus" – Falco (love that song)...Last night. It's weird I don't want to leave here. But I do. So much here that I love. So much at home...Aside from feeling fat, I am looking forward to having a sex life again. It may only be three weeks but I want it to be a very "interesting" 3 weeks. The same kind of sex can be so humdrum. Wonder how my sex life will be after those 3 weeks! If Ajey complains about the gut gain, the famous words "take it or leave it" will be said. I think I'm beginning to get horny – coming out of remission.

8/15/1985: Note: I've come to realize that one of my greatest pet peeves is speaking English in Germany to Germans. [*still is!*]. Airport buy: Stephen "Tin Tin" Duffy's The Ups and Downs. Second note: I HATE little kids who stare at you from the back of their chairs and constantly call out "Hallo Tante." (In fact, I don't really like this shit in front of me. 9-1/2 hours to go)...I don't know if or what I can say on my feelings for Ajey because to come out and say them right now wouldn't be fair. I'd be putting thoughts into my head, picking him apart. God knows I have done that enough without probable cause. So now I'm going to be fair minded because I was so happy with him before. Why should it all change? Tonight we're back in California and then I may have an answer or two. But is a few hours of time enough to make the judgment? ...As for the numerous pages I wrote on Denver, I was struck by the going away/love saga which will probably occur many times in my life before I settle down and have a life...When I found out last week that I was going, I was so ecstatic. That feeling hasn't left yet, either. I honestly cannot wait to go. I know now it's what I want and need to do. I feel it...As for Ajey, I think I'll try to break up when I go away – not on bad terms. But I don't know how he'll respond.

MORE

What is a satisfied heart,
When it yearns for more?
Is (some)one content
with mere essentials?
Do mountains grow
green with envy
Because another is
higher and greener?

Who wants to be small
When the others are tall?
Only so many exits exist
For those seeking coverage.
Hiding from humiliation
The others do not see.
They wear the mask
Becoming concealed.
Seeking remission.
Running to closed doors,
Ignoring the open,
Obvious escapes.

It is 8am USA time. ETA is 12:35pm. Almost there. Sometimes I think the drive to Greece was quicker. Imagine that: 3 weeks without travel before I leave for Denver. A break. Of the 1,080 hours we were in Europe, over 112 of those were either on a plane, bus, or train getting to temporary places of residence, over 1/10 of the trip.

8/16/1985: Today was a very weird day. Seeing Ajey yesterday for me was weird. I felt so much more grown up and different. Today started out the same way. I was very distant. We got into a gnarly fight over how I was acting. At one point I even said we could have sex right then, just real quick because I had to go meet my mom in an hour. He got up and said now he was pissed and said I might as well call my mom now. He goes, "Just get out." I went to get my stuff and then we said a couple of things. I asked him if he really wanted me to go. "No, yes. I don't know." I didn't go. I walked over to him. Gave him a hug and told him I still loved him. And he said, "I love you so much." We left on okay, ceasefire terms. (Later he told me he couldn't stay mad at me.) He picked me up again. And this time things were cool. We made love twice. He came so fast I couldn't even believe it. Both times even. It was the kind of sex we'd had when he first came back. Slow, easy, quick. But after both times we could lay there and joke like we used to. Even talked about Denver. We then went to frozen yogurt. And then came here. Laid on my bed for an hour and a half. It felt so good. It's always when he's gone again that I realize how good it feels to be back to him, with him. That love is really still there. Next week he's in the field. Comes back Friday. And then we're ours for the weekend. May even get to spend the night, because mom and Bobby (*a family friend from Germany*) are driving to Frisco...It feels good to be back. I'm excited about everything coming up...Wrote my roommate,

Emily. Signed my first loan papers. Turned in my film. Did quite a lot. I am very tired.

8/17/1985: I am just as tired tonight as last, if not more...Today was kind of neat. Went shopping with Bobby. Decided I want a couple more things for Denver. Went and said hi to Ajey's roommate. Took Bobby to the beach. Fixed my photo album. And went out with Ajey...We got along. Went to parents' friends for dinner. We were going to go to the movies but I suggested watching "Oxford Blues" on HBO instead, so I could run home and get the Germany video and my photo album. Mr. Hughes let me drive his 280ZX. That was so HOT. It's a thrill to drive a car like that...So Ajey and I watched the movie. Rob Lowe is gorgeous. Then he told me he wanted to stay committed whilst I was at school. We talked about it and came up with no conclusions. He just asked himself once why he was so much in love with me. We went to the bedroom...It was great at first. I had total control. I told him what to do to me. But when he said, "Now it's my turn," I lost most horniness. I don't like giving head, I realized today, because it makes me feel like I'm trying to make myself throw-up. That passed and we made love. I think he got the most pleasure when I started jacking him off. I would have loved to see him come then. But we had sex again. It was all kind of neat because I didn't feel shy or reluctant in bed...Tomorrow's it for the next five days. After tonight I need it because I am sore! Then he says he has all these plans for us next weekend – partying, which I am kind of beginning to look forward to. We'll see. But for now my tiredness is overwhelming me.

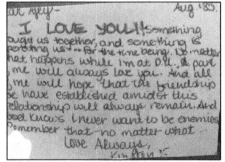 

(*At some point in August I gave Ajey this picture of me. On the back, I wrote: August '85 – Dear Ajey, I LOVE YOU!! Something brought us together, and something is separating us...for the time being. No matter what happens while I'm at DU, a part of me will always love you. And all of me will hope that the friendship we have established amidst this relationship will always remain. And God knows I never want us to be enemies. Remember that – no matter what. Love always, Kirsten... He*

shared this photo with me after we reconnected during the writing of this memoir.)

8/18/1985: Tonight was funny. Ajey and I had sex in my room and then Thor and Bobby decided they're going to sneak up on us. We jumped so quick. Thank God, we had our clothes on. We were all laughing so hard. Ajey's and my hearts were pumping...It was one of those times where I just had the sudden urge. So we did it. It was great. Heck man, I made him have a hard on before when we were watching TV. Glad we tried to carry it out. I was craving him...We went to the movies – "Weird Science" this afternoon. Then went out to dinner...My room is a national disaster. Partly from throwing things off my bed. The other part was already that way. But I'm enjoying getting things together...Ajey is gone now until Friday. Friday we're going to a party. Saturday we're going to Knott's. Sunday recuperate. I'm curious as to how it will all turn out.

8/21/1985: Today mom and I finished college shopping. My room is packed full of things. I discovered today that my schedule isn't exactly how I wanted it. I have total conflicts now. I am very pissed. I does not help that I am worried about mom. She's very emotional. She started crying today for hardly any reason at all. She says she can't control it. I'm worried about her...Talked to Ajey tonight. Still on for Friday and Saturday. I'm scared about Friday but being with people is something I too am going to have to overcome...My screwed up schedule has totally made me lose my train of thought. Shit, why me? There was so much more I wanted to say tonight. Sorry.

8/23/1985: Tonight Ajey and I went out and it was disastrous. All we did was rag on each other; chopped each other so low. It was fun at first and then it got bad. I think it almost got to the point of him hating me. God, that is the last thing I want. I love him so much. All I want to do is be with him alone. It doesn't bother me when we're in crowds of unknowns. There Ajey is all mine. We went to the drive-ins tonight. We hardly touched. It's weird, though, when we do touch or kiss it is so special. There's a certain electricity radiated. I love touching him; being with him. And I am going to HATE it when I have to leave him. He means so much to me. All I can hope for is that he and I can remain friends these next few months. And at Christmas if neither of us has new loves I hope we can try to be what we have been. Tonight we were enemies. A state I hate. Tomorrow we are going to Knott's Berry Farm. I hope it's fun and special. A day we can really enjoy each other. I love him so much, but I am beginning to get scared that Ajey is pushing away that love. I'm tired. I need to rest up for tomorrow. [Think of me, Ajey, because I love you.]

8/24/1985: Ajey and I went to Knott's today. It was alright. Seemed like we didn't have much to say after yesterday. But tonight we made love and it was cool. I felt like I came so close to having an orgasm. It felt good!! I was the total aggressor. The whole time we did it I was on top. It was neat. It felt like me in control. It was something new and I like that a lot. And we talked about everything. The evening was really cool. Tonight in the car on the way home he said the only way he could resume his old "roommate" lifestyle was if something bad happened between us (i.e. if I burned him). He said he's learned a lot from our relationship. I hope desperately that whatever happens whilst at DU that he and I can always remain friends. I part of me will always love him and the friendship will just add to it.

8/25/1985: Just got back from Ajey's. Watched TV and made love. It's been feeling especially good these past two times. Especially when I'm on top...I went to the beach all day. Can't tell, but the time went by quickly...Bobby leaves on Tuesday. Tomorrow we are having a BBQ at the beach for him. Suji, Deb, and I are all supposed to go out in the morning, too. Exchange of things. Finally...Mom is really worried about dad. And so am I. He hasn't called all weekend. Wish he'd hurry up and call us. I don't know what I'll do if something has happened...There's this killer running around California. And they call him the "Intruder/Nightstalker". I'm scared shitless that this maniac man is going to kill my family or come close to people I know and love. He's been working his way from Frisco, just hit Mission Viejo. I hope so badly he is caught before he can kill anyone else. It's a paranoid feeling and makes me hope no one else will get hurt...Aids is scaring me, too.

8/26/1985: Exhausted once again. Spent the entire day running errands for mom. Didn't mind, though. Went swimming. Always makes me feel a little better. Had Bobby's BBQ tonight. Think they enjoyed it. Hope mom did at least. She knocked herself out for it. Went to Ajey's. Watched part of "All the Right Moves." Remember my obsession with Tom Cruise? Looking back now it's weird. We then went to bed. Top again. I love it. Had a hickey war. My shoulder is a mess. (We got in a fight at the beach. I have to stop ragging on him. I think it might have to do with a lot of pressure from my leaving.) I love him, though. There are so many times I want to tell him that. But somehow I think I'd be hurt if he didn't say it back. Going to ask mom to let me stay over at Ajey's on Friday night...Dad's safe.

8/27/1985: Today Debbie, Suji, and I finally got together. Went to Denny's. It was fun. Something seemed a little 'off' between all of us. I can't help but wonder how it will be when we get together on vacations...Went swimming again today. Nothing much. But trying to maintain some physical shape...Ajey and I went to a movie again tonight. Saw "Teen Wolf". Definitely not fantastic, but it had its moments. "Back to the Future" was much better. Went to his house. Exchanged back scratches and then made love. It has been feeling so good these past few times. I can feel my insides trembling. I want it all and wish it would all cum (come) out...Tomorrow I am going to ask mom if I can spend the night at Ajey's on Friday. I'm old enough. Responsible enough. She knows we sleep together. I guess saying yes is openly allowing it. But I'll fight it. Ajey and I don't have much more time together. UNFORTUNATELY. I love him so much. Wish (sometimes) I could stay here and not be tempted by fate at DU. Hesitant (very) about leaving mom here. I'm very worried about her. I wish she could know how much I love her. And dad. But we ALL KNOW.

8/28/1985: I would say I am highly pissed right now. I'm probably being selfish but Ajey is going out with some guy tonight. Not me. And why? Because he figured that if I wasn't home at 5:30, why would I be home to see him tonight. Fuck that. I am going to be here ten more days and car shopping will always be there. He's coming by before he goes. I know I'm going to be a real bitch to him. Partly because I want to. I can see a fight start. And I hope he has a shitty time tonight. I've even contemplated leaving here and not being here at 7:00. I don't want to see him now. I'd rather be pissed at him until Friday, because I'm beginning to doubt I'll see him tomorrow the way it's sounding. FUCK him for making me sit at home...Okay...he came over. And as I said I'd probably be a bitch, I was. Ignoring him. Having "nothing to say." Then we got into a discussion. Things got cool again. Talked about us and things. Why do I have to love him? And him me? He left but said he'd call me when he got back so we could finish our talk.

8/29/1985: Today I went swimming and I saw that guy Brian that I went out with once this year. That was/seems so long ago. He was pretty cool to me. But I really had no interest in talking to him...Went out to eat with Ajey tonight. Then went to his house. I was in one of those weird moods. I had all these off the wall questions I wanted to ask, some I did. I laughed a lot. He asked me to give him head. I laughed while doing it. And, of course, I quit before he came. We then did 69. You can tell when a guy is getting into it because he gets so into it in you. Then we did it on top again. First, though, I was

233

facing his feet. I did it out of curiosity. Turned around and once again that incredibly good, non-orgasmic feeling overcame me. One of these days I'm not going to let him stop until I have an orgasm. It'll probably have to be some time this weekend. Time is running out. Very unfortunately. He told me he loved me tonight. I love him so much. I hope things work out for us in one way or another. Can't wait to see him tomorrow. I've been desiring him so much. Want all of him I can get before I leave. Mind you: despite leaving Ajey and the family, I am very much looking forward to going to Denver. I can't wait to start my future. And I'm anxious to see how it all will turn out.

8/30/1985: Distillery. Went. I literally had a great time. Dancing hasn't felt so good in a while. I liked the fact that I had someone for every slow dance. That's something I've never had. And I love dancing with him. But tonight I got this feeling he didn't want to touch me. I was the one touching, kissing first. He had a friend who went with us. His friend kept bringing up Ajey's illustrious past with women. I don't think he meant it badly. It's just weird to think of Ajey that way. Then again I can see it. It's flattering and scary now though. It's cool because it should make me feel special in that I have Ajey and no one else does right now. Next point, when I'm gone. I can only say "mess around" but I don't mean it. I can't stand the thought of him and someone else while I'm still deeply in love with him. And I'm sure it will be a while. He thought I was mad at him tonight. I wasn't. Just quiet. Thinking. Not even about his past. "The past is the past and I'm not going to dwell" – I'll try. I don't want trivial things like that to come between us. I guess what kind of bugged me is that he wouldn't touch me unless I touched him first. I don't know if I should take it as rejection – probably not. But if he's against my open display of affection, he should tell me. I enjoy touching him. He makes me so happy. I love him. And whatever part of him I can have and hold, it makes me feel that much closer to him.

8/31/1985: I hate when I tell Ajey that I'm going to spend the evening at my parents. It is now 8 o'clock. And I've discussed the pertinent matters with them. Now I have this desire for Ajey and he is not there...He and I went to the beach today. We fully ragged on each other. I HATE when we rag...It's weird when I'm with him I sometimes doubt us. But when I am away from him he is my every thought. I can't wait until the next time I can be with him. I know he is mine and I doubt highly that he is/was/will be unfaithful to me. Granted if the urge arises it arises. I don't think he will just as I don't think I will. Right now I feel so much for him. I'm going to hate leaving him. He is so much a part of my life right now. I would love for "IT" to work...I wish he could know how much I really do love him and believe in his love for me. I don't care about his past.

Honestly. I have realized it means nothing because I am not yet part of it. I hate myself when I make something come out wrong as a reference to his past. I don't want to hurt him but sometimes I get this feeling like I'm damn good at it. I'm just too curious, I guess. I don't care about anything but him, and the here and now...I want to be with him so bad right now, but he is not there. I hate when I want something and it is not there...I saw Bob at the beach today. He asked me if I'd heard from Terry. Felt dumb. Ajey was right there. Terry seems like it happened so long ago. A year. Sometimes I wonder how he's doing. I can't help compare that relationship to this one – very wrong vs. very right; curiosity vs love. Both were so different. I never really loved Terry and I very much love Ajey.

Why does it have to happen to me? All night long I needed Ajey so badly. I just wanted him there to hold. I all of a sudden feel like I have lost him. Like he's no longer mine. Said he went to a basketball game tonight. He just called from Poway where he went to some party. I was trying to sleep but kept having these visions of him and some girl named Mary Jo. The tears started to flow at that thought. Phone rings and he's spending the night at <u>her</u> house. I can't handle it. I can't. My God, what did I do? I hate myself for loving him. I hate it. I hate him. I just wonder how much else of this is a lie. I fucking need him tonight and Mary Jo got him. FUCK IT!

LEFT EMPTY

I could have used you tonight.
I was lonely; lost.
Needed a vitalizing touch.
Wanted your hands;
Your lips; your words.
Even hearing your voice -
I would have liked that.
Where were you?
(The tears didn't help).
Non-stop ringing of the phone.
Time is running low
I don't know how
Long I can stand it.
I miss you so much NOW.
Please, don't let the time change us.
I'm in too deep;
Care too much;

Love indescribably
But, tonight I am left empty.

[Labelled BTC, which I assume means Before The Call.]

WAITING

I am angry;
I am hurt.
Words I might try to write
Could not nearly describe.
I feel lost;
And ugly;
And very irrelevant.
An object in your possession,
dropped to ashes
on the pavement's crust.
I am a string
tied around your finger
for convenience sake,
or "just in case" you forget.
I have been dragged around
and been used.
A sort of second hand shop.
But the lies.
I will never be able to conceive.
What did I do?
I only fell in love with you.
Nothing more.
I never twisted the knife
And left it there.
Tonight I rustle in the sheets
Counting the hours
Until you call.
Like a compete fool.

[Labelled ATC, which probably means After The Call.]

9/1/1985: Saw Ajey this morning. I believe him now. No, he didn't mess around. I never really thought he did. I guess I am just not that sure of myself in these regards. I guess what clinched it is that he had written a note to his roommate saying where he'd be...I've come to conclude that I can definitely make this relationship harder than it needs to be. I must be very jealous and protective of what I want to be all mine – Ajey. The way I treat him at times makes me feel like shit. But I am too stubborn and pig headed to relent.

(PM) Today turned out to be really cool. From 2pm on until 9:30 I spent it with Ajey. We made love once in my room. That was cool. Took a shower together. Ate dinner. Then we decided to play tennis. I won! Came home. I then let him read what I'd written for the past two days in here. Said a lot. He was getting all into things I'd written. It was funny to see a guy get so into a girl's diary. But it was fun. Then we messed around in the kitchen. Pretended to have a fight - physical. It was kind of fun. A fight where my aim was to damage him, but to no avail. We had a truce. Went outside to say good-bye, but I dared him to have sex in his car. Wasn't really a dare. Was playing with his dick. Sooner or later he got a hard on. We jammed to the high school. Had sex. He came. (2nd time today). I told him I loved him, he told me back. Finally broke in his car. My body has been desiring him so much lately. I hope tomorrow is a cool day for us. Beach in the day. Together at night – for a while. We're trying to think of all these places that would be cool. Experimental sex. I love it. I love him. Can't wait to see him again. Tuesday and Thursday are shot. He has school until late. I start the rag Thursday. I pray that this rag is very minor. All I want to do is be with Ajey and make love to him, let him know how much I love him.

9/2/1985: Today was fun. Ajey and I went to the beach. Then came home. I took a shower. Then we went to a traditional A and K dinner – fast food at McDonald's. We then went to his house and the fun began. First we were kind of just messing around. He was touching me down there. Then the phone rings. It's some girl. For all of two minutes I could keep my hands off him and then I started touching him. Got him relatively hard and then started to give him head. He was still on the phone but told me later he could not remember much from the conversation. He looked like he was going crazy whilst still on the phone. He then got off the phone. We then proceeded to continue that scene. Me further giving him head. It wasn't so bad. And he fingering me. God, it felt good. We then made love sitting on the couch (1). Then laying on the couch (2). Took a break. Roommate came home. Chatted a minute or two with him. Shut the door and off we were. We got kinky then. Ajey tied my hands up and blind folded me. He then did it with a piece of ice between us (3). Then I tied him up and tortured him with ice. Took him a while to get hard. Jacked him off and did it to him from on top. Feels so good!! He said he likes watching me do that. Then I undid him and we made normal love (4).

Afterwards we were both two massive mounds of sweat. It killed to walk. And I was totally sore at the end. But I loved every minute of it. He then took me home. I gave him a journal for him to keep. Where he can keep track of us, what he feels, etc. I am chapter one (I said). I'd love to be the only chapter, and who's to say. I'm getting a new journal before DU. I want to start it for my college years, so this one is going to be left with some empty pages. No big. It's definitely had its share of adventure...Went out to breakfast with family and grandma today. I don't like her despite her giving me $1,000. She makes me so self-conscious. Today is the last day I will see dad until probably Thanksgiving. Weird. But I don't see him that much anyways. I'll miss him, though...In one week and a few hours we will be departing for Denver. It's so weird how that is quicky approaching. I'm so excited about the new experience, though. Hope my roomie's cool. It is so weird...I think I'm going to make this end on the 14th of September – four months after day one.

9/3/1985: I am starting to get really scared about going to Denver. I do not want to feel like an outcast. And then a friend who goes there was over making me even more nervous. I'll kill myself if I hate it. But seriously doubt I will. I think I'll probably love it. But I'm scared shitless to be a loner at first. Scared to leave Ajey because God knows I do not want to lose him. I am just lately realizing how much he means to me and how much I love him. I hope to God it all works out. EVERYTHING. That my life will have meaning in all aspects. I want to succeed in my DU adventure. With newly acquired friendships. I want me and Ajey to work out. Or I want us to at least keep the love and maintain a friendship even after it ends if it does. Right now I do not want it to in the slightest. I love him so much. I can hardly wait until the next time I see him again...I am just feeling very scared, lonely, and self-conscious right now because my life is going somewhere altogether new. Everything will be new again. I will have no family near and no boyfriend to hold me when I need it, which has been an awful lot lately. There is too much damn tension around here lately. Mom is totally nerving me. I feel like I may be going crazy. But I guess once I get into the swing of things, I will hopefully adapt. God knows, I don't want to disappoint anyone especially myself. That is most important...The luck of the Irish in me (must be some somewhere that I don't know of) must be with me. At 8:00 tonight Ajey calls from the mall. His class in SD was for mechanical engineering not premed. He was bummed because they'd told him it was regular physics. So now he has to drop the class. I'm kind of bummed for him because I think he was looking forward to having his time occupied while

I'm gone...Nonetheless, I wasn't bummed. I got him. And I get him (probably) every day until I leave. That makes me feel damn good. He came and picked me up. Ended up in the bedroom. We just touched each other lightly at first. I love that feeling. Then we made slow, calm love with me on top. He later made the comment that we go from extremes (i.e. last night vs. tonight). True, but it adds such versatility...Read part of his journal – honestly accidental – tonight. Saw a sentence that said he knows he's going to lose me. But I don't think so. Nor do I really believe I'll all together lose him. I love him too much.

9/4/1985: 159. That is how much I weighed today. I cannot figure it out. With the exception of the past couple of days, I have not been eating much. I start the rag tomorrow. Maybe? I doubt it. My legs are gigantic, though. That they have gotten. I can't figure it out. I definitely do not want to gain the freshman 15. I can't picture me at 175 pounds. Its weird because I can wear a two piece and feel relatively comfortable. Not fat. Today I feel fat. Knowing how much I weigh. That is as much as mom. But I look so much slimmer. Why did I have to be born big boned? I hate it!!...I am getting very scared about leaving here. I wish I never would have talked to my DU friend. I'm sure what interests him won't necessarily be what interests me. He and I are two different people who are going to find pleasure in opposite things. What I get out of DU will probably be so much different from what he gets out of it. God, I feel like I am being intimidated. I don't want that. I DO NOT want to be a little wallflower like I was in high school. I want to make it all work out. My way. To fulfill me and my future requirements. No one knows me there. I can be totally aggressive academically, socially, just in all. As for my friend, I don't think he'll pay any attention to me. And if he does he'll just have to withstrain from saying "you're different." I want to establish some excellent relationships and connections there. If things don't feel right at first, I will adapt and try to use things to my advantage. Despite how damn scared, paranoid, etc. I am feeling now I am going to make the best of things. I do not want to sit back and just be an observer, intimidated by the beautiful ones, the doers. God, if there's ever a time in my life where I'm going to have to strive for more than personal recognition it's going to have to be now. And I definitely am going to have to learn to tolerate a broad amount of people. All I want is to make it. These are my goals: good GPA; make it work with Ajey – because it's too good to let go of; make friends for a lifetime; let go and be me; lose weight; and simply enjoy myself at something.

PM: Ajey and I spent a couple of hours together tonight. We went to the mall and then to "the most important place of all – bed." It was very slow and quiet. Ajey didn't even say anything. He usually does. All I think about in that case is how much I really love him. It's weird because I really do love him a lot. I love the time that I spend with him so much, even if it's just for a couple of hours. I know he loves me which is also a great feeling. I think Ajey and I will make it through Christmas vacation. That would be fantastic. There is an incredible magnetism I feel towards him and I think him towards me. That will keep us together a while...Talked to Lisa...People change, I guess. And that is weird. I hope Ajey and I can withstand them for the time being.

9/5/1985: Really don't feel like writing tonight...Spent the day doing nothing. Bummed around Ajey's tonight. We just watched TV. Sometimes it's cool like that. Tonight wasn't extremely satisfying but I enjoyed being with him none the less...Tomorrow we are going to play tennis and what not. I am on the rag right now which is an incredible bitch. Not much hope for adventurous sex. But if I can run to bathrooms quick enough – who knows.

9/7/1985: My headaches are really beginning to scare me. They are too painful and recurring too often. They happen even when I wear my glasses and when I feel no stress. Aspirin don't even really help. Tonight it just put me to sleep. Last thing I want to do because I was with Ajey...Yesterday from 3:30 on we were together. Made love even though it wasn't the most flattering due to ole aunt Flo (Hate that bitch)...Today we were together from eleven on. Just bummin around. Would have loved to have made love to him. But we didn't. He because of my headache. I because I thought he wanted to sleep. Sometimes we are either just too considerate of the other or not at all. I love him, though, despite the whatevers, with all my heart.

9/8/1985: Spent the entire day with Ajey, again. We played tennis. I played pretty good. He played terrible. I killed him. Left him in a bad mood for a while. Went to the movies. Saw "Compromising Positions." It was a good movie. Sometimes I wonder where screenwriters get their ideas. From dreams? Mine are so obscure usually. I couldn't even try writing them. After the movie we went to his house and made love. This girl, with her perfect timing, called. Couldn't believe it. She's done that before. I'm beginning to get over that jealousy. His birthday kind of worries me. But fool that I am, his words of reassurance seem to take away the doubts for a while. We then took a shower together. Making love there, too. That was fun. Killed my knees. Because I was on top they kept pounding against the back of the tub. There were times when I felt like I was going to explode and cum all over him. I wish I would. I think that's something that would bring us even closer than we are now, which is pretty close. For him as much as me I wish I could. The sensations I get now are incredible. Just wish they'd be all the way fulfilled...It's weird to think that tomorrow is it for a while. I know I am going to sob tears to no end. I love him so much. Leaving is going to kill. It already is. It's really bothering him, too. I think Ajey and I will make it. The love is definitely there...Tomorrow we leave. I leave for college. It is finally here. That is weird to think. I WONDER how it's all going to be. Anxious – definitely – to find out.

9/9/1985: I am now on the phone talking to Suji. We are gossiping for the last time locally before I leave...Said good-bye to Debbie, too. I wonder how it will be when I get home with us. Sometimes it was cool. Sometimes not. These past couple of weeks since we've been back haven't been so great for our friendship. Couldn't really tell you who's at fault. Or if anyone is...Ajey and I said our good-byes tonight. God, it HURT. I love him so incredibly much. I wish I could record some of our conversations. He told me that he doesn't want to lose me. I poured tears tonight. He teared. And then poured when I told him that I love him so much. What we have is so deep. I hope to God neither of us blows it. Our love is too special (it is so different from when Terry left)...We went out to dinner tonight. Then we went home and made love. I couldn't believe how close I came to an orgasm.* This incredible sensation overcame me. It was fantastic! I felt like I was going to explode. And then Ajey starts to giggle because something was tickling him. I came so close. And then later again I almost did. These incredible feelings kept coming over me. No sex for 2-1/2 months. No Ajey for 2-1/2 months. That is going to kill...No matter what happens between us I thank him for letting me know REAL love. I LOVE YOU, AJEY. REMEMBER IT. HOLD IT. I WILL BE BACK TO YOU...Off to Denver in one hour. I cannot believe it is finally here. (God, I don't want to leave Ajey.)

[*Sex Ed and Cosmopolitan should have taught us that there is more than one kind of orgasm instead of making us believe we should be trying for the big, most elusive one right off the bat! And because I have no doubt inquiring minds will want to know, this would not be an issue for long. It takes some of us longer to figure this out.]

9/10/1985: Mom and I are sitting here in our motel room after driving for about 16 hours. We are only three hours away from Denver. I cannot believe I am almost there. And you know all I think about is coming home at Thanksgiving. Then I think about how I think things will be at school. I think about Ajey, Ajey, Ajey. How I already miss him. But how I really believe things will work out between us. I think about the time we'll have together. AND then I think about how I hope to God I like DU. And everything about it. Most of all I hope I don't fail myself. There's so much keeping my mind occupied. Haven't slept much. Looking forward to tonight's sleep. Good night from Glenwood Springs.

9/11/1985:

> *There is an immense power*
> *Holding me to you.*
> *The love I feel,*
> *It is strong enough*
> *To endure the test of time;*
> *To withstand distance;*
> *To keep us as we are.*

Damn, I love you, Ajey. God, do I love you. And I tear at every thought I have of ever having left. I hope to God that you and I can remain as we are, and possibly grow to be more. You are my every thought. Every dream. And I want to hate you for making me want to come home...There's so much here. My roommate is cool. A total jock. I'll probably never see her because of that. I guess that's where I'll just have to grasp out and make new friends. I am going to have to take the initiative. People seem really friendly though. I hope I meet some neat, fun people...There were times today when I was so frustrated. I felt bad for mom because I just jumped all over her. I don't mean to. I am also trying very hard not to feel guilty about all the money being spent. It is so hard, I just want to cry at the thought. I love mom so much. I don't want to hurt her in any way. God, I love my family so much. I love Ajey so much. (Please let everything work out for us ALL.)...I'm staying the night with mom in a hotel in Denver tonight. Tomorrow I will be back in the dorms. Good. I hope I meet more people then. I'd really like to get involved and meet people...I can't believe how many gorgeous guys infest this campus. And not that many pretty girls, but then again I haven't really seen that many people on campus. BUT I really have no desire for anyone but Ajey. Sometimes I think November won't be soon enough. But I haven't given here a chance yet. (I'm going to apply to SDSU just in case of economic sanctions.)...Got a job in the University Relations department. I'm kind of excited. Won't be making much, but it's going to be a great experience...I am really going to make an effort to meet people here. I want to know I can make it somewhere else, too. I don't ever want to regret this...I'm thinking of joining aerobics here. If aerobics doesn't work out, I am going to swim and MAYBE do some jogging. My knees have been killing. Probably the only good thing abstinence will bring – no body pain...Ajey wasn't home tonight when I called. And you know, I'm not even worried or jealous he might be with someone else. I honestly believe he loves me. And I do love him...Talked to Ajey tonight. I didn't want to hang up. Just wanted to hear his voice forever. He said he's going crazy without me. All he's doing is playing tennis to try and keep busy. All I'm doing is going crazy with thoughts of him. He's already counting down the days until I am back home. Man, I love him so much.

9/12/1985: (AM) Had a couple of dreams about Ajey last night. One was at a carnival. We were there with Debbie and her boyfriend. They got off the ride and Ajey and I made love on the ride. Constantly telling each other how much we love each other. The other was at the beach. All these goings on were happening around us. All we could do was desire to make love. Once again there was so much love involved. There was so much passion.

9/13/1985: I am now on my own. It is a lonely feeling not having mom, dad, Thor, or Ajey. I miss them all so much. The being alone part would have been so much easier had I not fallen in love. Damn, I love him so much. Sometimes I feel there is nothing I wouldn't do for Ajey. God, he was my life. He still is. He's just a thousand miles away...Aside from that, I really think I am going to like it here. Once school starts, I think I am going to be kept very busy (at least during the week)...My roommate, Emily, is really cool. So far we've gotten along great. Last night we went to a couple of parties around campus. Frats are so wild. Gorgeous guys. But for once in my life there is absolutely NO desire to be with one. But, as I told Emily, that will not stop me from having a good time. She's a total partier. As soon as I relax a bit more I may come to enjoy it more...She plays soccer so she already knows quite a few people. She's cool about introducing me around to people...I hope this year is fantastic. I hope Ajey and I make it through the year and beyond. I love him so much it's incredible. I hope I do great in school and that I don't let my parents down. Most of all, I hope I will be happy no matter what...Time to write letters...I wrote all my letters. Seven to be exact. I even got mail today. Ajey wrote me. I've read it about five times. Each time it brings tears to my eyes. It was a totally cool letter. Makes me miss him all the more. The first thing it said was, "I have this incurable desire to make love to you."

(Excerpt from that letter – dated 9/10/1985:) Well not even a day gone by and I find myself with the incurable urge to want to make love to you. At this point, I'd even settle for an argument. As long as it resolved like they all do. Needless to say, I don't hate you for leaving me. I thought I would but it's quite the opposite. I've decided that I should dedicate myself to school so maybe the time will go by fast. God it better. I cried all the way home. I didn't think I would hurt that bad when you left but I was wrong. I miss you terribly…I'm hoping you get this letter after you have unpacked so you can relax and read it. I figured that this relationship will work for the simple fact that our egos won't let either one give up. Lucky us, right?…Going to play tennis. I need to take out my frustrations on someone…Needless to say I'll be thinking of you while I play. I Love you. Love, Ajey PS I want your body! PPS Wish you were here.

What did I do? I cannot believe how much I love him. That love is so intense. So real. There's practically nothing I wouldn't do for him. I used to countdown the hours in a day until I'd see him again. Now I'm counting down months. I love him so incredibly much. It's almost crazy. Here I am at the school of my dreams, the place where I wanted to start anew. All I want is my Ajey. I want his body, his touch, everything about him. I want him  to make intense, passionate love to me again. I want a best friend back. And he definitely is that. God, those last few weeks we were each other's existence. Always together. It was fantastic. Because of Ajey, I know what love is. Right now, I can say I never want to lose that. Depending on how we are at X-Mas break will definitely decide what I'm going to do…Staying faithful to Ajey is not going to be hard, not at first. And I doubt it ever will be. Celibacy is not going to stop me from having a good time here at DU…Emily is totally funny. I think they're all out to look for scams, which makes it kind of hard for me. But I'm sure I can think of things to compensate for that…I want school to start so as to help the time fly by. I want Ajey so badly. I miss him so much. The emptiness of not having him around is incredible. I love him! I love him! I love him! Damn, I want him back. Would I be a fool to go here only a quarter? God, I can't even believe those kind of questions are crossing my mind. Hell, I must love Ajey more than I'd ever recognized before…I don't know if I'll be able to shake some of these guilty feelings I have. I hate myself for having been so selfish. I love my family so much. They have sacrificed so much for me. I do not want to let them down. I'm worried about mom and hope that she'll be okay. Hope we'll all be okay, if not better…Broke down and called Ajey tonight. It made me so happy talking to him. Made me feel like a completely different person. Why does he make me feel so good? Why? Because I love him too much.

(Excerpt from letter to Lisa dated September 13, 1985:) Dear Lisa, I owe you the greatest apology. I am so sorry that I did not call you when I said I would. I had been going crazy through sheer frustration trying to get my act together for college. Needless to say, I made it here with relatively few problems. The greatest problem was leaving Ajey, because I love him so much. God, Lisa, it's weird because I never thought I would start to regret leaving California. I was all ready for the independence movement. But now I want to come home to Ajey, to California. It's weird because it's totally cool here. Gorgeous campus. Really cool roommate. She's from NY. A total partier. She's also a jock. She already knows so many people from soccer. She's asked me to do things. Last night we, plus a couple others, went to some frats. They know how to party – WILD. Gorgeous guys infest this place. But I can't believe me, these guys are everywhere. I'm sure if I set my mind to it it wouldn't be too hard to scam around. But I just don't want anyone here. I just want Ajey. I never thought I would be able to feel so much love for someone. There is so much passion in our relationship. Terrific sex life. I'm thinking of transferring to SDSU next year so that we can be together. It seems like it will last that long. There's such intensity. So much emotion. We had a crying session before I left. But what I do depends on how Xmas break is…I can't believe how much it seems you've changed. Who would have ever thought Lisa gallivanting around Europe? It's totally cool that you are still a virgin. You haven't done it for the wrong reasons. You'd better make sure you tell me everything that is going on at UCSB…Starting everything on Monday. It's so weird to think that we are finally in college. No longer awaiting it. I guess we must be getting pretty grown-up. Write soon. God knows, there will probably definitely be times when I need to hear from a best bud. Take care. Love Always, Kirsten

9/14/1985: Fourth month of this journal: Last day of it, too. Strange…Today I discovered that I have to drop a class. That sucks. So now I am down to 14 units…I am so fucking ready to come home. I don't like the way things are working out. I just cannot believe me. I wanted to be here so badly…When I think about going home I think of all I could be doing there. Granted, I would have to miss a semester of school. I'm not unhappy here. Last night, I met a couple of nice girls and we've been kind of hanging out together today. They're down to earth and aren't obnoxious in the slightest. My roomie is inconsiderate, but I don't think it phases her in the slightest...I've been trying to call dad, but I never know what I'm supposed to say. I am ready to plea with him right now. I am living with so much guilt over money. I know mom said not to worry about it. I just think about how much money we could still be saving. This is what I'd love to do: come home (kick myself), go to SDSU next year, buy a used car, and Ajey and I could be together...I guess I'm doing all my realizing long after the appropriate time. What a dumb ass I have been. Why do I always do that? The folks are going to say stick it out. I seriously doubt they will contemplate letting me venture home. I think of all the money I could be saving them. I am also worried shitless about mom. She doesn't seem very happy. And then there's Ajey. I can hear it now. Dad's first reply will be, "Ajey." Partly. I am being such a hypocrite...I don't know what I want. I wish I did. This is a shitty feeling. How the hell would it be? I'd be a damn fool. They'll all say, "You haven't given it a try yet," or "we're committed." I know I'd be letting everyone down. Why me?

Tonight, I end this journal. Today was okay. Hung around these really nice girls. Tried calling dad to no avail. I'm going to stick it out this quarter, guilt and all, unless tomorrow turns out otherwise. My roommate is making herself at home to all my stuff. Pisses me off. She's explored my closet and is already wearing my clothes. Never again. She can be nice but is more often inconsiderate. I want it to work out here, but I am so confused. And I already know the answers to things. Oh well, this journal will now end. And imagine, we had one boyfriend through it all. I love you! Kirsten

The Last One: The Nothing Book
(1985-1986)

9/15/1985: (AM) Today, I start my new journal, and how do I start it? Depressed as hell. I want to like it here so much. I want to try, but all I can think about is being back home...I called mom this morning and copped the plea. She says financially things are really great right now. I hope she didn't say that just to make me try to feel better. If I don't like it here or feel these feelings after the first quarter, I think I am definitely going back...Being away from Ajey is killing me, too. Mom knows that. She says she went through the same thing when she had to leave Germany. I can understand that.

(PM) I am beginning to get used to this school. I feel more relaxed again. I think I may even like it here. Today Barb and I went on a bus ride to downtown Denver. That was kind of fun. She's really nice and so are Janet and Chris. Emily can be okay. Very careless, but I think we'll make it...Ajey called me today. I was very happy. I love talking to him. Today I did a lot of realizing about us. I am so much in love with him, and I believe he is with me. I think that we won't break up for a long time despite the distance. I trust myself and I trust him. That love is so strong. I don't think he needs to worry about losing me and right now I'm not worried about losing him...Just had a floor meeting. We were informed of all policies, etc. I'm bummed because this weekend is Geneva Glen but it is also little sister rush and a floor volleyball game/kegger at CU. A definite bummer. I'm going to have to contemplate further what I want to do...Starting tomorrow I am going to make time for exercise. I think swimming and racquetball maybe with Barb. Looking forward to being busy starting tomorrow. Yeah...Already feeling better about things.

9/16/1985: School started today. I was busy all day long. Up at 7:30. Ate at 8:15. Class at 9:00. German will probably be educational. Got out early. Signed loan checks. Dropped a class. When to work for two hours. Typed the whole time. Should be kick back. Went to English. Came back. Played racquetball with Barb. It's free. It feels great to play. Ate at 6:15. Now relaxing. Going to read my English and start a rinky-dink journal for it. Then read my newspapers. Time to be educated...Got a letter from Ajey today. Yeah. I love getting mail from him. Because I love him.

(*Excerpt from letter dated 9/12/1985:*) *Hi babe, what's new? ... So when are you are coming home? 73 days I think? I had this killer dream that we got stuck in a motel and ooooh it was so rough. After we got out, we both had to go the hospital for treatment. (sounds good)...Well, I still haven't gotten a good night sleep and I'm still messing up at work. Is this some kind of weird side effect?...Why don't you write SDSU soon so you can find out if they still want your ego then if we stick together you might consider going if you could hang with me as a roommate. I wish you were here right now. Not because I'm bored but just lonely. I never realized just how much time we spent together. But I can see now it was a lot...Well, I'm still writing in my book but nothing really except tennis scores and dreams about you...It's boring going to bed by yourself, but I know I can hang till you get back. Behave.*
                    Love always, Ajey

Oh, wait, I discovered hockey players. They are so damn gorgeous. Practically all of them. They have HOT bodies. Incentive to head over to the field house and workout. (No touch. I love Ajey too much) Being here is definitely getting easier, though.

9/17/1985: Ajey called me tonight and told me he'll be out here on the eleventh. He's already made the reservation. I am so happy. I can't believe he's going to be here so soon. He told me he couldn't stand being without me anymore so he's coming to see me. That weekend is totally free, too...I do have a major exam on the 15th (my Bday!) that I'll have to study for. Hopefully no other classes will be effected by it. I am so happy...I really like it here. I am having fun with Barb, Janet, and Chris. We skipped parties tonight because of massive homework. Going tomorrow though. So we took a break and ate popcorn with beer. It's 11:15 and I still have to read this massive thing. Welcome to college!

9/18/1985: A long day...Learned how to sort of use a word processor at work. That was fun. Played racquetball...Mom called me. Surprised. I felt good talking to her. I miss her. Told her all was well here. And all is. Really beginning to enjoy it, even without the parties. In time...Thinking of trying out for cheerleading. Going to a meeting tomorrow with Janet. Sounds like fun...Ajey wrote. Questions whether he is very much in love or lust. Not too bad a question. Probably both. Buying a teddy for when he comes. Gonna go socialize.

(*Excerpt from letter dated 9/15/1985:*) *Hi sweetheart, this letter is coming to you at the most important time of the day, dinner time. And as you already guessed I'm eating my traditional meal. Big Mac, large fries, and large diet coke. But this time no salt...I'm home by myself right now. My roommate left. His latest girlfriend is a stripper at some bar in San Diego. I wonder if that makes a good living? ...I'm left here trying to figure out how I managed to get left behind while you are in Denver seeking higher education...So I think I miscounted. I think it's 73 days from today if you come home on 28th of Nov excluding your birthday trip...Tomorrow I've got to get back to working out...I need more to keep me from trying to think of ways to kidnap you. Who knows maybe one of these ways would really work...You know sometimes I have trouble getting to sleep. I find that you are always on my mind and with that thought I toss and turn. But hopefully soon I'll have someone to toss and turn with. Think you can hang? HaHa. All I can say is take your vitamins. You'll need 'em guaranteed. I'd write more but I told you it all on the phone so I guess it's a short letter but at least you know I'm still madly in love with you. Or is it lust? Probably both. So be good. Love Always, Ajey PS I miss you!*

9/19/1985: Tomorrow is Friday and if I make it through tomorrow then this week will have been dandy. Actually, it would have been very cool. Very busy. Very tiring, but I basically enjoyed it...Tomorrow night is Geneva Glen (*camping in the mountains*). I do hope it's fun. As for cheerleading, I went to practice tonight. It was frustrating but seems like it would be fun. But I don't think I'll do it. It requires a lot of dedication...Three weeks from tomorrow, Ajey will be here. I can't believe it. I can hardly wait. I was getting/have been getting some incredible cravings for his body. I think of his entire body – from head to toe. I think of his every facial expression – from anger to delight. I think of his gorgeous chest. His incredible eyes. That look of 'let's go make love' or 'I want to make love to you.' I think of his body parts and of how much pleasure I got from them those last three weeks. Sex was fantastic those last couple of weeks. He brought me so much. And he never left me feeling empty. There was so much passion to our love making. Now in three weeks for a few short days I will have Ajey back in my possession. Back to please him and him me. I miss him so much. I miss his touch. Everything he possesses. He's gorgeous. He's fun. He's mine. I don't want that to change. I love him so much and lust him, too. A cool but incredibly lonely feeling. In a sense people who have never had sex are lucky because they don't know how the craving can be when they haven't had it for a while. Unlike me, I became quite fond of it and desired it from Ajey, because he's the one that makes me feel so good. Three weeks, huh? I'll make it. I'd better. It's six damn weeks after that until I am with Ajey again. I am definitely not going to start masturbating. I'll just keep watching those hockey players. Keeps my mind off of the satisfaction Ajey brings me.

(Letter from Ajey mailed 9/18/1985 telling me his flight plans for my birthday weekend, that he got a new stereo for his car that "really makes it shake" and telling me "the most important part which is I love you.")

9/21/1985: Geneva Glen wasn't much. I was with Kirsti and Sarah. Square dancing was fun. It was a way of being sociable...I've been thinking about Ajey a lot. Been desiring to talk to him all weekend and tonight when I tried calling he wasn't home. So now I am bummed. He is probably out partying, forgetting briefly about me. It is just incredible how much I miss him. I wanted to talk to him about a more serious matter, though...I wanted to talk to him about us. I want to know what he really thinks about us. If he's losing his love for me. I don't think it's purely a sexual reason Ajey wants me. I mean he could sleep with girls while I'm gone. So why does he say he wants to remain celibate? That's it. Obviously, there is more. I can't help but worry that that something more (love) is disappearing. My love for him grows stronger as each day goes by. But what if his becomes more questionable, less in love? I mean, my letters should definitely tell him how I feel. Maybe they're intimidating. Actually, I think they're flattering. His kind of make me wonder. But I don't want to doubt anything until I talk to him. Gotta go shower. I feel gross.

9/22/1985: Well, I did talk to Ajey last night for like an hour. It was pretty reassuring. I don't know why I get in the phases where I doubt us. The love I feel is tremendous. We talked about making love again. And how fantastic it's going to be. I have no doubts about that. Next weekend I am going to go out and buy a teddy. Starting tomorrow watch weight again. So help me if I'm on rag when he's here, I'm going to be so fucking pissed...Having sex again has become this major thought process. I can hardly wait for Ajey to be here so that we can bring our bodies to the point of total physical exhaustion...I am now into the routine of DU. I am also ready to go out and meet people and to party. I want to meet more people. I'm not going to withdraw from guys. I trust myself well enough. I know I wouldn't do anything to jeopardize my relationship with Ajey. He's already thinking of what he's going to get me for Christmas. Maybe a diamond ring. Ha, ha. Just being with him for a long period of time will suffice.

(*Excerpt from letter dated 9/21/1985:)...flying with two guys from Denver. I told him we would stop by if we could walk. Which I'm not counting on walking...Did I tell you I went and saw your mom? She asked me if I was keeping busy. I told her yes but not doing what I would like to do (hint). Thor and I are going to the Oingo Boingo concert...Wish you were going with me...So do you miss me? Needless to say I am going crazy. I now know what my roommate must have felt like when you were here because we were always together...now he's got something to do and mine is in Denver. God I hope you decide to go to SDSU. I'll be your roommate. Love Always, Ajey PS I hate sleeping alone.*

TEMPTATION

The words of this faded song linger on.
Momentary lapses in the forbidden zone.
Tapping of your heart triggers the predator's spark
Malice is the mark,
Insignificance the start.
Momentary distraction
Temporary insanity
at what fraction?

Tempting fate.
Building the hate.
Ignorance recedes.
Realization proceeds.
The final knock,
Last ticking of the clock.
Stop the beat.
Sense the heat.
Taste the sweat.
(Place your final bet)
You smile.
He just glares a while.
"Come closer," you say.
Then he moves your way.
The passion still exists.
The preexisting visions still persist.
It is he you wish;
He you want to kiss.
With each exulting thrust.
A new sensational rush.
The temptation for another
Becomes smothered.
It is him, your him.
It is his power you thrive to discover.
And that of no other.

9/23/1985: ...I'm beginning to get motivated to really physically exhaust my body. It's already mentally. No big...I want to look hot in my teddy – when/if I get it. Maybe I'll go run the steps...Had Freshman Experience tonight. Boring...It's so weird. I was telling Barb and Chris about this guy who intrigues me. I said wouldn't it be weird if he was in my group. Five minutes later we were in the same room. Weird. His name is Al or something like that. He seems kind of dumb, but that's okay. It's only that he's intriguing...(37 degrees outside. Never that cold in California.)

(Excerpt from letter dated 9/22/1985:) Hi good looking! What's cooking?...So are you counting down the days? Well as of this letter there are 452 hours till I get to hold you in my arms or 27,360 minutes...I'm going crazy waiting for you to get back to stay. But I know that one day you will be here and there will be nothing to take you away, which sounds great...Well, I'm still trying to figure out why you said it sounded like I

*doubted us in my last letter. God knows that's about the last thing I
would do and especially when you're so close...I hope SDSU is ready for
both of us...I need to know the information for hotel. No waterbed. It will
not survive our first night. How close is Mickey D's in case we get the
munchies?...Soon class will start and I will have something to do besides
be bored and that will make the time go by faster for me at least. So
hopefully before I know it I'll be in your arms, my kinda party...I miss
ya and am deeply in love with you and your body. See ya in 452 hours.
Love always, your lonely boyfriend, Ajey   PS Should I bring my yellow
belt? Remember?*

9/24/1985: I called Ajey tonight just to tell him I love him. I get that urge
often. He was sick with some kind of flu. He sounded awful but he
sounded better the more we talked. A five minute call turned into 20 min.
My poor checkbook. But I miss him. An awful lot. I love him more. And I
guess that love is what is making me believe in this. We're both counting
down days until he comes. I can hardly wait. Until then I will continue
to look at the hockey players. Rugby players aren't too bad, either. I don't
agree with Emily's theory on soccer players. They're kind of assholes if
you ask me. Tomorrow I start to diet. Worked out for a while tonight.
Now we're going to eat popcorn and study further. What a hypocrite.
Heard from Deb yesterday. Wrote her a kind of mean letter. Cold. But I
can't figure out and maybe she can explain it to me.

*(Excerpt from letter dated 9/25/1985:) Well, how did I sound yesterday?
I felt like shit...This letter has taken me two days to finish. I have been
getting sidetracked lately, but nothing to worry about. You're always 1st
in my mind. Needless to say by the time you get this letter my birthday
will only be something of a bad hangover to me. I think that out of all the
people I could spend a birthday with I would choose you. I feel like part
of me is missing when you're not around. And I'm afraid that I'll learn
how to cope without you. And that's something I don't ever want to
learn...I will probably call you Sat for the basic reason I miss you...UVA
said they'd reconsider me. No thanks. I know this killer looking girl who
said she would be my roommate at SDSU if I don't mess up. Could be
interesting. I miss ya and love ya lots. See ya in 14 days. Love, Ajey*

9/29/1985: Today is Ajey's 21st Birthday and I really wish I were there
with him, but I'm not. Twelve days. Been kind of busy. Partied Thursday
night, some of Friday night, and Saturday night. Been tired and not in a

writing frame of mind. It's been showing. Had a snowball fight last night. It's been fun. A relatively cool, non-boring weekend.

9/30/1985: I am in so in lust with this guy named Al. He's a hockey player and does he send my heart pounding. It's like I look at him and I can actually stop thinking about Ajey – as bad as that may seem. He is just so incredibly intriguing. Damn hot body. I was relatively intrigued by the bulge in his pants. God I hate Freud! What is he doing to me? It's like I have sex on the brain. (It's like I want to see other people). I have wanted someone for a while now. I don't want to be a sleaze. I really do want to get and be with other people. I honestly STILL can say I love Ajey. But right now my mind is obsessed with Al. And hockey players. And. And. And. Sometimes Ajey will say things that just turn me off. Sort of in a threatening fashion. He's not doing this/or he's not doing that because of me. It's high time to crash. Me.

(Excerpt from letter dated 10/1/1985:) ...Well, 10 days left. 10 nights till I get you back in a compromising position (do you mind?)...Of course I missed you at my birthday party but I was so drunk that I passed out. Not too exciting if you would have been there, but in no means does that mean I wouldn't have enjoyed your presence. (on the margins he wrote 'I miss ya' and 'A+K'). You know I'm going crazy waiting to get to Denver. All I can think about lately is you. I've got Kirsten on the brain syndrome. I hear it's a permanent problem so I guess I'll need lots of therapy. I think you have the qualification. If you choose to accept you must hang till the end. Oh I forgot totally important stuff. I got a job down @ the med center on campus starting in June...And the only thing I'll need is a roommate (hint). I talked to the premed advisor...I miss ya and will see you soon, right? Of course. Always missing you. Love, Ajey PS Nine more days

10/5/1985: The past two nights I have gotten totally trashed. Last night being the definite worst...Thursday night I was foolish enough to call Al. Out of boredom. Then last night his roommate, Dan, who is HOT, and I started talking. He walked me back over here and we sat and talked. I wish to God I wouldn't have been wasted. The guy seems so ultimately cool. I feel like calling him up and asking if I can redeem myself. But that kind of seems childish. I'm confused. Just down right confused. Ajey called me last night. I was so rude to him. I can't believe or comprehend how I'm acting. I kind of want to be careless. It's kind of how I feel right now. Somehow the response I'll get from Ajey will not be too hot and he'll not let me forget it. Ok, what now? What do I want? What do I need? ...

I am embarrassed about Dan. It's like the guy is so ultimately cool. There are things I said I can't remember. Nothing happened. I feel sorry for the guy. God, what does he think about me? FUCK THIS.

10/6/1985: Today was basically a shitty day. Fucked up at that. I called Ajey and we talked about seeing other people. In essence, Ajey and I are broken up. Like put on a very long hold. He told me that he hated me and if he never saw me again it wouldn't phase him at all. It was awful. I told him I loved him so many times but he just kind of blew it off as well as me. It's like why did I try to be honest with him? I lost everything tonight. I told him I'd come knocking on his door when I got back. And that I would fight for him – if I discover he's what I've wanted all along. That's just it. I don't know what I want. I didn't want him to hate me. But I managed that one, of course. How can I just be such a master of screw-ups? Seems like all I've been doing lately is screwing up. My forte I guess. I am so damn frustrated. Why couldn't he just accept my confusion and me for me? My God, I am so young. I do not know what I want exactly. He said if he could have it his way, I never would have gone, and I'd be his forever. But I can't say that's what I want. I couldn't have coped with not being honest. (Heck, I haven't even found anyone interested in me.) And I couldn't have coped with lying. I think I've really lost Ajey. I feel like crap. But maybe what this will eventually lead to will be for the best. I don't know. Right now I am just so damn confused. I have this feeling I won't hear from him for a long time. And even then it will be negative. It is always me who seems to do the wrong thing for a semi-right cause. Approximately one year ago Terry and I broke up. What the hell is wrong here? As Sting says, "Free, free. Set them free." I still love you, Ajey. I may have been a fool but if you are what I really want I will fight to have you back.

10/7/1985: Well, last night Ajey called me back. He said that I was probably basically right. But he just sort of apologized. He told me he's never been so mad at anyone before. But eventually it came out that he's so in love with me and probably always will. So now he says he's coming out to talk to me. He says he has to because he's put too much time and effort info the relationship. He even called my mom to talk to her about me. And me? What do I want? What do I feel? I love him. I am interested in Dan but know not how to go about it. And what if the response is bad? I need the break from Ajey. But I don't want to lose him. I am so confused. Scheisse (*shit in German*).

(The letter from Ajey in its entirety dated 10/7/1985:) Dear Kirsten, Well, needless to say, the more I think about it the more it sounds like a good idea. I guess we should see other people so we can make sure about how we feel for each other. And for that reason I won't be coming to Denver this weekend. It's not because I'm mad because I don't think I am anymore. But I want to know that if you knock on my door in November that it's because you're sure of yourself and I don't think me coming up to Denver when you're trying to establish who you are and what you want would help...I guess we should see other people. It will probably help us, me decide on how I want to spend the next year. And for you it will give you the chance to enjoy DU. And who knows maybe in December we will be able to meet on equal terms. I hope that I don't lose you. But I'm sure that whatever happens to us it will be for the best. You know I'm so in love with you. But I don't want you if you're unsure so I'll just hangout and wait and see. Oh yes. Go out with other people. You know actually the more I think about it the better it sounds...Of course, I'll keep in touch. I'm not that much of a geeeeeeek. And don't worry about me saying anything like I do about (a girl) because you're not even close. I'm sorry things are turning out like this but I'm sure it's for the best. And who knows it might even work out. I love you and I'll miss you lots. Take care and don't party too much. Love always, Ajey PS Good luck! PPS See you in November.

10/16/1985: HAPPY (BELATED) 18th BIRTHDAY! Well, I am now a legal adult. I can buy 3.2 beer in Colorado. Gnarly stuff. But hey! My birthday was a lot of fun. We had strawberry daiquiris. They were great. Think I may become known as the daiquiri queen in this joint. It ended early too so that I could finish my "wonderful" English paper. It was a lot of fun. My friends here are great. Thor, Deb, Mickey, and Lisa (mom, too) all called yesterday. Talking to Thor was fun. We seem a lot closer. Ajey didn't call. We've worked things out pretty coolly. I miss him and the love I feel for him is still there. If anything, it might be stronger because the relationship has matured, it seems...There's this guy from Sigma Chi who likes me. But I don't like him. He might be a cool friend and I hope that somehow that'll be the outcome because I can see us as nothing more. As for Dan, I am basically over the obsession. He is still incredibly "hot" and if I had it my way, a hockey player and I will get together once before my freshman year is over*. There is just something incredible about them...I haven't gone to work in nearly two weeks. I am so fucking bored with it. I want a career where I won't be bored...I'm confused about what I want and how I might achieve all of it. Oh man the pressures of being eighteen!

[*Spoiler alert: I never had it my way.]

(Birthday card from Ajey. On the front it said "Because I love you." Inside Hallmark wrote: Today, I'm thinking fondly of the many things we've done, the happy moments we have shared, the laughter and the fun – And with each new tomorrow I'll be warmly thinking, too, of just how much it means to me to have your love and you. Happy Birthday With All My Love" then he wrote: I wish I could be with you. Maybe in December? (right) Love Always, Ajey)

10/20/1985: I am so depressed tonight. I feel so alone. Life can be so damn confusing and lonely. I hate being alone. And I desire the closeness of someone again. I am obsessed with an untouchable. I have so many friends and acquaintances, but I feel so unnoticed. I feel like I am nothing. I miss being touched. It's not even so much Ajey I miss. The fourth floor to the ground isn't such a long drop. Ha. I'm not suicidal anymore. I'll work out my depressions. I always seem to one way or another. I hope this time it works out quicker than the other times. Mid-terms tomorrow. I have got to get my ass in gear. My personal life cannot wreck the rest of comprehensible life. Hup to it.

[At some point in October, I walked on to the Denver swim team at the encouragement of Sarah. Swimming at Denver was the most fun I would ever have doing the sport. No one knew anything about my past accomplishments. I contributed and was part of the team. They were not great, and the girls were way too serious, but Sarah and I definitely had fun.]

(Excerpt from letter dated 10/18/1985 from Ajey:) Hi good looking, what's new now that you are of age? I guess this means you're legal now, A?...This letter comes to you from 35,000 feet and somewhere over Iowa. I couldn't deal with Ohio much longer even though my grandmother was there, I had to leave...So how's the party life? I guess now that you're 18 you can do all the things you think you've been missing. Is it exciting or what? Well, I hope you get home soon. Although I never tell you on the phone, I do miss you a lot. And I would probably like nothing better than to spend all my time with you when you get home...My sister and I both caught the same plane to Pittsburg but then split from there. God she's fat...and she smokes. What a nasty habit. Maybe she'll change. My mum asked if I was going to be home for Xmas. I told her I couldn't make it...How's the swim team? Your mom said they're not that good. Actually she said they were closer to stink...Got to go write a policy paper...I'll see you when you get home. Love, Ajey

A second letter was also included: ...I would love to come over for Thanksgiving dinner. Thanks for the invitation...We'll see you in 38 days. Love, Ajey)

DARKNESS AGAIN

A silence shed light
on the scene.
Two lovers unclothed,
Shivering to the touch.
Nestled beneath the sheets
they lay still.
Momentarily glancing at
their naked bodies.
Flushed with embarrassment
(there will be no next time)
Staying with the dreams and visions
That it will get better
They hold each other through the blushes.
One staggers from the bed.
The other watches-
fascinated by the body which moved.
A little lonely.
A little longing.
A little nothing -
For something which seemed more.
The shades are shut.
Light is drown out.
The room is dark.
The room is empty.
One sneezes.
"Bless you," says the other.
The door shuts.
Curtains shudder.
Brief light on one's rolling tear.
Darkness, again.

10/26/1985: Of me: "You have to be the most obnoxious person I've ever met. But I like you a lot." -Dave.

Talked to Ajey tonight. Not the coolest conversation. Like talking to a stranger. I think it's pretty much over. I'd like to see him at Christmas break, though. I guess it is then that I will know what I feel for him...Tonight we're going dancing. We're going to a new club. Yeah.

11/2/1985: Last night I had my first one-night stand. I was so trashed. But the guy I was with was someone I find more than just desirable. It was Adam, a volunteer coach. He is 25. And he is so awesome. I must have had some sort of power. He kept saying he wouldn't because he didn't do that sort of thing. We started making out and eventually found our way to the bedroom. Messed around there. And then it happened. Very fast and he even apologized for that. The bad part is I don't even remember if it felt good...I don't even feel guilty. This is terrible, but I felt this certain power. I had a guy that I find too ultimately desirable. In fact, all the swimmers do. Me. I'd wish for it to happen again but I know it won't.

(Excerpt from letter to Lisa dated November 3, 1985:) Dear Leaky, Loved that last letter...Things are going better for me. I'm not so depressed anymore, if at all. It's more a thing of being alone guy-wise. This weekend wasn't bad. Or hasn't been bad...Last night was great. Went to a swim party. We were the only 4 girls there, swarmed by gorgeous men. I got so thoroughly wasted. I only remember parts of the night. Well, Lisa, last night I had my first "one night love affair". It was with Adam, a volunteer coach. He's 25 and one of the most gorgeous men I've ever seen. I've melted over him for weeks now. And last night I scammed on him. I don't remember a lot of it – it's too bad. Remind me to tell you about that little one nighter some time. It's funny and it's kind of depressing. I don't regret it at all. He probably does. God, I had so much fucking power over him last night. It's weird to think that every other one-nighter turned out to be more, but Adam was a conquest. A desirable piece of man – so off limit, but I had him. Lisa, he is so incredible. But I know there won't be more. Somehow I wish there could be because there's so much more to him. I guess the first real one night stand is the toughest to deal with. But I guess it just makes the others easier. I was too wasted and he, too. It'll be weird if I ever happen to run into him again. God, Lisa, he is awesome; intense; hot!...How was Halloween? We went over to this guy's

room and drank beer bongs – or Kate did and I watched her get wasted. I had morning practice the next day. Some guy named James scammed on me. That was brief. I wanted Dave. Still do. I know sometime that will happen. It's practically inevitable. Physical attraction...That's all guys are – physical attraction. Except for Adam and Dan, guys don't turn me on otherwise. Dan is a mere everything attraction. Adam had the whole well-roundedness. Dan, god, he is my dream. The extent I desire him is incredible. But, like Adam, he is what I will not have in my clutches again. It's all shit. So I'm learning the one night scene. And with guys not in the same circle. Adam won't talk. "Oh well, Kirsten, you must learn. You are a woman now; full of insatiable desires."...I do not want to get wasted for a long time again. I'm still burping up beer. I'm beat tonight, too. I guess if I really wanted to be alive, I could get some speed. They say it works. Recently, I've discovered people who have connections. I'm not stupid enough to buy that crap. Alcohol alone drains me...Love always, Kissten

11/4/1985: What I realized from Adam is that it's the first one nighter I had to accept. It's kind of weird knowing that it will never become anything, that it really was just one night. I feel better now. But I do keep looking over my shoulder waiting to see if he's there. End...I guess the experience helped me. Kind of feel grown up. Have less desire to talk about sex. The desire to have it is still there...I have so many desires. I have so many tests tomorrow and I have procrastinated long enough now.

11/5/1985: There are some things that are so hard to grasp. They are unescapable, and they hurt like hell. Yes, I am speaking of Adam. Why is it bothering me? No, stupid question. I know why...I was talking to Sarah tonight. She told me how the assistant women's coach hated Adam for that night because in her eyes Adam was perfect. I still think he is in every sense of the word...I know I did all of the pursuing and I should be the one blamed, he shouldn't. I'm a jerk.

11/7/1985: Well, guess who I saw today, Adam. He made me melt all over again. There's so much magnetism to the guy...When I walked into the pool area, he gave me this wicked grin that just made me melt. He watched me walk all the way to the office. Embarrassed me...Later we were on a long, non-stop set. Our coach told me he was going to stop and say hi but she wouldn't let him. Saw him watch me swim (shitty) for a while…Sarah said he told the coach to tell me not to feel dumb because he was just as embarrassed. Said he'd like to talk to me sometime. Sober.

(The last real letter from Ajey. Mailed 11/5/1985:) Dear Kirsten, I love you and I wish I could help you make up your mind. I know that eventually you will decide what it is you want. But I'm afraid that by the time you decide it will be too late. Please let me explain. I want nothing more than to know that I can depend on you, and I would love to plan my next summer with you in mind., but I'm not sure that next summer will ever get here for us. I want to give you a chance to make up your mind. And pressure I know you don't need; but the fact still remains that I can't be expected to wait forever. So far I haven't been able to even go out with other women mainly because I'm so in love with you. But I'm slowly realizing that my life must also have a direction to it. So maybe I do know where I'm going to school, and maybe I do know what I want to do. But I also know I want to share it with someone. God! I wish it was you. I doubt you will ever understand how I feel, and maybe that is the way it is supposed to be, but I figure I have one more chance to try to convey my feelings to you; that being Thanksgiving…This Thanksgiving is going to be very important to both of us. I can only hope that you decide that what has been missing is me. If not, then I'm sure we will be able to deal with this too. I would ask you to call but as you yourself stated you're too busy. And I guess maybe that could be a statement right there. Don't call me if you're going to be indecisive. I don't need that. This is the hardest thing I've ever done but I want you to know that I'm still here if you need me, and I hope things will return to what they once were. Love Always, Ajey PS I have Thanksgiving day off plus Friday, Saturday, and Sunday, so we can figure this out, okay?

(Excerpt from a letter to Lisa dated November 13, 1985:) Dear Lisa, I am home two weeks from today. I can't believe it. The time has gone by so fast. I think I'm sick. Gnarly headaches. Off to doctor right now…I'm back. Such the speed demon. Still aching. But life's just been a pain lately anyways…As for men, I am madly in love with Adam, my one nighter. But I will never have him. Probably mainly because of age. But I've only seen him once since then. He said, though, that he'd like to talk to me sometime. He makes me drool…I haven't really met any people here that I am interested in. Granted, there's physical attraction. It's weird but people here, or girls, aren't very open about talking about sex. They think it's so California. Isn't that weird? At home, I never would have thought twice about talking about it to my friends. Even strangers. I guess we

just aren't as conservative...Ajey and I are pretty much over, even though he says he is still deeply in love with me. I like messing around. Wish I could find some guys with interest. Hey, bud, when we get together we're going to have to go out and get some MEN. Real California MEN. None of this wanna-be crap. We're women now and we have earned the right for our bodies to be loved *...I will call you on Thanksgiving. Love always, Kissten*

[*Sometimes even I want to cringe at what I wrote to Lisa. I was overly obsessed with boys/men.*]

11/27/1985: I go home today. Very psyched. Nervous because I have to end it with Ajey. Long time coming...Messed around with James* today. We had sex. Let me tell you, it was easy because we were sober and friends and still are, which is cool. He's got a nice body and soft skin. I'm sure it could have been a lot of fun if it weren't so quick...Next quarter looks to be cool. I'm really looking forward to it. Hopefully, it'll bring on a lot of changes in my life...I'm home in 12 hours. The time has flown. It's weird leaving friends here. We've all gotten to be so close. So much I want to do at home, though. Can't wait to see mom and dad and Thor and Deb. I have a feeling the time is just going to fly by. I'm anxious for everything. Tomorrow marks the start of something new...No homework for six weeks! Rejuvenation time. But for now I still have one more final. Can't even concentrate. HOME!

[*James. He is a great mystery as I cannot remember him at all, but he comes up several times. I swear that it was Dave I slept with before I headed home. That is what/who I remember. James is the only person in this college saga of messing around that I cannot remember.*]

12/8/1985: Been home nearly two weeks now. I miss my friends. I've seen Debbie twice since I've been home. I'm kind of bored. I enjoy all the time with mom even though she worries too much about me and I get irritated for no reason. But I love her. Thor and I get along pretty well. Car conflicts, etc. Dad and I get along great. As for Ajey, we are friends. The big conversation wasn't as tough as either of us had expected. We went out as friends a couple of nights later. It was tough not being able to touch him. But it was easier by the end of the night. There are still quite a few feelings felt mutually. He told me that no one has ever hurt him that badly and that no one has ever driven him as crazy as I do – sexually. The desire to be with me sexually he has never had with anyone else before. We reminisced and talked about our relationship. He only had good things to say.

[I wish I could say that I got my shit together and recognized how much he loved me, but alas that is not how I worked back then. I wish I could end 1985 with our story continuing, figuring out how to be together when we were apart. It has been painful on so many levels to read that someone could love me so much and that I could hurt him so badly. I would get two more letters from him in April 1986. They were very friendly letters with no more mentions of us. He left the military and had been accepted into college. Was playing tennis. Roommate updates. He had clearly found a way to move on with his life.]

1986 – and the end of this story

[I have no doubt that my confidence flourished in college because of my relationship with Ajey, so much that it meant I needed to see how much more I could conquer. This definitely became a reckless time period. I was like a pinball bouncing all over the place, as evidenced in some of the letters I wrote to Lisa. Many of them during this time period served to fill in gaps, especially since my journal writing was sporadic at best.]

1/5/1986: Back at DU. Missed this place and my friends. Looking forward to classes again...The year of '85 ended good. Ajey and I never spoke again. It kind of hurt, but it's what he wanted, I guess...I've given up trying with Debbie. It's all about her boyfriend. Maybe one day she'll realize the extent of our friendship...Spent New Year's with Lisa. Had a great time partying at the Rose Parade. I have never had so many guys acknowledge me like that. Ego booster, especially this guy Kevin from UCSB. Gorgeous. There was a mutual twinge, but our paths never crossed again after our brief encounter at Lisa's...Have a lot of personal plans for '86. Like to lose 20 pounds or so. Remain confident. Went off the pill. No urge to sleep around, no one nighters. I feel much more attractive to others. I won't take it personally if no guys show interest. Mr. Right will come along soon enough and at the right time. I'm a dreamer. Have so much I strive for and want. I've realized it is nothing personal when they don't knock down your (my) doors. – I have a good feeling that my personal goals are going to be reached and maintained this '86 and on (I hope!).

(Excerpt from letter to Lisa dated January 10, 1986:) Dear Leaky, I hadn't planned on starting this until later this weekend, but it seems

boredom has overcome me completely in the half hour I have before calculus. This is the first time this week I have had two minutes to myself. I'm taking 18 units and so far it has been anything but fun. Lots of hard work. Yes, granted, I added a math class. It's a requirement. It's hard. And I hate math. Tonight starts w/the hockey game. One generally consumes before, during, and after. Tomorrow I have a swim meet. Then there's another hockey game and a party at Sigma Chi. I kind of dread going because that guy Steve that liked me is a Sigma Chi. I have yet to face him after blowing him off. Oh well, a party is a party (most of the time)...It feels good to be back here. Kind of depressing, too, because we always seem to get into these discussions on men and what the hell drives them. I feel really good about myself right now, so as of yet I am not worried. Granted, a guy would be fun but the way things are going so hectic in my life I'd have about 1.3 hours a day to spend with him...What is it about guys, Lisa? What makes them tick? I still wish that Kevin would have found us that night. There was something about Kevin that really intrigued me. Not just his looks. And I know what you think about the notch in the belt stuff. I used to play that game, too...It amazes me how much I feel I have changed in regards to sex. Lisa, save it for someone you feel is special. There is no real satisfaction to casual sex. It doesn't bring friends closer because you never talk about it and it isn't something you usually tell your school buddies, especially if they're befriended with him (James). And with virtual strangers, it just makes it stranger – and eventually talk becomes cheap (Adam). So here I stay, off the pill, and determined to know there is someone for me out there. Now, granted, if Mr. Irresistible should say 'hey, hun' then a run to the drug store might suffice. It's weird, though, because summer doesn't seem to fit that bill. Casualness seems to accompany the meaning of summer. Odd, isn't it? Maybe because people are at the height of desirability and some tourists are incredible. And no one has to know...There are a couple of new lookers on campus this quarter. One guy is a swimmer from South Africa. Very intriguing. Another guy is unknown name-wise to me. But he looks very much like a luscious Californian. I'm almost to shy (or embarrassed) to even say 'hello' to him...the clock says I have just enough time to make that trudge across campus and be adequately punctual to calculus...I'm psyched. I passed the calculus test...And so we cruised through swim practice. Mr. South Africa was there. His name is Nick. I think he keeps looking at me. I'm terrible at figuring those things out. There is a swim team party next Friday so that Nick can meet us girls, which in essence is only Sarah and me. We seem to get the most attention. Perhaps because we stick around the longest and mingle the most. It's neat, though, because that makes us the most known among the guys, not in a bad sense. Only one person knows about me and Adam, but you never know how guys talk. They can gossip just as much as girls...I am in a very good mood tonight. I have to find a way to sneak into the hockey game. DU hockey is just so popular. It's incredible how much people get into that sport. Actually, it's pretty neat...Then we're off to Beta for a party. It sucks, though, because the parties have to end before one due to the frat fire scares (still!). I don't even care how I look tonight. Scum is the evening attire code. Men are men whether you look like crap or not...Right now I'm living on the memories of all the luck I had New Year's Eve. That was probably it for the year. I still don't know what it was that night. Probably never will. If I'm ever able to radiate that again I'll be sure to take notes for myself...I think I have given my arm adequate exercise. Write soon...I miss ya' and take care of yourself and, as my mom always says, "watch out for your body." She doesn't mean food. Love Always, Kirsten

(Excerpt from letter to Lisa dated January 19, 1986:) My dear Lisa- It seems as if my life has reached some sort of predicament. Yes, it's men. God, Lisa, I am having so much fun this quarter. I've been partying massively. Don't give an actual shit about guys. They're only good for playing with your head...Quite is the case with me. The South African, Nick, Sarah, and I are having conflict. The story: Sarah is totally and madly in love with him. I put him out of thought for that reason. The other night they sort of got together. Last night was the swim party. At the party, he tells me he's liked me long before Sarah. But everyone said go for Sarah. Okay fine he does. He tells me he's massively confused about who to be with. To make a very long story short he is with Sarah because I can't give him the guarantee that it will be a long lasting relationship. I don't know why. But Nick and I totally made out at the party. Damn he is sensuous. And I had frickin' power. Didn't go to bed with him. Power prevailed. And Sarah's guilt trip worked on him. This morning they come into breakfast and she's wearing what she wore last night. Bang! ... (Tonight) I went to Nick's because Sarah said he totally had the wrong impression of me now – like it was totally him who did all the move making. So we're talking and Lisa he fuckin' wants me so bad. He said no one has ever turned him on like that before. I must have been damn erotic, but I was being myself. He is very desirous. Fabulous long fingers. They turn me on period. He's all "I desire you, but she can give

me the relationship." He told me that when Sarah spent the night the past two nights they did nothing. I go no way because he was horny as hell last night. He said he was but Sarah doesn't turn him on in those ways. So now I get to be the practically best of friends with Sarah and know that Nick is thinking inside about me...Everyone says fight for him. But how am I to know it's not just some game? Two for one. God, he's a temptation that is very hard to resist. And I don't know if I can do that to Sarah and I don't know what I really want. I want him once, Lisa. Hate myself for it. He told me, also, that the desire probably won't go away. So now I'm going to wait. Make him want me. And then blow him away. Just once. It's like he wants me so bad. If you could see the way he looks at me. He had a hard on the whole time tonight. Had to use a frickin' pillow. Oh man. Maybe I'll start the rag soon and that desire will be overcome. I should just say 'what the fuck' and give in. But I can't let my guard down. And I have a hard time when it concerns hurting a friend. What the hell am I to do?* I'm having such a good time. Feel so much more noticed by guys. Changed my ID. Now I'm 21. Go to the campus bar on weekends and love it. Sat outside until 3:30 this morning telling scary stories. He (I don't say a name!) has no physical interest in me, but the more I'm with him the more I enjoy the person not the body and face. Theory: Men cut you like a knife and leave you to clean up the mess...How is Kevin? I still think about him. Crazy and foolish as it may be. Something about him was totally intriguing...School's going good. Swimming too. Both irrelevant at this point...Why can men be such problems? Love ya, Kirsten

[*I would choose friendship over the boy.]

(Excerpt from a letter to Lisa dated February 18, 1986·) ...There has been so much that has gone on...Nick is a jerk. He does not even talk to me anymore. Gives me dirty looks and then there are times when he gives me looks of regret and he'll stare at me. What a geek, though...Right now I am lusting/liking/loving no one. Haven't been with anyone thus far (scammed on Nick once). Sometimes I wonder if my guy is any where around this campus. And when the hell are our paths going to cross? In time, I guess. I hope. But I am basically content with my life right now. I've made so many more friends this quarter. I can't believe that it's almost over. In four weeks, I leave for Mazatlán...I've kind of been blowing off this whole quarter. Sometimes I don't even care. My motto College is not for an education; it's for the experience. Great, aye? Cal *me sometime. I'm broke and I'd love to chat with my pal. I miss and love you. Love always, Kissten*

(Excerpt from a letter to Lisa dated February 23, 1986:) My dearest Leaky – Thanks for the call. It was definitely what I needed. The weekend was shitty nonetheless. Hate to think how it might have been minus your call – HELL. My mind is basically a jumbled mess right now – guys, summer employment, school (10pm and I have yet to study for my 9am German test), etc...Tomorrow there's no more swimming and I am going to start my diet so that my body might look ok on a beach. I'd lost 11 pounds since I've been back, but gained a few back...Anyways, here's a definition/explanation of the songs on Side A (we would send each other cassette tapes of our favorite songs) and how they apply: #1 THE BEST IS YET TO COME – because it really will come one day; #2 LOVE IS THE LAW – no matter how badly it may suck at times. And then you'll be #3 ALIVE AND KICKING – love'll do it; when it's right. People say it's a fact; I'll let you know when I find out. #4 SOONER THAN YOU THINK – it'll all come your way – it will (I hope for both our sakes). #5 SOMEBODY – is out there. Where? Hell, I'm still waiting, too. #6 and that somebody will SHAKE THE DISEASE and love will be abundantly ours. #7 JUST CAN'T GET ENOUGH – is what you'll be singing because it allegedly feels so good. #8 MY TIME – is when it all comes together for you and works. The BIG, LUCKY time of our lives...We just have to remember the best is really yet to come. Think I made this tape for me, too – HOPE, I guess. Write soon. I miss ya, kid. Hi to Kevin. Love Always, Kissten

(Excerpt from letter to Lisa dated March 11, 1986:) Dear Lisa- I have decided to take a few moments out of my states of frustration and write. It must just be that time of the quarter (finals) or that time of the month. I never know about that one anymore. Ever since going off the pill my body has been going weird...Nothing has come up with the opposite sex this quarter. I was a very good kid. But all of a sudden my body's beginning to feel starved and is looking for some definite affection. This may sound queer but I can just imagine all this passion in me lately. I have been celibate too fucking (oops!) long. If temptation should cross my path in Mazatlán I may have to – rag or not (probably rag). But I hear maids do the sheets in Mexico, too. Gross, I know. Being sexually frustrated right now doesn't help. It just adds to other frustrations...I may end up going under a 3.0 for the first time in my life. Ouch! That hurts, but it was a tough course load. And, yes, I will admit that I did not

do nearly the studying I should have. I guess I just fell prey to the freshmen college party scene. Hopefully, spring quarter will be better. Ha! I hear this place is pretty hoppin' in spring. Maybe someone will volunteer affection then...DU announced an 8-1/2% tuition increase. Guess who may not be back next year? I'm bummin'. It's too late now to transfer to a UC school. I may have to try for winter quarter. It's a mess...I am so psyched to go to Mazatlán. I need this break badly. All I want to do is dance and maybe get some passion here or there. I could care less if it's an Iowan (as long as he's got what it takes)...I took a three hour nap today. Felt damn good. Time to study now...Love always, Kissten

3/15/1986: [*I have no idea what motivated these poems. My writing feels really confusing and disjointed.*]

ME

I am very good at hurting people,
Getting them back more
powerful than they got me.
(If words of power could kill)
When I've been stabbed,
I strike back with more
than I knew possibly existed.
I am a fighter.
And I hate to lose.
So I hurt instead -
inside, and others.
Sometimes I feel like I just can't win.
And that I never will.
Too bad: Sometimes it's a
crime to care too much.
Too bad: Sometimes it's not safe to say
what you feel to others.
Slip of the tongue-
'Oops, it just fell out.'
Time to lock it all inside,
Until redemption of trust occurs.
A walking zombie-
now, that's me.
(Pretend not to hurt or show a care;

never been burned or ever shared.)
A locked up mannequin
with only one goal –
survival.
(Sorry, I do the best I know how).

BLOW OVER

Emotions simply do not just blow over.
Clouds blow over.
Winds blow over.
Tumbleweed blows over.
Hurt does not blow over.
Perhaps, had the storm hit all at once
and not been a long, unknowing procession.
BANG, it hit!
Ha! and to think it can blow over
JUST like that.
Vengeance is a funny thing.
Hurts like hell.
But works, right?
What's one more scar on my belt?
Hell, by now I should be expecting them.
Does everything JUST blow over?
Or is there hope of reconciliation
before another storm hits?
But, oh that's right,
storms just blow over, too.

Spring Break – Mazatlán, Mexico 1986

[*What happens in Mexico stays in Mexico! Unless you write it in a letter on Hotel De Cima stationery and seal it up. You put it away with the promise that the contents will not be revealed until you and Sarah do it in person. Flash forward to 2021, the writing of this memoir, and a day trip to Colorado to reveal the contents. The contents long forgotten, but clearly confirming that our spring break rivaled that of no other and was a complete display of reckless abandon and alcohol fueled confidence. I never had a single regret about what happened that trip: the good, the "drunk" night stands, or the unknown.*]

Tuesday, 3/18/1986: Arrived in Mazatlán but not without difficulty. Plane delayed. Lost luggage. Found it. Everyone but Sarah and I was too tired to go out. So we (Sarah and I) went out and had an incredible time. First, we went to Valentino's but it was having some private thing until 11:30. Tried to con the sleazy Mexican at the door. No luck. The guys were incredibly friendly. Some tried to sneak us in. Then we went to El Cid where the line was a mile long. Saw three guys and were going to approach them but they approached us first. They were pi psys from Texas Tech. Five of their friends came up. So now we are 8 guys and 2 girls. 4:1! Anyways, we ended up with these two guys who were totally cool. Royce and Ely. Royce had a gorgeous looking face. Ely is funny. Spent the evening until 3am with them. Royce and I proceeded to get very physical after returning from our walk back from Joe's and Valentino's (incredible place). Royce and I did a lot – basically. He's different in his ways of being physical. We didn't go to bed together. I was on the rag so he did all I'd let him and I did all I could do. Thank God he came fast. Hate that taste. Anyway, they got us a taxi back and Sarah and I went to sleep. One night down, six to go.

VALENTINO'S – awesome nightclub. Major pick-up joint. Good dancing and drinks. Expensive cover.
JOE'S – A good time. Dancing on tables. Pick-up again.
ED CID – Fantastic. Slides. Great dancing, three floors. Fascinating. Could do it every night.
EL PATIO – too long of a wait. Very expensive. Fun if you're drunk and with a lot of people.

Wednesday, 3/19/1986: First day in Mazatlán. Beautiful. Like home. Spent day getting regretfully fried. Shopped a little. Went out. First went to Senor Frogs where the line was too long. Then went to El Patio's and was very bored. Sarah and I took off to El Cid's and had a great time. Ran into some girls from DU. Got sort of picked up by these high schoolers. Blow off. Then went dancing with some Spaniards who spoke only enough English to say, "He thinks you are very beautiful." My guy spoke no English. Whilst blowing them off who should we run into but Royce and Ely and this guy named Chris, who was funny as hell. Actually, all these Texans are cool and funny. We ended up with Royce and Ely again. Royce was totally drunk. We had a good time, though. Didn't do much of anything physical. Kind of glad. Royce has this thing where he does not look at you after he kisses you and he doesn't get very physical (kissing wise) in public. He doesn't seem to like to do more than one thing at a time. It's kind of an awkward situation because I'm very outgoing, adventurous, and free-spirited compared to him. Not the type I'd spend the rest of my life with. Maybe not even the next couple of days. He needs some confidence. It's strange, too, because he is very good looking facial wise. High cheek bones. Cute smile. His eyes are set perfect and are this neat shade of blue. Short, blonde hair. Neat looking. He needs to do some sit-ups and I have yet to see the rest of his body (almost). There are flaws, granted. But I guess Kirsten is just trying to grow up a little. I'd like to be 7 for 7 by the end of this trip. So far I'm 2 for 2 (Same guy, but that doesn't matter). Ely was neat. Total ex-swimmer with a great personality. Cute, too. Mike was drunk and funny. Seemed like he hadn't quite made puberty yet. Chris was a riot. Couldn't stop laughing in his presence. Jeff (Spaz) is a looker and has a great personality. Could have gone for him. He was too drunk, though. Have yet to see the 3 guys who originally picked us up again. This trip is being totally incredible. No hockey players (but sometimes I miss lusting after them. Royce sort of looks like one of them.) Yo ♡ Mazatlán.

Thursday, 3/20/1986: To relate tonight's experience: We went to Senor Frog's. Incredible. Loved every minute of it. Waiters were cute and very flirtatious, food was great. Danced on tables and the walkways at Froggies. Met a guy named Greg from University of Alabama. Blew him off. Went to Joe's. Had a great time. Danced for hours. Met a couple more guys from Texas. One TCU (Mike). One Texas Tech (Greg). Greg and I danced and then walked on the beach. Kissed. Went to his room and went to bed. It was fun. The guy had an awesome body and was good in bed. Gorgeous smile. Sort of reminded me of Ajey, but not. Blonde. And totally different in bed. Weird when you've been with one person for so long that when you're with another guy you almost expect it to be like before. Wrong. Anyways, I had fun with Greg (Sr; Marketing; ex- SAE ha) and we went back to Joe's where we mutually kind of blew each other off. Tons of good-looking guys were looking at me. Look out Friday night. So far 3 for 3. Sarah's with Ely again tonight. She's fallen for him and I think it's very mutual. Lucky, kid. Anyways, I'm beat and it's time to sleep until Sarah gets back and we gossip. WHAT A TRIP!

Friday, 3/21/1986: NEVER AGAIN WILL I GET THAT DRUNK! Last night was too much. I'm ready to go back to DU on account that I was just too out of hand. The night went something like this: We bought 18 beers between six of us. I had four. (Sarah and I decided we'd get wasted). Then we got on the bus and went to Joe's. This guy comes up to me and said he'd buy me a beer if I kissed his friend. 1st free beer. Finished off that. Went to the bar where this old man bought us a beer (Sarah and me). Went back and danced on tables. Saw Greg and his friend, Mike. Then went with Sarah and Ely to the other TT-ers where Chris and I had a contest that I won so I had to kiss him. Good kisser. So I was with him a while. And then Greg and Mike came up. Took off with Greg to his hotel for a repeat of last night only this time I was so drunk that I passed out and when I woke up there were two guys on top of me – Mike and Greg. I made Greg make him leave the room. He did. Thank god. I'm so embarrassed when I think back on that. Yuck. I can't believe I did that. Greg and I walked back. Blew each other off. Then I lost Sarah. I had no money to get back with either. So I became a mooch. Finally Chris took me home. Too cool to do that. Could have really liked him, too. Glad that ALL of the Texans are now gone, and I am cleansed of them. Got home last night and passed out until this morning not remembering conversation with Sarah and Ely who got intense while I snored away in my drunken state. NO MORE.

Saturday, 3/22/1986: Very mellow day. Exhausted as hell. I think I managed to cram a whole week into four days (six for four). So last night I very tiredly went to Joe's. Picked up on no guys. Didn't get drunk. Came home early. Paid my own taxi fare. We ate dinner at El Patio which was a lot of fun and good. Came back here. Danny and Jack bought us beers. Then we went to Joe's and just kind of hung around. Danced. Met some people. Left. Had fun none the less. And if I fail to be with another guy on this trip, I won't mind at all. My system is cleansed for a while. Kind of missed having those Texans to hang around. They were cool. Not looking forward to going back to DU and hockey. Think about Dan but not obsessed with it anymore. I miss California. I've noticed that DU has mellowed me out. I'm not as rowdy and self-assured as when I was back home.*

[*I cannot read this statement and not think, "What am I saying?" I was completely wild and out of control at DU. And self-assurance? When did I ever have that at home? I guess I wanted to believe it even though all my writing would contradict this especially when describing me in Oceanside.]

Sunday, 3/23/1986: Another fun day. No scams either. Rather kind of liked it that way. Met these guys from Stanford (Rob, Dan, Jeff, and Jeff 2) and CU (Grant). Sarah and I got some beers and were sitting on the balcony drinking when these guys asked us to come over. So we did. I instantly lusted for Dan. Nada We then went to Joe's. It was so packed. So Sarah and I left for El Cid, which was incredibly $$. It was so packed. So we went back and ran into Dan and Grant who we talked to and then we went inside where the crowds were incredible. Gorgeous men strewn out everywhere. Danced on tables and then these guys bought us beers. After getting the beers, Sarah decides it's time to run. So we ran and successfully blew them off. Grant made the move on Sarah while Jeff 2 was trying on me. We walked down the beach – didn't let him touch me. Got us all in trouble with the police because I was harassing some little kid. We then went back to Joe's. Then Grant and Sarah and I came back here and sat around and talked for a little while. And then I crashed from exhaustion. Had a good time, though.

Monday, 3/24/1986: What a day it has been so far. Sarah and I took the Sobalo to El Cid. We went parasailing. That is one of the most incredible experiences. It's a total high to be up in the air like that suspended over the ocean. Ecstatic feeling. Then went shopping. Had such a good time. Don't want to go home…We went to some restaurant called Las Terazas, or the like, for dinner. Good food. The waiters came around and made us do tequila shots through this mug container in the shape of a man's genital area. Funny. Then we decided to all go to Joe's and drink these awesome strawberry-banana daiquiris. Sarah and I had a long talk about guys, of course. And then we went to Joe's and saw Danny and Jack. The others in our group said they were leaving so we stayed with those two (Danny and Jack) and danced. I had my last little scam to be 7 for 7, but it was very minor. The guy's name was Dave from CU. Great dancer. Summoned me out and we were dancing on this table. He gave me the ultimate compliment. First he goes, "You're a really great dancer." Then he goes, "God, you're a damn great dancer." He hugged me and then this girl was all over him so he went but not without giving me a small kiss first. Sarah said he'd been wanting to get back up on the table the whole time but this girl wouldn't let him. Oh well. So I danced the rest of the night and had a great time just dancing away for three hours. Think Jack may have developed a slight crush on me. He's cool, though. Grant is lusting for Sarah. All the luck.

Tuesday, 3/25/1986: One week later and it's back to the US. Damn, I had the best time. I've never experienced anything quite like this. I pity anyone who never goes on a Spring Break. It's going to be hard to find anything that will ever compare to the experiences here in Mazatlán.

Now I need a vacation. I'm very psyched to be going home to California. Hope I get to see Lisa – don't even really care about Kevin because I'm kind of burned out on guys. Everything that I didn't do last quarter, everything I didn't have, I did have and do. Now what do I want? God. A relationship. Fun. Sun. California. (Miss that place). Want these guys (*the friends other than Sarah*) not to hold a grudge against me because that's almost what it seems like. So glad that Sarah went. Might have been a very drab and BORING vacation otherwise. YEAH! I will never in my life forget my Spring Break 1986. Incredible. And it should get me through this spring quarter. Here's to keeping secrets!! Love Ya Mazatlán! Kirsten

(The airplane ride). I don't want to go back to reality. Shit. I have been living in a dream world for the past week. Nothing mattered. Now all of a sudden I have to think about things realistically. It's scary. Same old questions, problems. They don't go away. They just get prolonged. Like before: What do I want? Honestly? To be happy and in love and loved back. I want to be a jet setter. I don't think I ever really want to face reality. But it's inevitable because in a few hours I will be back at DU. And then see how I was there. Just had an incredible time. The personality I was was me. Outgoing. Carefree. Free spirted. Sometimes I wonder if DU prohibits me from being the total individual I am. Maybe that's why I need to go to a bigger school. So I'm a number, but it doesn't seem to be the great competition that DU is. Fit a certain mold bit. I miss California. I miss Mazatlán. I hate caring. And I hate wanting so much. And waiting. I'm impatient. Restless. Sometimes intolerant. I want to scream. I want to cry. I want. I want. I want. (I want to hold Bixby – *my bear*). Sarah: I want my teddy bear too!!

3/26/1986: It's already a new quarter. Third one at that. Incredible...Kathy is in my speech class. Maybe I'll get the chance to figure out what Dan sees in her...

Point: I wonder if I will ever know love long enough to keep it. If I don't pull away and get distracted by other things going on around me like I often do. There's got to be somebody out there who's like me in that respect. Definitely a free spirit. But I don't know if that's good. Could be hazardous to a relationship situation...Second note: I'm pretty protective and almost possessive of a guy. I don't like to share. And that can interfere in understanding one another...I really don't know what kind of guy I like. Good looking, yes. It ranks rather high. Personality is the most important, though...I tend to like the person I am. Sometimes I feel very intimidated by those here at DU. There are certain pedestals that people do not allow others on. But I haven't really tried, either. Guess I want to know the person I am first. Right now I feel like me. Very content. Carefree. An observer in the halls of the 3rd floor GCB...I'm a Californian, too. Very much. Just the lifestyle. What DU is helping to do is let me discover who I am. And who I want to be. I'm getting there, though. At least I'm trying...Feel like writing.

THE LOG

Walking through a forest,
came upon a swamp.
A musty, moldy log
lay across the top.
Didn't care to move it.
Or even stop and stare.
Just jumped on top of it,
Only to cross with flare.
Sank my foot below the mud;
Damped with much despair.
Wanted to hit it.
But didn't much really care.
It popped back to the top
After I jumped off.
Bobbed up and down -
Still so seemingly lost.
A sudden urge had hit me.
I slowly turned around.
Only to see, the log had
safely hit the ground.
'Not without a friend"
the thought ran through my head.
Guess there's really no need
For an unhappy end.

SOMETHING TO DESIRE

Looks like a little boy;
Body of a man
Smirk of a child;
Power of his hands.
Drifts of arrogance

(Proud like only the elite).
The dimple when he smiles.
The stern brow when he thinks.
A mind of his own.
A will of intent.
A heart that's pure-
But has never felt.
The love, the passion he could live.
We'd have it all.
What a thought to ponder;
What a plan to scheme.
Something to desire-
A never ending stream.
Something to desire -
My never ending dream.

(Written while pining over a hockey player from afar.)

4/7/1986: "Some situations I get myself in are very awkward. (Shall we just say the two SAEs.)" ...Things seem to be going pretty good in my life right now. I handled the situation with seeing Carlos and Will this morning pretty well. I think I'm beginning to become a master in the art of blow-offs. They must think I'm a total bitch. Probably am to guys I don't much care about. I wonder if they know about each other's association. Sad thing is Carlos was more attractive in manner, but then in my extreme state of drunkenness, who's really to say...I'm trying to get my butt in gear for this quarter. So many other things seem to be occupying my mind, especially lifeguarding and Kevin (of all things. Me and those damn obsessions) ...

[There are no prior entries, but I actually remember some of this saga. Carlos had a huge crush on me and was pursuing me at some SAE parties. Will was also pursuing me, literally. He followed me out when I was leaving the nearby bar, drunk, and we went to his room. No recollection of what happened. If we did or didn't. Thought about stealing his SAE sweatshirt but darted without it.]

4/12/1986: *[My Oma in Germany died on 4/12/1986. I was shitfaced when my mom called me that night. My friend somehow got the call from her the next morning because I had knocked the phone off the hook. I knew the second she said that my mom was calling that my Oma had died. Strangest feeling ever. I would get a letter from her a couple of days later.*

276

I was shaking from the realization that she must have known that she was going to die and needed to reach out to me one last time; Making sure I knew she was thinking about me. It was like her spirit had come to see me. I cried all day. She was not an affectionate woman, but I knew she loved me.]

4/24/1986: "Fate up against your will, through the thick and thin" – Echo and the Bunnymen.
A letter to myself. Be good to yourself because nobody else will.
A Streetcar Named Desire.

> Things to do:
> -Don't ask if there's food on your face.
> -Don't look in the mirror.
> -Show a little more of your shy side.
> -Don't ever give off that you are confident around your friends.
> -Blow yourself down in front of them, they can't accept the person you are, so fuck them, because you are who you are and almost proud of it.
> -Lastly, don't talk about yourself or how you feel, especially about others because some people aren't to be trusted.
> (I'm on the streetcar named desire, and right now I don't like who I'm riding with. They're lies and cheats. I'm surrounded by these people and I have no one to turn to.)
> -Don't catch yourself glancing in the mirrors.
> (Yuck, why don't they take me for who I am? Fuck it all. And that's really how I feel.)
> -Never ask anyone how you look!
> (Fuck it all.) (Fuck it, fuck it, fuck it.)

[I wish I knew what led up to this journal entry. Too many periods of not writing during this time to try and figure out this outburst. Ultimately, it probably had to deal with navigating my friendships and how I fit in. Evidently, I had taken it quite personally.]

(Letter to Lisa dated April 29, 1986.) Dear Leaky – I am sitting here at the library jamming to Depeche Mode and not doing any homework. Yes, I am bored. I have nothing to do tonight. I'm wondering if I could fly to Las Vegas for the evening and entertain myself. I don't have much of anything to do. I actually feel like partying but I have an 8 o'clock class and there's really no one to party with. There's always Carlos, but that's kind of an odd situation. Remember me ever telling you about him? Well,

he's this really cool SAE who isn't half as gorgeous as his friends – in fact, he's not too good looking at all, but everyone thinks he's great. Well, Carlos started talking to me again. We went out Friday. It was a lot of fun. First we went to a car wash and just laughed. Later that night we went and partied with some SAEs. A bunch of high school girls were there. The SAEs were so mean to them. I talked to this guy Jeff the entire time because Carlos was pouring beer on the HSers. Then we went to the campus bar. Some guy tried to pick me up. Scary. Then Carlos and I went to my room and talked. And this is what he said: I like you a lot and could really go for a relationship with you. I said wrong bud, because I do not have those kind of feelings for him. We could easily be the best of friends and I wish we could be. The thing is though that I don't want to become an association of his w/in the house as his girl, because I would love to go out with some of his friends and he knows it, esp. this guy named Jef, but he has a girlfriend and Carlos makes this quite clear. Waa!! But that doesn't matter because I'm not very good at being assertive. – So guys continue to be weird. – My friends here are being weird, too. I don't know what's up their butts and I'm not one to just knock on someone's door and say let's go out. I would to Carlos but he lives at the house – too far to go for a casual conversation. – It really pisses me off how little my friends here like to party. They can be such deadbeats. But it's too late now to change 'em. I can hardly wait to party w/the guards this summer. Actually, my roomie for next year loves to go out so things might look up then. I'm not having a bad time at all, though. Just kind of burned out. Last Sat. there was a road rally. I was shitfaced by the 3rd stop at 2pm. Passed out at 4 and slept until the next morning. I had beer, champagne, wine, vodka, tequila, and 10 million hits of pot. I was shit. Did shrooms the weekend before. They were cool. - My hand kills...Miss and love ya. Kissten

5/10/1986:

OF LOVE AND LUST AND LIKE

Amidst a field of cluttered confusion
Simple, childlike illusion
Lies a lust, a like so deep
the ultimate love to seek.
In rows of roses thorns which prick
Hides the seed of tomorrow's pick
Cut in half the rose's stem
Separation – new life is formed
Emerging from that rose, that thorn

In prairie fields with farms out back
Even there, lurks this incredible task
Of love and lust and like
Behind barnyard doors on wooden floors
Flames become ignited that which becomes excited.
A power like no other
In depth emotions to uncover
Feelings bound by satin shields
Warrior codes no longer suffice
Love is the ruler – the ultimate device.
Lust is the keeper of the flame,
That which inspires to stay in the game
And like, the giver of trust
He who prompts that love, that lust
Of love and lust and like
Be it such
Give so little, take so much.
Against the odds feel the might
Make love with that passion tonight.
Live it, lust it, love it.
Feel that passion ignite.

BOMB DROP

And if a bomb drops tomorrow
I beg to be at the center of the blow
Torn to pieces,
Never having to know.
No good-byes, or tears of pain.
Simply turned to ashes;
A painless cremation;
Never needing to feel again.
And if a bomb drops tomorrow,
I pray to already be dead.

5/13/1986: Things in my life are good, really good. And I can say that I am honestly happy. Ever since Carlos has resurfaced. I've met so many of the guys this past year that I lusted after. And Carlos and I are on the way to a very close friendship. The best part is we are under no obligations to each other. I have the best time around him now because he has agreed to be "just friends". I think we're both pretty psyched about that. I think he still likes me as more but it's not showing as much, just in occasional statements. He's not going to be here next year, so I guess I'm going to have to work on the men of SAE on my own. Will is being really cool. He's a really nice guy. I think he's intrigued by me. He looks at me a lot and asked me if we could talk some time. – Jeff, I am majorly in love with. I love the person he is so much. Carlos says I should go for it. He thinks we'd make a great couple. Maybe next year. Attracted to Danno and Kevin and especially Andrew (I can't really tell if he is looking at me. Our glances have met, though). I wouldn't mind scamming before school is out; it's hard to be with any of these guys. Most of the SAEs think Carlos and I are sleeping together, except Jeff. And I don't know what he thinks of me. – There is always next year. And I am getting really psyched about that. I'm hoping that this summer will really help me in regard to having a positive attitude in approaching guys, especially like Jeff and Andrew. I know I don't need to impress Jeff; it's just getting away from this big brother thing we've established lately. We have a very special relationship. We get along so well, too. I'm hoping to see him a lot next year. I'll just have to make sure that I do. And I'll have to go for what I want. And knowing that there's the whole summer and having somethings to come back for here helps, too. – I can't wait for this summer. Carlos and I are going to hang out on occasion (*we never did; just talked on the phone*). Then there's Lisa and the possibility of Kevin. I would love to have a summer of just dating and scamming, being highly careful not to get a reputation around the other lifeguards (*I actually managed that! They tried though.*) I bet Tim and I become really good friends (*we did*). I hope this job works out. I may go crazy (and get fat) without it. I'm not looking forward to going home to my old friends. We've all changed so much. I don't know if it would be much fun to hang around them. I want to party this summer, all summer. I don't think Deb will get to into that. I'll probably see Suji on occasion but just to kid around and laugh. I almost think I'll date this summer. A summer lover would be fun. I'd love to date a variety of guys. The SAE type. I'm so attracted to them. I want to work out a lot for next year. I want to keep in shape and lose weight. I want to keep on jogging and swim at least 5,000 a day. At least. I'm hoping my hair will grow and that I can keep the weight off. I just really want to be happy and right now I really am. I am so excited about next year. Sarah and I are going to be roommates. Both of us are going to go through a reconstruction of friends. Our current friends don't like to do what we do. Hopefully more people that enjoy partying like we do. I love that lifestyle so much. Next year is going to be my year. I have this neat feeling about it. It could end up being quite an experience. And now that I know how to go about it, I'm going to do it. Three weeks left in this quarter. – I feel good and despite the bad that may happen between now and the end of the quarter, or the super great of the summer, I'm going to make the best of next year! PROMISE! – Doing what I want, my way.

5/15/1986: Sometimes desires subside to mere nothingness as is the case with "Something to Desire."

(*Excerpt from letter to Lisa dated May 17, 1986:*) *My dearest Leaky – Happy 19th Birthday!! (such an old woman)...Howz it going? Better? You didn't sound too happy in your last letter. I'm doing really good. Things are progressing in my life. The best part is that summer vacation is less than three weeks away...I got the lifeguard job unless I fail the physical. They'll probably say I'm too fat and a hazard to my health. Ha, ha. Actually, lately I've been running 3 to 4 miles and playing tennis. Sometimes I swim. Always do sit-ups. I eat a lot of desserts so the fitness doesn't really show yet. Tonight is the Modern English concert and I'm so excited. I love them. The best thing is it's right on campus so I can get drunk and not worry about it. Kappa Sigs are having Beachcombers today, but I didn't have $15 to go so we're going to MiniMart and getting chilly willies and drink them w/vodka. Carlos, a friend, and I did that last night and got a great buzz. I have the best time partying with him. And we've started this great friendship, but he still likes me a lot. Lisa, it's scary. He really likes me a lot, but I am so in love with Jeff. We're really good friends, too, but he doesn't know I like him as more. Carlos says I should go for it. It's like Carlos likes me. But I like Jeff. But Jeff doesn't know. Actually, I can see Jeff liking me and not admitting it. So we have this circle – and it involves all my SAEs. Yeah. Anyways, I've decided this summer's going to be awesome...Carlos and I are supposed to hang out together. So you'll meet him. Everyone thinks he's so great. Total partyer. And I'm also going to make myself feel really good about myself so that I can go for Jeff next year...Have a super birthday!*

5/17/1986: [*Hands down my all-time favorite 80's song was "I'll Stop the World and Melt with You" by Modern English.*]

[*The school year would end, and I was super psyched about the next year. Definitely felt like I had finally found a way to fit in more at DU. I think it had a lot to do with recognizing that hockey boys were never going to be a thing for me. My personality fit much better with the party happy boys in fraternities. They were fun. And they were interested. Only took me the whole bloody year to figure that one out.*]

[*Of course, not all great plans end accordingly. Kevin and I would start talking regularly on the phone as soon as I got home that summer. After our first meeting that summer, an overnighter, my grand plans to date and play all summer went quickly by the wayside. I still partied a good deal when I wasn't with Kevin.*]

6/25/1986: I spent the night at Kevin's last night. I had a really good time. I'm scared to like him, although it may just be too late for that. Would think it mutual, but I don't know yet. We didn't sleep together. Close, very close. Due to my being on the rag and wanting a little respect in return. I thought we had a very cool time. Kind of weird to spend that much time with a person on the first encounter. I had to keep reminding myself that it was the first one. I wanted him badly and am pretty psyched that it didn't go to that complete extreme. What happens next could be pretty intense, though. I hope this one works out for the complete best. Please.

7/2/1986: Spent Monday night and Tuesday with Kevin. I had the best time with him. I spent the night Monday. And, yes, we had sex. It was really cool. I could really like him and it scares me because it's a weird situation (I'm really scared he may go back to drugs and alcohol). It's not that I doubt his sobriety, but he talks about the good times of drugs a lot. But I'm sounding more like a girlfriend than what we really are, which is what? I don't know, either. Yesterday morning he told me that I'm the best thing that's happened to him in a long while. He's always hinting at things, too. But I don't know if it could be called hinting. I'm falling quickly for him. I won't deny, but sometimes I'll try and hold out from saying things. He's a cool lover. And he doesn't talk. I like that. It's fun and if it ends tomorrow I'll be bummed but I'll move on – opportunities may come up in other places, too.

(*Excerpt from letter to Lisa dated July 9, 1986:*) *Dear Leaky... discovered that a letter is much cheaper than the phone and we all know how expensive "dial 1" is. Just wanted to let you know how things went with Kevin...I think Kevin and I are going to try and take off for a couple of days – if we can ever synchronize our schedules. Once again, I had a really good time with him. I'm beginning to feel quite a lot for him and it kind of scares me. Lisa, he makes me feel so good – not just in bed, but as a person, too (don't worry, we've been using protection). I don't think I made the best impression on his mom, because we slept in the same room, only he slept on the floor. I'm hoping for redemption. I'll just have to impress them next time. His mom did invite me back. Lisa, I'm really liking him. I'm not stopping myself. I guess if I'm going to be hurt it'll happen anyway. I totally get the impression that it's mutual, too. Things he says to me; the ways he looks at me. All he has to do is smile and I break down...My parents are away for the weekend. Maybe Kevin will come stay with me. It'll be great to have the place. Talk to you soon. Love always, Kissten*

8/14/1986: I am in love with Kevin. Very much so. And he is with me. He makes me feel so good. He is honest. He compliments me. He always tells me I look nice or I'm cute or I have a "hot" body. I love him so much. But I have to face that whatever happens happens because of fate. We'll see. Right now, the feelings and emotions are intense.

[*I was shocked I did not write more about him. My accounting of our relationship virtually non-existent. I was busier during that time, too. The journal, I am sure, was no longer what I needed. At some point at the end of that summer, I made the decision to apply to California schools and transfer.*]

(*Excerpt from letter to Lisa dated September 12, 1986:*) *Dear Leaky- Heading out to Denver for what looks like the last time. It's kind of a weird feeling, but I'm psyched to do well this quarter. It should be pretty exciting and busy. Keep my mind from being obsessed (too much) with Kevin...I don't know where I'm going to go yet. If I go to UCSB, I know I'm going to get side-tracked. The men I saw were beautiful, too. I know, I have Kevin but looking never hurts. And I can still fantasize!! The summer was great. The end was a little emotional. Zits and the rag prematurely account for that – and a slight weight gain. One comment from anyone and I'll seek them out...I hope someone is at the airport to pick me up. I'll probably go out tonight and party. I can dig that. And in a week I'll wonder where all my money went. No problem. I'll survive somehow. It's weird going out with an alcoholic. I hope Kevin can stay sober. I think he wants to enough but doesn't trust himself around it (parties, etc.). Hopefully in time he will...Plane is beginning to descend. I'm psyched for this quarter and the ones "wherever" following. Love always, Kirsten*

[Kevin was from an affluent family and had been exposed to drugs and alcohol early on. He was smart enough to recognize the problem, or his parents were, and was already living sober by the time he got to college. This would sometimes be hard for me and our relationship because I still liked to party and have fun. He just never went to lifeguard parties with me. Probably a good thing.]

FALL 1986

[There are no journal entries from this time period. The only evidence of what I was feeling documented in several letters to Lisa. Excerpts from those letters follow.]

September 22, 1986: Things have been going great here. My brain is already being overworked, but it's cool because I'm being challenged. I have some pretty tough classes, but I'm also sitting down and studying, but mind you, my social life has not been neglected...For the first time, guys have shown an interest in me. It's so weird. I haven't been with anyone. Kevin plagues my mind. But remember Jeff from last year? My major lust – he looks hot – very. When he saw me the other night he hugged me, kissed me, and then hugged me again. It was weird. God, Leak, if anyone could make me question my loyalty to Kevin, he could and that's very hard. But I think Jeff is content at being friends, as I will be. He's a temptation though. As for others, they're just fun to lust after. I really do miss Kevin a lot. I can't wait to see him again. I am so in love with him. I just hope that we can make it through this period.

284

Sometimes, by my own dumb reactions, I feel like he might want someone else. I know he doesn't (now at least), but still. You'll have to spy for me…If I go to UCSB it will probably kill me when it comes to guys and dealing with Kevin and my desire (wrong word) to drink. But I won't worry about that yet. The next few weeks will be the crucial determinants.

*September 30, 1986: Dear Leaky, I know that you'd never mention any of what is to follow to Kevin, but if you'd like burn this letter because if he finds it, it's over…Yesterday, I got a letter from Kevin. It was heavy. God, it seems like he's so in love with me and is scared to death to lose me. He was thinking of breaking it off in order for him not to have to deal. I'll let you read it sometime. It was a trip. He talked so much about God controlling his life. It's hard to deal with him not accepting the person he is. He is controlled by God. Lisa, I love him so much but sometimes it's so hard to deal. I don't want to break-up because I'd like it to work…Okay, so why burn this? Because I want to embark on a new relationship (perhaps). My Saturday night was just as good as Friday, except I didn't scam on anyone. I was shit-faced (had all memory, though). But I met this guy named Alex who's an SAE. He's a senior and gorgeous. We hung out all night. Actually, I hung out with everyone but always went back to him. I'm weird. I can't remember why I didn't let him walk me all the way home. He walked me half way. I don't even think he tried to kiss me good-bye. He was just so cool. I want to see him again. I want him to get to know me sober. He's so cool…Made an ass of myself in front of Jeff. I can't remember if I spilled my guts to him. I think I came damn near close. I haven't seen him yet so I don't know what his response will be. [I totally remember spilling my guts to him, even telling him I would leave my boyfriend for him!]…I met so many guys that night. Mostly SAEs and pledges. This fag tried to pick me up. And all the other guys say hi. I'm so physically friendly when I'm drunk. Shit, I'm having the best time…So you see, Leak, I am normal. I love Kevin, but I love the freedom, too…I want multiplicity in my life. Kevin will be the hardest part to deal with if I go to UCSB. No, I take that back, AA will be the hardest. I love him so much, but I want it all…The rest of my life is boring. School's tough. Swimming's started. At least I'll be in shape. I am having the best time…Take care. Love always, Kissten *This letter will now lose itself! **Do you think I'm a tease? Will does. Jeff thinks I'm a clepto – I am!*

[The letter from Kevin was a pretty dark one that delved way too much into personal demons that aren't relevant to this story. Most of his letters that fall had the same theme: He loved me, and he was always struggling as a recovering alcoholic. They were deep on many levels.]

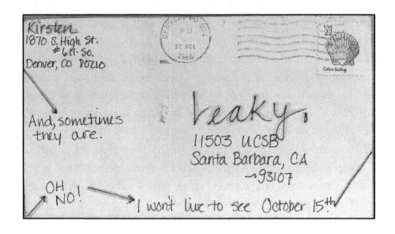

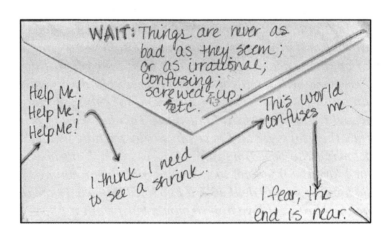

①

Sarah Schultz

Hi Lisa!
Kirsten has found a new love! Yeah! Tell her to go for it.
Bye - Sarah

9.10.86

yes, she's found a new love, but she majorly fucked-up last night. Wah! I want to call you and tell you all this but I don't have a voice. I am so confused. This letter will be in confusing little abstracts.

PART I. I still love ████ and I miss him. Sometimes it's hard dealing with an alcoholic. But then again sometimes I think I belong in A.A. too. Esp. as of late. (NO WAY!)

PART II: Scooter. Stands for ██████████ ████████████████████ 6. Sophomore. Brown hair and eyes. 6'0". Totally cool.

And I fucked up last night. (SCOOTER IS VERY CUTE!!)

Story line.

We met Tuesday night and hung out the entire night at Kappa Sig. Had the best time. Totally clicked. Walked me home. Kissed me good-night. End. 1:30 am.

Wednesday afternoon ran into Scott (KE friend). Said, in response to inquiring about Scooter, "Are you kidding, he's fucking in love with you!" Rad, I thought. The night before he said he'd go out to dinner with me on my birthday. He said he was

287

Sarah Schultz

totally psyched. God knows, I was.

Wednesday night: Wine and cheese party at K's. Kirsten gets _wasted_. Scooter's there all night. Talking to lots of people. Looking at me alot. Exchange of words on occassion. I wouldn't have been wasted had I not had medicine in me. God, I became a <u>bitch</u>, first class-to everyone. Scooter blew me off. Later (TOTALLY) I'm like, "Scooter, I fucked up, hah?" He said "no." And still kind of blew me off. Said he wanted to talk to me today (Thurs.). Haven't talked to him.

Damn it, Leaky, I could really like him alot. But I feel anything that might have come about was thrown down the drain last night. He makes it easy to forget about ~~Keith~~. It's crazy. Now I don't even (YES, WE ARE!!) know if we're going out to dinner or not. God, I want a chance at redemption. He's to awesome, and I fucked up so you see my position?!

PART III: ~~Keith~~ knows nothing. (cool) Scooter knows nothing about ~~Keith~~ or that I'm supposedly leaving. If he comes over he'll see ~~Keith~~'s pictures, because they hang in my room. Lisa, I know I have ~~Keith~~ around my finger and that kind of sucks.

P.S. Sarah had fun last night. (WEE!!) We never have fun on the same nights. Her Tuesday sucked. (Next Wed. we are BOTH having fun!)

③

PART IV: So you see, Lis, there is hope for me yet. I am just in a sticky situation and don't quit know how to deal with it. It plagues me day and night. Sometimes, it's like, "████, ████ who?" Bad. But when I tell him I love him I do mean it.

PART V: The humdrum of D.U.

My classes are going pretty well. I had a major exam today. Except for one question, it was pretty basic (I hope).

Swimming is going really good. The coach doesn't want me to go. I'm so confused there, too. He's all, let me see how much money I can bribe you with. The folks are kind of psyched. But still. Damn, Lisa, I am so torn.

→ I have to go to class and then practice. Yuck. Until later.

HELP ME!

I wish it would be easy for me to just blow things off. It would save so many of my problems. When it gets right down to it, I'm the one that screws everything up, esp for

④

myself. I think I'm the reason why I'm bumming. I was just the most major bitch And Scooter saw that, so did others. I think maybe I learned a very hard lesson last night. Too bad it had to be in front of Scooter. Maybe it's not hopeless, but sometimes it's easier to believe that it is. I AM SO STUPID. But, I'm beginning to feel a little better about it. I should see him tomorrow for sure. (I hope).

Oh, we didn't pledge SAE. We got bids but have been having more fun at KΣ. So now we're rushing there. They have better parties, although I'm never drinking again. — Ha!! If I should get a bid, I may not accept it. Who knows.

Question: Who knows anything anymore? Answer (God knows) I just feel like a confused and demented little kid, who doesn't know anything anymore.

Well, I'm going to go jamn down to dinner. I'm hungry. So what's new! Write soon or call. My laryngidice should be gone soon. I hope. Miss ya.

Love Always,
Kirsten

October 14, 1986: Dear Lisa, Sometimes things get totally fucked-up. Like birthday dinners. Scooter bailed on me. Tell me my self-confidence is at about zero right now. He totally leads me on then blows me off. I think it has something to do with his very independent spirit and, I don't know. But I handled it well in his presence. Oh well. Blow it off. I have Kevin and right now he means a lot to me. It's just hard dealing sometimes. But I guess the situation will have to be made dealable no matter what the eventual (good or bad) outcomes will be…The final decision has been made and I will be in Santa Barbara come next quarter*…I'm kind of scared to be going to a new place like UCSB. God, I won't know anyone. I'm going to feel like a freshman all over again. Why am I scared, though? I can totally meet people, right?…Kevin invited me to go to Hawaii for a week over break. I'd be stupid if I didn't. I should see how things go with us in November…Tomorrow is my birthday. I hope it's fun despite Scooter. So fuck him. I don't need that in my life. My 19th year is going to be great and mark the start of great things to come. It'd be about time for that to happen in my life. I'm going to get wasted. I've earned it!…You know it really does not feel good to be screwed over by a guy. Sometimes I wonder what males are good for until I get a letter from Kevin saying he loves me. At least someone holds an interest in me. WAH!…

October 16, 1986: My birthday was cool. I had a lot of fun. Went to dinner with a friend, Scott. He's a good guy. And Sarah and Kevin. Partied!! Went to the pub and danced. Scooter was there. Turns out, as I was told, that he really liked me at first but then the second time it didn't click, it wasn't there. Well, I'm not bummin'. Things are cool. Kevin sent me the most gorgeous roses. I was majorly missing him last night. My grades are doing shitty this quarter. Oh well. Love ya!

[*I had originally planned on UCSB but when I really sat down and thought what I wanted academically I made the smart decision to go to Cal State Fullerton and pursue my "dream" degree of International Business. Socially a terrible decision – or maybe it wasn't! My extreme partying went by the wayside only to be occasionally awakened in the summers with lifeguard parties when I wasn't with Kevin, which was most weekends. I was a loyal and faithful girlfriend to him. The wild child had been tamed with the return to California. Probably for the good of everyone, most of all ME!]

[I would continue writing Lisa for years. It's sad that the art of letter writing has virtually disappeared. I sent her this card with a letter at the end of November, just after I returned from Denver. It is a fitting close to how I felt at that time.]

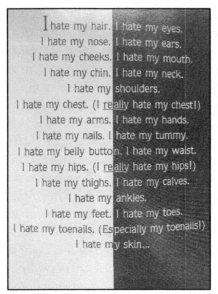

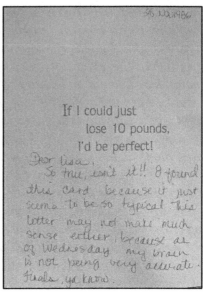

November 28, 1986: Dear Leaky! Once again, I feel like a creature of habit. The writing must look familiar – like someone trying to write whilst on a moving train! Yes, it's off to Kevin's for the night...This will be the third time we'll have seen each other since I've been back. The first time we saw each other was kind of awkward. There's like a major readjustment period that is going to have to take place. The worst part about Wednesday night was having sex with him. It was awful, and in his car. It just wasn't right. Last night we didn't and tonight we probably will. I think it might be cool this time...We're both kind of stressed because we had this fantastic relationship this summer and now we both kind of would like that again, esp. Kevin. It just doesn't work that way though. Parents don't help. I hate having sex in his car. You can't share enough when you're being paranoid about cops and peeping Toms. Tonight we get to be paranoid about his parents. I love him so much and missed him more than I realized, but I hate this constant fear of being discovered whilst loving him. It's just great being with him, too...I'll probably be up to UCSB this weekend. It'd be cool to see you and talk my brains out while finally being alone with Kevin (and his roommates).

Sacrifices, sacrifices...Kevin looked so awesome when I saw him. Too bad, I feel like shit! My face is a major zit from stressing over school. It really does feel good to be home. I can hardly wait to see you again so we can party and talk. I need reassurance right now because my whole life is up in the air and who knows which way it'll come down? Until soon.

LEAVING DENVER

Despite seemingly having found my footing by the end of freshman year I still struggled with the decision to stay. I wish I wrote down my thought process to leave DU back then. I know there was Kevin, but I also feel like I still carried this tremendous guilt of burdening my parents with the cost of a private school education. Once I had told the swim coach I was leaving, he offered me full tuition to stay. I had already made up my mind. And it seems when I do that, there is not much use in trying to change it. In hindsight, I wish I would have stayed. I made some great friends and have such good memories (the way my mind lets me remember them) of that short time in my life. Maybe deep down I feared losing another person I loved by staying far away. I know I would have been tempted had I stayed. And my partying ways were going to be an issue long term. Even then I had "kissing friends", but I never considered that being unfaithful the last quarter before I left.

This was undeniably a wild time for me. It's probably good I didn't stay in Denver based on my letters. I definitely had a pattern of behavior with men: Pursue. Discard. Repeat. I was even guilty of keeping options open despite having committed to leaving Denver. I was always "in love" with someone from an early age and, once I got to college and was confident enough, definitely discovered I liked playing the game and keeping my options open.

I wish we all possessed the power of hindsight, but life has a way of happening to us whether we take the steps, or they are taken for us. I know for a while I struggled to feel I fit in there. My free-spirited thinking about sex was too much for some girls – at least in the beginning before many of them would become equally corrupted. I just never shied away from talking about it. But when I did finally leave, I do feel like I had found my place. I would not find that again in my next college experience.

I was so excited to get to the last journal, The Nothing Book, in this process of telling my coming-of-age story. But I was extremely disappointed in the end to find so many empty pages. The entries sparse, all over the place, not cohesive in its narrative. It felt choppy and like I

293

struggled to put the words on paper. I had saved some pages from notebooks that I would randomly write my thoughts in or exchange thoughts with friends. Those were included. I was definitely not done growing as a person.

The last gift to this project was the fact Lisa had saved all her letters. I thought I had finished with this book when she reached out and told me she had all my letters to her. While I may have stopped writing my life down in a journal, I spared no details in sharing my escapades with her.

I clearly still had not figured out who I was or what I really wanted. I guess I did not feel this journal call out to me to be written in anymore. Maybe because I made friends that I could talk to about what I was feeling (if only I'd written it down, I'd know!). There was a lot of drinking, laughing, discovering during that time. Seems it was just time to stop. And end the story there.

The years from 1986-1989:

While I only stayed at DU for four quarters, I made some truly remarkable friends. I could not tell you anyone's name from CSU Fullerton during my time there. I wish I would have been strong enough to stay as true to my convictions as I was when I was initially struggling with the decision to go there. But I do not believe we should ever regret decisions we made. They helped shape the future. One is not always mutually exclusive or inclusive.

I became a beach lifeguard starting that first summer after I started college. I was one of only a few women and enjoyed a lot of attention, most of it unwanted because I did have a boyfriend. My last summer would end in a fling with another lifeguard. It was unemotional and just about sex. As far as I know, we were the first ones to have sex in the pier lifeguard tower. The view was pretty amazing. I think it was the first time I did not want more from the situation.

I recognized years later that I also experienced some definite sexual harassment during my time as a lifeguard. One lifeguard made such repulsive comments that I think if I saw him today, I would still want to tell him to fuck off, which is pretty much what I did anyways. I was tough and it generally didn't faze me.

EVER AFTER

Why didn't I write for chunks of time in those years? And then stop completely? I could speculate on the reasons. Maybe I did not need the crutch of putting it all out there, my head spinning in circles, overthinking, overwhelmed, over-everything. I worried about letting people down whilst (I used that word A LOT back then) ultimately and sometimes recklessly doing what I wanted anyways. Maybe I felt embarrassed looking back at what I wrote. Maybe I would stop because of the depth of my emotions. Maybe on a deeper level I knew I had put so much to paper, tortured myself in a world of what if's/had I only. Maybe it was time. Or maybe I was just content moving forward living in the moment. Nonetheless, my writing stopped when this story ends.

I embarked on this project remembering some things so differently than I wrote about them. It has been a cathartic process, made me realize that I was destined to end up okay. I remember how much weight played a role while swimming, but I do not remember how skinny I really was to be the weight I kept hitting. Weight is just such a warped concept. It can create such a convoluted sense of self based on a series of random numbers that can dictate emotional satisfaction or shattering complexes. I would like to believe that coaches have evolved and understand that weight is not purely a number, and the consequences can be tragic to sense of self long beyond the weekly weigh-ins.

I had a strange obsession with wanting to be an actress/model. I had so many insecurities with my curly hair, acne blemished skin, the weight. I was always trying to find something in myself to like. I look back and think I probably wanted to be an actress/model because I equated that with being beautiful. Even today, I do not always look in the mirror and see myself positively. I did learn that my body was not the issue I thought it was. Stupid perceptions! While it sounds petty to admit, I am thankful to those boys early on who made me feel wanted. It did instill some confidence.

And those countless fantasies I would write about. They would sometimes go for pages. I generally only provided snippets of those. For me, those became an alternate reality; so different than the life I was leading at that time. I needed those to feel normal, loved, and valid. For me, they were a coping mechanism I needed to survive. Ultimately, I think the real experiences I write about, both emotionally and sexually, trumped any of those that I fantasized about.

Then there was the time at Denver where I seemed to have discovered my sexuality and exploited it. I have no doubt I was likely overcompensating for the years I felt I was not worth noticing. Or just finally comfortable in my own skin. Selfish undoubtedly. I was obviously not perfect. I was wild, deceptive with the guys I had and reckless with the ones I wanted. I know I savored this newfound power over them. Sarah remembers me telling her that sex made me feel powerful. I was using my "power" way too much and am lucky, in retrospect, that I didn't get myself into more trouble!

I have always believed that you cannot regret the ones you do not remember, and I have always taken full ownership of my behavior. I do not even regret the ones I vaguely remember. And I regret none of the ones I vividly remember. I am grateful to have been such a prolific diary writer, journal keeper, letter hoarder, and poet in those teenage years. I tucked away memories and forgot details. I look back now and think I have not given myself enough credit for getting through and that much of it was not nearly as bad as I have sometimes wanted to remember it.

I can reflect on those likes and loves and say I do not know that I believe we have just one soul mate. I think if we are lucky, we get to have more than one true love. As much as I love the concept of love, I do not believe we are supposed to love only one person forever. We are lucky if we find people along the way that help shape and define us, help us recognize what we like and dislike, make us feel whole or a part of something. Love, as in life, is not simple.

Letters to Lisa after college graduation would show that I had finally settled and mellowed, no longer distracted by what may come my way next, living in those moments rather than looking for the next best thing. I asked a lot of questions of myself, recognized my weaknesses, had fun in the moment, and never lamented any of it.

I have made good decisions, bad decisions, irrational, spontaneous, and misguided ones. But none of those changed where I ended up. The most important people during those times are still there for me today. We rack our brains sometimes trying to put faces to names. Cringeworthy moments reminders we were young and dumb once, but we were living, experiencing, discovering like so many people at that time. Most of us ended up with "normal" lives.

My high school English teacher, Mr. Brooks, wrote in the back of my senior journals that I should hold onto them, that someday it would be nice to look back. I forgot about them for decades. They added to this story of me in those years when not knowing who you are is pretty much what everything is about.

Throughout the years, I would pull the journals out and glance. My reaction to myself was not kind. This time, though, it was a wild ride back in time. I could feel all those emotions, remember some of those kisses, touches, intimate moments. I can even laugh at myself for some of those crushes I had along the way. It has been a journey. My journey in those amazing eighties was not that different than that of so many of my classmates, teammates, and friends. In the end, we turned out okay; our experiences making us better versions of ourselves.

EPILOGUE:

TIME DID NOT STOP WHEN MY WRITING ENDED

One of my all-time favorite movies during this time of my life was "The Breakfast Club" with its aptly titled theme song "Don't You Forget About Me" by Simple Minds. Maybe because I saw myself and people I knew in those characters, I have always wanted to know what happened to them. It is absurd because they were just fictional characters. Mine is a true story with real people that affected my life in countless ways. I know much of how their stories went after this one ends.

My Heart

So many infatuations, obsessions, lusts, and likes over these many years. But only a few truly got a piece of my heart. I think I am lucky to have had my first sexual encounters be with two men (they were definitely not boys) that had experience. They made any insecurities I might have had disappear in their confidence. They made it exciting and about me.

Terry...ended faster than it began. While I know I was never really in love with him, he was my first time and an accelerated sexual experience at that – and it was fun in the moment. I am pretty sure I wrote him a few letters trying to rationalize my feelings and break-up. He called me a couple of years later to tell me he was out of the military and that he still thought about me. And that he said he had told me he promised he would come back for me. That kind of scared me. I remember liking his bad boy persona but was momentarily mortified by the thought he might actually do it. He did not fail to make me feel good when he complimented the memory of my body. To this day, I do not know what happened to him. But he was my first time and a willing teacher. And I never felt anything but grateful for the experience.

Ajey...Turns out I would never write about anyone like that again. He was the great love story of those years. I locked so much of that relationship deep and far away in my memory. It is the relationship that has struck me most reflecting on that time. I look back on those journal entries and the letters and realize that I was so in love with him. But it was painfully clear that time was never quite in our favor. Maybe that is why it was so intense: we were always racing to catch up only to have to let go again. I am guessing it is why I wanted to fight it but fell so hard anyways. It was a relationship that did not get to be what it might have been because of the constant challenges of time, distance, and reality. It was intense when it was not supposed to be. It scared me in ways I can only see clearly now. It was raw, honest, emotional, passionate, and educational.

The last time I saw Ajey was when I came home for break that first year of college. I could not handle seeing him; it was hard. I tried to look him up a couple of times over the years but did not find him. We finally reconnected when I started this memoir. He really did become a doctor. I do not think at seventeen that I would have seen that drive and determination in him. Makes me so happy for him.

Kevin...and I broke up in person on the beach in Santa Barbara after nearly two years together. It had been a while in the making. In hindsight and from letters written after this book's timeframe, it was a complicated relationship more because he had to deal with a lot of personal stuff, and I ultimately did not want to. I remember driving an hour towards home after a fight and telling myself I needed to turn around and just break up otherwise we were going to drag it out. We broke up as best we could. No hard feelings. He called me when we both graduated the next year to tell me about his new car. We caught up many years later and still keep in touch every so often.

And of my friends, crushes, obsessions, parents, and mo...

Sarah...My best and closest friend to this day. She has always believed in and supported me and deserves much of the credit for encouraging me to pursue this story when I had just been playing with the idea. My everything friend.

Debbie...We get together for breakfast or lunch a few times a year. There will always be a bond between us of some very dark, deep, emotional, painful, and absolutely great times. Truly a forever friend.

Lisa...Will always be my oldest friend. She, too, saved all the letters I had written to her over the years reaffirming that I shared intimate details about my life, and she always provided honest feedback. A loyal friend and a friendship that has withstood the test of time even though we only talk a few times a year.

Suji...She doesn't get as much journal coverage relative to the importance of her friendship at that time. To this day, I still mourn that friendship ending. She was the most eclectic, interesting person I knew. So above the high school drama, but so conflicted with herself. Her last letter to me in our early 20's was cryptic at best, and we never saw each other again. Well, at Debbie's wedding where she avoided me. I tried hard to get to the bottom of that one. She saw in me things that others did not at a time when it meant a lot to be seen.

Britta...My German soul sister. One of my favorite people in the whole world. It is a friendship that has transcended time, oceans, and initially language. We have always found a way to laugh ourselves through everything even when language was no longer an issue.

Mary/Chris...Mary and Chris dated all through college, married, and had five beautiful children together. Tragically, Chris would die shy of his 50th birthday. Mary and I remain close friends despite being on opposite coasts.

Mickey...I wish I knew what happened to her. We kept in touch for a couple of years of college, but then lost contact. She was a fun person and understood me so well back then.

My DU friends...We wrote letters for many years. Barb even sent wedding and baby gifts. Sweetest person and I was so happy when she finally met someone. I have reconnected with others through Facebook, and it's been fun to see how their lives played out beautifully for them as well. Sadly, Janet passed away way too young.

Emily...She moved out quickly to live with her soccer friends our freshman year. That was for the best. I learned she committed suicide years later. A sad and tragic end.

Jim B...The first boy I ever knew I "loved". I was ten. I would write him letters telling him how much I liked him. Sadly, for me, he never reciprocated those feelings. He did call me once and asked me to call him back. I didn't have a pen or paper and ended up forgetting the number. Who knows if that was the chance that got away?! Jim never really paid any attention to me even though we had mutual friends. I'm pretty sure he made out with just about all my swimmer friends. Even years later if I heard he might be somewhere I was going, it still made my stomach turn a little. Sadly, Jim died just shy of his 45th birthday. A little piece of my heart died when I found that out. He was my great unrequited love.

Paul...My high school obsession that lasted way too long. We are "friends" on FB. He is engaged to be married. Never had kids. Played in a punk band. Got lots of tattoos. Never had any ill will towards him – even if he never liked me like I liked him.

35 Degree Angle Man...I do not believe I ever had a romantic thought about him. He was just the absolutely most fascinating person I had ever encountered. He forever remains a mystery. He had a very generic name. While I have tried looking him up, I have not uncovered how his life turned out. Hopefully, always true to his nonconformist self.

Lutz...No one understood that one. Probably least of all me. When I moved to Germany after graduating college, a friend told me he wanted to give us a chance, but I was already dating someone by then. Oceans, distance, and timing.

My Parents...The most important people in my life. I am not sure who had the harder part looking back: them or me. They stuck by me, did not resent me, and have loved me unconditionally all my life. We overcame the hard parts, moved forward, and embraced that I turned out just fine after all. Just like they knew  I would. They were a near daily part of my children's lives when they were growing up, and I am grateful that they could be.

Me...I would graduate from college in 1989 and move to Germany to begin my career. Two long term relationships would follow. One my German love. And the other my husband love. We all have a history. I married at 27. I had a successful career in marketing. I got my MBA. I had three beautiful children who have gone on to be amazing adults. I was lucky enough to get to walk away from my career and be a full-time mom. It surprised a lot of people that I could do that given my drive to succeed. I channeled that by actively involving myself through volunteering and coaching. It was truly the greatest 20 plus years of my life. There is no part of me that is not grateful for this life I have been given.

That is all. My final words. On becoming me.

The Memory Vault

I lived;
I loved.
I buried the memories
Deep in the hallows of my mind.
I opened the books;
Turned the pages;
and unlocked my mind's vault.
I refresh;
I remember;
I hold on tight
Never wanting to forget again.

July 19, 2021

Kirsten Hegberg Pursell in 2021...
being the best version of herself.

Kirsten lives in Oceanside, California, currently navigating the waters of an empty nest. In addition to *On Becoming Me: Memoir of an 80's Teenager*, she has published two additional novels: *Harvard* and *Company Clown*.

Color photos and bonus content for *On Becoming Me* can be found at www.kirstenpursell.com.

Made in the USA
Las Vegas, NV
13 November 2021

34359922R00174